THE MAN
I KNEW

THE MAN
I KNEW

THE AMAZING STORY OF
GEORGE H. W. BUSH'S POST-PRESIDENCY

JEAN BECKER

TWELVE

NEW YORK BOSTON

Twelve
Hachette Book Group
1290 Avenue of the Americas, New York, NY 10104
twelvebooks.com
twitter.com/twelvebooks

First Edition: June 2021

Twelve is an imprint of Grand Central Publishing. The Twelve name and logo are trademarks of Hachette Book Group, Inc.

The publisher is not responsible for websites (or their content) that are not owned by the publisher.

The Hachette Speakers Bureau provides a wide range of authors for speaking events. To find out more, go to www.hachettespeakersbureau.com or call (866) 376-6591.

Library of Congress Cataloging-in-Publication Data
Names: Becker, Jean, 1956?- author.
Title: The man I knew : the amazing story of George H. W. Bush's post-presidency / Jean Becker.
Other titles: Amazing story of George H. W. Bush's post-presidency
Description: First edition. | New York : Twelve, 2021. | Summary: "As chief of staff, Jean Becker had a ringside seat to the never-boring story of George Herbert Walker Bush's life post-presidency, including being at his side when he died and subsequently facing the challenge—and great honor—of being in charge of his state funeral. Full of heart and wisdom, THE MAN I KNEW is a vibrant behind-the-scenes look into the ups and downs of heading up the office of a former president by one of the people who knew him best. This book tells the story of how, after his devastating loss to Bill Clinton in 1992, President George H. W. Bush rebuilt his life, found a way to make a difference, and how, by the time he died in November 2018, was revered by his country and the world. Bush's post-presidency journey was filled with determination, courage, love, hope, humor, fun, and big ideas. He became best friends with the man who defeated him; developed the odd habit of jumping out of airplanes; and learned how to adjust to life in a wheelchair, after having lived most of his life as a high-energy athlete. He joyously saw two sons become governors of their states, one of whom would go on to become president of the United States. What happens when you go almost overnight from being the most important and powerful person in the world to a private citizen? THE MAN I KNEW tells just such a story, of one man's humble journey from president to man of the people."— Provided by publisher.
Identifiers: LCCN 2020054046 | ISBN 9781538735305 (hardcover) | ISBN 9781538735299 (ebook)
Subjects: LCSH: Bush, George, 1924-2018. | Ex-presidents—United States—Biography. | Presidents—Retirement—United States. | Bush, George, 1924-2018—Friends and associates. | United States—Politics and government—1989- | Houston (Tex.)—Biography. | Becker, Jean, 1956?–
Classification: LCC E882 .B43 2021 | DDC 973.928092 [B]—dc23
LC record available at https://lccn.loc.gov/2020054046

ISBNs: 978-1-5387-3530-5 (hardcover), 978-1-5387-3529-9 (ebook)

Printed in the United States of America

LSC-C

Printing 1, 2021

*To Joe and Dorothy Becker, who gave me all the love, confidence, discipline,
and support I needed to seek a life of purpose and adventure.*

*And to George and Barbara Bush, who generously shared their extraordinary
lives of purpose and adventure with me, therefore giving me the same.*

*I selfishly imagine now and then that the four most influential people
in my life have met in heaven and maybe even gossip about me
now and then. "Why did she just do that?!"*

Contents

Author's Note

A few hours before he died, I was sitting at President Bush's bed-side, holding his hand and talking about nothing in particular. He was not in a coma, but his eyes were closed, and he seemed far away. So I chatted about this and that and kept him company. People had been coming and going, but at this moment in time, we were alone.

Thanks to a small tickle in my throat, I coughed ever so slightly. His eyes flew open, and he squeezed my hand and asked, "Are you okay?"

Those would be the last words George Herbert Walker Bush would say to me. I can think of no better ending to a friendship that had begun twenty-six years earlier when, after he lost his reelection bid, I followed President and Mrs. Bush back to Houston to help her write her memoirs.

The question "Are you okay?" was just so him. He was dying. But as always, he was thinking of the other guy.

I squeezed his hand back and assured him I was indeed okay. And yes, I do think, on a deeper level, the question was bigger than about that cough.

And I really was okay. He was ready. And if he was ready, I was ready.

His was, after all, a life well lived.

Much of it you know. He was shot down in the Pacific during World War II but was rescued by an American submarine; married his sweet-heart, Barbara Pierce; graduated Phi Beta Kappa in two and a half years from Yale, where he was captain of the baseball team; moved to Texas to enter the oil business; went into public service, serving as a congress-man, an ambassador to the United Nations, an emissary to China, the director of the CIA, and the vice president and president of the United States. When he left office on January 20, 1993, he moved back to Houston with Mrs. Bush to retire, with every intention of staying out of the public eye.

That was not to be.

This book will tell the story of how—after leaving the White House—President Bush rebuilt his life, found a way to continue making a difference, and, by the time he died in November 2018, was revered by his country and by the world.

His post-presidency journey was filled with determination, courage, generosity, love, hope, humor, fun, and always big ideas.

From his partnership with President Bill Clinton to raise money for disaster relief to his very public parachute jumps, the forty-first president never quit living life to the fullest, even after Parkinson's disease put him in a wheelchair. In between his more public adventures, he devoted himself to a wide variety of causes, including cancer, volunteerism, leadership, patriotism, and to what was his life's mantra: faith, family, and friends.

And he lived what he preached: "Any definition of a successful life must include serving others."

And then, of course, two of his sons would become governors of major states, and one the forty-third president of the United States.

How lucky was I to be along for the ride for all twenty-six years, the last twenty-five as his chief of staff? As the daughter of a Missouri farmer who never finished high school; as a graduate of a country high school with a class of only fifty-seven; as a news groupie (brought about by the whole Watergate affair) who wanted nothing more than to be a reporter when she grew up; and who, by the way, grew up a Democrat—you could say it was an unexpected ride. Somewhere along the way my life took a sharp turn. I never once looked back.

Working for George H. W. Bush taught me so many things: to live with joy, think big, be humble, make a difference.

I loved him but was often fearful when he came into my office and said, "Jean, I have an idea." They were sometimes little ideas—"Let's go get pizza for lunch."

But often they were BIG: "I would like to go back to Chichijima, where I was shot down. I need to close that chapter. Let's go do that soon."

One thing was for sure: It was never boring.

I am excited to share with you some of my favorite stories about George Bush's life after the White House. Some will seem like fairy tales, but others range from broken toilet seats to broken hearts.

The stories are based on all the emails, notes, essays, occasional journal entries, and work files I kept over the years. Sometimes I had to rely just on my memory, which as we all know can be tricky. (President Bush once complained that as much as he loved his World War II squadron mates, he hated going to their reunions. "They all remember that we won the war single-handedly.")

So, when possible, I asked the other players in these episodes—George Clooney comes to mind—if my memory was their memory, just to keep me honest.

Occasionally, I have reconstructed a quote from President Bush, but only if I felt positive that it was almost exactly what he said. Many of the conversations seem like they took place yesterday.

While I did everything possible to make this a fact-based book, I should note that the George H. W. Bush Presidential Library and Museum—which contains all of his records and files and some of mine—was closed because of COVID-19 while I was writing this book. (Thankfully, I brought some key files I needed home with me when I closed the Office of George Bush in March 2019.) I assure you I didn't make anything up, but you might notice that sometimes I am a bit vague. For example, instead of telling you how many campaign events the Bushes did in 2000 for their son George W., I just tell you it was a lot.

I also cannot claim the book is objective. I was and am the biggest fan of George and Barbara Bush. So if you are expecting deep, dark secrets or tabloid gossip, put the book down now. (For the record, I have read both of their diaries. There were no deep, dark secrets.)

But I promise it will be a fun ride.

Since I have shared the last words George Bush said to me, I am fairly sure I remember the first words. It was 1987. He was vice president of the United States and running for president. I was a reporter for *USA Today*, a junior member of the paper's election team. I was assigned to travel with the vice president on a trip to South Dakota and had been asking the press staff all day for a short interview. Finally, late at night on the long flight back to Washington, they said I could have five minutes.

I was scared to death. He was by far the most important person I had interviewed, unless you count a phone interview with Billy Joel. I made my way to the front of Air Force Two, introduced myself, and sat across from him with my notebook in hand. He gave me an exhausted—and slightly exasperated—look. "What do you got?" he asked.

And we were off and running…

Jean Becker

Glossary of Names

To help you keep track of some of the recurring characters in the book, here is a list of the people (and some places and things) that pop up more than a few times. The biographical information is as of March 1, 2021.

Family First

Bush, George W.: Oldest son of George and Barbara Bush, he was elected president of the United States in November 2000 and reelected in 2004. He served as governor of Texas from 1994 until 2000, when he stepped down to become president. Before entering politics, he was a businessman and co-managing partner of the Texas Rangers baseball team. Now an author and artist, and an active participant at the George W. Bush Institute in Dallas, he is also an avid mountain biker and golfer. He and his wife, former First Lady Laura Bush, live in Dallas. They have two daughters and three grandchildren:

- Jenna Bush Hager and her husband, Henry, live in New York City with their two daughters and one son.
- Barbara Pierce Bush lives in New York City with her husband, Craig Coyne.

Bush, John Ellis ("Jeb"): Second son of George and Barbara Bush, he was governor of Florida from 1999 to 2007. He is a member of the board of directors of the George & Barbara Bush Foundation and chairman of the foundation's board of trustees. Active in business and education reform and the author of multiple books, Jeb and his wife, Columba, live in Miami. They have three children and five grandchildren:

- George P. Bush and his wife, Amanda, live in Austin, Texas, with their two sons.
- Noelle Bush lives in Orlando, Florida.
- Jeb Bush Jr. and his wife, Sandra, live in Miami with their three daughters.

Bush, Neil: The third son of George and Barbara Bush, he is engaged in international business development with a focus on Asia. He is active in promoting Bush family charitable legacies, serving as chairman of the board of Points of Light, the George Bush School of Government and Public Service Advisory Board, and the George H. W. Bush Foundation for U.S.-China Relations. He is founder and chairman, with his wife, Maria, of the Barbara Bush Houston Literacy Foundation, and a member of the George & Barbara Bush Foundation board of directors. He and Maria live in Houston and are the parents of six and grandparents of two:

- Lauren Bush Lauren and her husband, David, live in New York City with their two sons.
- Pierce Bush and his wife, Sarahbeth, live in Houston.
- Ashley Bush and her husband, Julian LeFevre, live in Los Angeles.
- Lizzie Andrews lives in New York City.
- Pace Andrews lives in Houston.
- Alexander Andrews lives in Houston.

Bush, Marvin: The fourth son of George and Barbara Bush, Marvin is managing partner of Winston Partners, an investment firm in Arlington, Virginia. He serves on the boards of the George & Barbara Bush Foundation and the Virginia Athletics Foundation. He is a past board member of the George W. Bush Presidential Library Foundation and the University of Virginia Alumni Association. He also is a former trustee of the College Foundation of UVA. He and his wife, Margaret, live in Arlington, Virginia, and are the parents of a daughter and a son.

- Marshall Bush lives in Charlottesville, Virginia.
- Walker Bush and his wife, Lora, live in Fort Worth, Texas.

Koch, Dorothy ("Doro") Bush: Youngest child of George and Barbara Bush, she is the cofounder of BB&R Wellness Consulting; the honorary chairman and a board member of the Barbara Bush Foundation for Family Literacy; and a member of the board of the George & Barbara Bush Foundation. She is the author of *My Father, My President*. She and her husband, Bobby, live in Bethesda, Maryland, and have four children and one grandchild:

- Sam LeBlond and his wife, Lee, live in Washington, DC.
- Ellie LeBlond Sosa and her husband, Nick, live in McLean, Virginia, with their daughter.
- Robert Koch lives in Nashville, Tennessee, and is engaged to Kitty Montesi.
- Gigi Koch lives in Washington, DC.

Friends

Baker, James A., III: He served as secretary of state from 1989 to 1992, and also was Ronald Reagan's White House chief of staff and secretary of the Treasury. He is the only known person to run five presidential campaigns for three different people. The author of numerous books and chairman of various boards and committees, he is an active participant in the James A. Baker III Institute of Public Policy at Rice University. He and his wife, Susan, live in Houston. Between them, they have eight children and eighteen grandchildren.

Card, Andrew: He served as White House chief of staff under President George W. Bush from 2001 to 2006. He was deputy White House chief of staff under the first President Bush before being named secretary of transportation in 1992. He got his start in politics serving in the Massachusetts House of Representatives from 1975 to 1983. His post–White House career has included serving as acting dean of the George Bush School of Government and Public Service at Texas A&M University before becoming president of Franklin Pierce University in Rindge, New Hampshire, resigning in 2016. He and his wife, Kathleene, live in Jaffrey, New Hampshire, and have three children and six grandchildren.

Gates, Robert M.: He served as the twenty-second secretary of defense from 2006 to 2011 and is the only secretary of defense in U.S. history to be asked to remain in that office by a newly elected president. Gates worked for eight presidents and has been heard commenting that President George H. W. and First Lady Barbara Bush's White House was the most fun. Before becoming secretary of defense in 2006, Gates was the president of Texas A&M University; before that he served as interim dean of the George Bush School of Government and Public Service at Texas A&M from 1999 to 2001; and before that he was director of Central Intelligence. The author of numerous books, he and his wife, Becky, live in Sedro-Woolley, Washington, and have two children.

Heminway, Betsy: Betsy and her late husband, Spike, were among the Bushes' closest and oldest friends. They lived in Kennebunkport, Maine, in the summer and Hobe Sound, Florida, in the winter. Betsy still does. Betsy was active in President Bush's campaigns, serving in Connecticut as co-chair of '84 Reagan-Bush, and '88 and '92 Bush-Quayle. She has one daughter and two grandchildren.

Major, John: Prime minister of the United Kingdom from 1990 to 1997, Sir John was knighted by Queen Elizabeth in 2005. Previously he had served as foreign secretary and chancellor of the exchequer under

Prime Minister Margaret Thatcher. He was a member of Parliament until he retired in 2001. He and his wife, Dame Norma, live in London and have two children.

McLane, Drayton, Jr.: A businessman and philanthropist, he worked his way up in the family's wholesale grocery business from the night shift to president and CEO, developing the company into a multibillion-dollar corporation. Following the McLane Company's merger with Walmart, Inc., in 1990, he became vice-chairman of Walmart while maintaining his position as president and CEO of the McLane Company. He later resigned from Walmart in order to devote more time to the McLane Group, a parent company consisting of family-owned companies operating throughout the world, which until November 2011 included the Houston Astros. He and his wife, Elizabeth, live in Temple, Texas, and have two sons and five grandsons.

Meacham, Jon: A presidential historian, author, and professor at Vanderbilt University, Jon wrote *Destiny and Power: The American Odyssey of George Herbert Walker Bush*. In 2009, he won the Pulitzer Prize for *American Lion: Andrew Jackson in the White House*. He and his wife, Keith, live in Nashville, Tennessee, with their three children.

Mulroney, Brian: Elected in 1984 and reelected in 1988, Mulroney was Canada's eighteenth prime minister. From the Canada–U.S. Acid Rain Treaty, to NAFTA, to the first Gulf War, to the end of the Cold War and the reunification of Germany, there were very few issues of importance upon which he and President Bush did not work closely. He and his wife, Mila, live in Montreal and have four children and fifteen grandchildren.

Scowcroft, Brent (Lt. Gen., USAF, Ret., Deceased): He served as national security adviser to Presidents George H. W. Bush and Gerald Ford—the only person to have held this position twice. He was a 1947 graduate of West Point and received his master's and doctorate from

Columbia University in 1953 and 1967, respectively. His twenty-seven-year Air Force service included postings at West Point; Belgrade, Yugoslavia; U.S. Air Force Academy; Office of the Secretary of Defense; and Joint Chiefs of Staff. He has said that President George H. W. Bush was "one of my dearest friends and the most prepared person ever for the presidency." He is survived by his daughter, Karen, and granddaughter, Meghan.

Sidey, Hugh: Hugh covered every president from Dwight Eisenhower to Bill Clinton—first for *Life* magazine and then for *Time* magazine—becoming a respected observer and chronicler of the presidency. He and President Bush became pen pals in 1993, exchanging letters about current events and their life philosophies, including Hugh's love for his native Iowa. He died in 2005. He is survived by his wife, Anne, a son, three daughters, and nine grandchildren.

Simpson, Alan K.: He served from 1979 to 1997 as a United States senator from Wyoming. He was elected the assistant majority leader in 1984 and served in that capacity for ten years. He wrote *Right in the Old Gazoo: A Lifetime of Scrapping with the Press*, which chronicles his personal experiences and views of the Fourth Estate. When asked, "Have you lived in Wyoming all your life?" he replied, "Not yet!" He and his wife, Ann, live in Cody, Wyoming, and have three children, six grandchildren, and two great-grandchildren.

Updegrove, Mark: Mark, a presidential historian and author, is president and CEO of the LBJ Foundation. His book, *The Last Republicans*, about the two Presidents Bush, was released in 2017. Mark lives in Austin, Texas, with his wife, Amy, and their four children.

Personal Aides to President Bush

Appleby, Jim: As a high schooler, he began working as a "summer lad"—President Bush's job description—for the Bushes in Kennebunkport in

2001. He eventually became President Bush's personal aide, serving from 2006 to 2012. Today Jim works for Shell in external relations. He and his wife, Lauri, live in Houston with their two children.

Dannenhauer, Michael: Michael first worked for Vice President Bush in 1985 at the age of seventeen, volunteering in the file room. He returned to Washington every summer to work in various vice presidential and White House offices, becoming President Bush's last White House personal aide, moving to Texas with the Bushes in 1993. He continued as his personal aide for five years, then was his chief of staff for two, followed by a year at the George Bush Library Foundation. Michael returned to Washington to work in the second Bush administration, where he still resides today working as a realtor.

Frechette, Tom: Tom began working for President Bush while in high school as a "summer lad" and then as an intern, then served as President Bush's aide from 2000 to 2006. He currently is a managing director at Avenue Capital and a member of the George & Barbara Bush Foundation Advisory Council. He lives in New York City with his wife, Jennifer, and their two daughters.

Lapointe, Coleman: After working at Walker's Point as a "summer lad," Coleman became the personal aide to President Bush from 2012 to 2015. He joined Governor Jeb Bush on the campaign trail during his 2016 presidential bid. Between 2017 and 2020, Coleman worked at the Pentagon, where he served as the director of travel operations for the secretary and undersecretary of defense. He and his wife, Sarah, now happily reside in Maine where Coleman works for General Dynamics at the Bath Iron Works.

Peressutti, Gian-Carlo: Aide to President Bush from 1996 to 2000, he left in 2001 to join the White House staff of George W. Bush as associate director of the Office of Public Liaison. He currently is director of public affairs at IFM Investors and serves on the advisory board of the George Bush School of Government and Public Service. He lives in Ridgefield, Connecticut, with his wife, Amanda (whom he met on the job in Kennebunkport), and two daughters.

Sisley, Evan: Evan served as President Bush's personal aide and senior medic starting in 2015, supervising the medical team who cared for President and Mrs. Bush until their deaths in 2018. Evan began working for President Bush as a medic in 2013 after being recruited to the job from a Marine Corps Reserve company in Houston, where he served as a Navy corpsman. During his time in the Navy, Evan was deployed to Afghanistan, Eastern Europe, and Israel. A paramedic for seven years, Evan worked on ambulances in Kentucky, Maine, and Texas. Prior to serving in the military, Evan was a photojournalist who covered national politics, including the presidency of George W. Bush from 2005 to 2008. He is currently working on prerequisite courses in anticipation of applying to medical school, where he hopes to further his medical career and become an emergency physician. He and his husband, Ian Carrico, live in Washington, DC.

Office of George Bush

Lamoreaux, Melinda: Melinda began working as a volunteer for both President Bush and Mrs. Bush in 1994. In 2000, she joined the staff, sharing job responsibilities at the front desk with Mary Sage and taking on special projects. During the funeral, Melinda was in charge of administrative logistics in the Office of George Bush, including heading the phone bank of twenty volunteers. Today Melinda works for the George & Barbara Bush Foundation as the liaison with the Bush Legacy Groups. She and her husband, Scott, live in Houston and have one adult daughter, Leslie.

Lisenby, Nancy: Nancy started volunteering in 1997 and began working as a part-time receptionist the following year. In 2000, she became my assistant, and among her many jobs was to listen to me vent and help me decipher my handwriting. She was my No. 2 on funeral planning and execution. She and her husband, John, live in Houston. They have three children and ten grandchildren.

McGrath, Jim: Jim served as President Bush's post–White House press secretary and speechwriter and was in charge of all media operations during the funeral. He started at the White House in 1991 in the Office of Presidential Messages and Correspondence, and later served as vice president of the George & Barbara Bush Foundation. He and his wife, Paulina, live in Houston with their three children.

Pears, Laura: After working for the 1990 G-7 Economic Summit and the 1992 Republican National Convention—both held in Houston—Laura joined President Bush's staff in 1993 when he returned to Houston. Initially a volunteer, she joined the full-time staff in 1995, working on special events and later serving as director of scheduling. She was in charge of the Bush family's schedule and logistics during the week of the funeral. She lives in Houston with her husband, Dan.

Poepsel, Linda: Linda worked for President Bush for thirty-seven years, having joined his vice presidential staff in 1981. In 1989, she went to the White House to work with Chief of Staff John Sununu and Deputy Chief of Staff Andy Card. She left the White House in early 1992 to serve as executive assistant to Andy, the newly appointed secretary of the Department of Transportation. She followed the Bushes to Houston in 1993, where she served as President Bush's director of correspondence. She was in charge of invitations and RSVPs for the funeral. She lives in Houston with her husband, Jim, and their three dogs—including Mrs. Bush's two dogs, Bibi and Mini-Me.

Sage, Mary: A full-time volunteer on President Bush's 1992 campaign, Mary joined the staff first as a volunteer, then became the part-time receptionist and the office administrator, overseeing technology issues and serving as the liaison with the federal government oversight agency. She oversaw the ticketing system for the funeral and assisted with RSVPs.

Volunteers: You will see many references in the book to the office volunteers. When the office closed, they were, in alphabetical order: Carolyn Anglum, Melza Barr, Danna Burkett, Barbara Comee, Tina McClellan, Caroline Pierce, Meredith Powers, Mickey Schwab, Janis Sullivan, Lorelei Sullivan, and Margaret Voelkel. Longtime volunteers Annyce Duffin and Susan Mowry had retired. President Bush's great friend Jack Steel was the dean of the volunteers until his death in 1996. Some of the other deceased A-listers: Marjorie Arsht, Betty Baker, Ellie Bering, Dot Burghard, Beverly Chadd, Nancy Crouch, Ida Fahey, Mary Louise Knowlton, Alicia Lee, Willie McCullough, Kerry McGee, Barbara Patton, and Marianne Sawyer.

My Siblings (from oldest to youngest)

Aulbur, Millie: Millie is a teacher turned lawyer. For the twenty-three years prior to her retirement, she was the director of citizenship education for the Missouri Bar, which was the perfect blend of lawyer and teacher. She now does volunteer law work for the Samaritan Center. She is married to Mark, and they have two children and four grandchildren. They live in Jefferson City, Missouri.

Heppermann, JoAnn: JoAnn practiced law for several years in Louisville, Kentucky, where she lives with her husband, Ken. They own, race, and syndicate thoroughbred racehorses. JoAnn is active in Rotary and currently serves as district governor. JoAnn and Ken have two sons and three grandchildren.

Becker, Edward: He practiced law for nearly ten years before entering seminary to become a Catholic priest. Ordained just before his fortieth birthday, he is the pastor of Our Lady of Guadalupe in La Habra, California. His sisters call him Eddie; his parishioners call him Father Ed; President and Mrs. Bush called him Father Eddie and were very supportive of his second calling as a Catholic priest.

Places, Things, and Pets

All the Best: Instead of writing an autobiography, President Bush published in 1998 a book of letters written during his lifetime: *All the Best, George Bush: My Life in Letters and Other Writings*. The original idea was to do a coffee-table book with some of his more memorable and historically important letters with photos and commentary. But when I started my research to find those letters, I realized he was such a prolific letter writer, we could tell his entire life story, starting from when he was eighteen years old. The book was reissued with a new chapter of letters in 2013.

The Dogs: Millie, Ranger, Sadie, Bibi, Mini-Me, Sully.

Fidelity: The name of President Bush's powerboat, which he kept in Kennebunkport, Maine. *Fidelity 1*, the boat he had when he was vice president and president, is now on display at the George Bush Library. The older President Bush got, the faster his boats got. *Fidelity 1* was a cigarette boat with two 280-horsepower engines. His last boat, *Fidelity 5*, was a Fountain boat with three 300-horsepower engines.

The George & Barbara Bush Foundation: Headquartered at Texas A&M in College Station, Texas, the foundation is dedicated to preserving the historic legacies of President and Mrs. Bush by supporting and promoting education and service-oriented programs at the George H. W. Bush Presidential Library and Museum and the Bush School of Government and Public Service at Texas A&M University. The foundation is the successor to the George H. W. Bush Library Foundation.

The George H. W. Bush Presidential Library and Museum:
Opening in 1997 on the campus of Texas A&M in College Station,
Texas, the library and museum are part of the National Archives. All of
President Bush's presidential papers, and most of his personal ones, are
housed in the library. The Bushes are buried on the library grounds. In
this book, when I talk about the library, I mean this library.

The George Bush School of Government and Public Service:
Part of the library center, the school also opened in 1997 and is part
of Texas A&M University. The Bush School offers master's degrees
in International Affairs, International Policy, and Public Service and
Administration, plus an online executive degree in Public Service and
Administration.

Walker's Point: President and Mrs. Bush's summer home in Kennebunkport, Maine. It was purchased by President Bush's maternal
grandfather, George Herbert Walker, in 1900. Shortly before he became
vice president of the United States, President Bush bought it from the
estate of his uncle Herbie Walker, which prevented his widow from sell-
ing it to the Howard Johnson hotel chain. Walker's Point is now owned
by the five Bush children.

THE MAN
I KNEW

PROLOGUE

O ne night in 2012, Margaret Tutwiler—a former ambassador and top aide to former secretary of state James Baker—called me at home to ask if I knew anything about President Bush's longtime friend, Prince Bandar of Saudi Arabia, being assassinated by the Syrians. There were rumors everywhere, but she could not confirm. She asked if I could "check my sources."

What she really wanted was for me to call the CIA, which maintained a special relationship with President Bush. After all, he once was the top boss there, and CIA headquarters in McLean, Virginia, is named the George Bush Center for Intelligence.

So I called, and my point of contact told me they were aware of the rumors; they were trying to confirm; they had "boots on the ground," checking sources.

By noon the next day we had heard nothing. Then Margaret called to update me that the French press was reporting that Prince Bandar had indeed been assassinated.

This was tough news to break to President Bush. Prince Bandar had been the Saudi ambassador to the United States from 1985 until 2003. They were very close, and I knew President Bush would take this news hard.

We were sitting outside President Bush's office in Kennebunkport, enjoying the weather and going over some work, when I told him. I explained that the CIA had not yet confirmed that Bandar was dead but feared it was true, since no one had seen or heard from Bandar in months.

Then of course he had an idea.

"Did you think about calling him?" he asked me.

The answer would be NO. It never occurred to me to call and ask Bandar if he was dead or alive.

"Well, let's get him on the phone."

I hollered through an open window to his aide, Jim Appleby, and asked him to get Bandar on the phone. Jim leaned out the window and mouthed to me, "Haven't you told him?!"

"Yes, I told him," I assured Jim. "Ring his cell phone."

A few minutes later an incredulous Jim leaned out the window again, saying, "Prince Bandar on line one."

President Bush picked up the phone and literally asked his friend, "Hey, Bandar, dead or alive? Everyone here thinks you are dead." At some point, he covered the phone's mouthpiece and whispered to me, "He's alive!"

Yes, I got that.

As it turns out, Bandar knew the Syrians were trying to kill him, so he was in hiding but safe.

When the call was over, President Bush rang his friends James Baker and Brent Scowcroft and assured them Bandar was alive. Then he turned to me and said, "See, Jean, that's the best way to figure these things out. If you aren't sure if someone is dead or alive, call them. And if they answer, they are alive."

And with that he triumphantly drove off on his golf cart, on his way to the house for lunch. His work here was done.

A few hours later, the very apologetic CIA officer called to tell me they still had been unable to confirm the rumor, but they feared it was true. I took a deep breath and told her Bandar was indeed alive.

"How would you know that?" she asked.

"Because President Bush called him," I replied. "Bandar confirmed he was alive."

There was a long pause, and she said, "We have to put that man back on payroll."

That was the day I knew I had to write a book.

CHAPTER ONE

THE MORNING AFTER

George H. W. Bush once said to a friend who was bemoaning the fact he had been fired: "I know how you feel. I was fired by the American people. It hurt."

Then he said, "It will be okay."

As it turned out for the forty-first president of the United States, it really was okay, because he made it so.

Not that it was easy.

President Bush could never really describe how it felt to go, literally overnight, from being the most important and powerful person in the world to a private citizen. You lose not only your power, but also your house, your plane, and a large, devoted staff.

How does it feel when the last strains of "Hail to the Chief" fade away?

The first word that comes to mind is "devastating."

For President Bush, it did not help that in early 1991, after his successful campaign to free Kuwait from Iraq, his approval ratings hit 91 percent, unheard of for a sitting president. So what happened after Operation Desert Storm ended? How did he lose his reelection bid to Bill Clinton, the governor of Arkansas, who at the beginning of the 1992 campaign wasn't even a Democratic front-runner?

Depending on whom you ask, the reasons range from the third-party candidacy of Ross Perot; the eleventh-hour Iran–Contra indictments; his breaking the "no new taxes" pledge during the 1990 budget crisis; a momentary economic downturn and credit crunch; and the fact that the Republicans had held the White House for twelve years. Many voters felt it was time for a change.

And of course it didn't help that President Bush had begun 1992 with the unfortunate incident of throwing up on the prime minister of Japan during a state visit. As it turns out, he had the stomach flu and had tried to power through the dinner. Unfortunately, Mother Nature prevailed.

Determined to leave the office he cherished with honor, President Bush put this handwritten and now well-known note in the top drawer of his desk in the Oval Office:

January 20, 1993

Dear Bill,

When I walked into this office just now I felt the same sense of wonder and respect that I felt four years ago. I know you will feel that, too.

I wish you great happiness here. I never felt the loneliness some Presidents have described.

There will be very tough times, made even more difficult by criticism you may not think is fair. I'm not a very good one to give advice; but just don't let the critics discourage you or push you off course.

You will be our President when you read this note. I wish you well. I wish your family well.

Your success now is our country's success. I am rooting hard for you.

Good luck—

George

With that, President Bush returned to Houston and to private life.

The changes were abrupt.

There was no household staff. No coffee waiting in the morning. No meals on the table. No schedule.

No nuclear treaties to negotiate. No crises to solve. No cabinet meetings.

It was a rough beginning.

Mrs. Bush loved telling the story of how one day early on she was attempting to make a vegetarian smoothie for then nine-year-old granddaughter Lauren, when the top came off the blender, and suddenly carrots and tomatoes were dripping from the kitchen ceiling.

Somehow that very same day, she managed to knock over a large jar of spaghetti sauce that President Bush had bought on his first of many visits to Sam's Club.

They ordered pizza.

Before we go on, I have to share this side note about the Bushes' love affair with Sam's Club: They became frequent visitors to the store, and despite the fact it was just the two of them, they bought everything in bulk. (There still may be Cheetos left over from those early visits.) I once went with Mrs. Bush, and as she pushed her flatbed cart around the store, I could tell people were amazed to see her there. I was an eyewitness on that visit to a habit that she developed where she told people who asked if she was Barbara Bush: "No, I am much younger and prettier."

But the best Sam's Club story ever, as told by Mrs. Bush, is the day she needed to buy some copies of her autobiography, *Barbara Bush: A Memoir*, which she had started writing almost as soon as they left the White House and which was published in 1994. A few months after it came out, Mrs. Bush had given away all her copies, so she decided to buy some from Sam's. There were none in the book section, but the clerk offered to check in the back. Much to Mrs. Bush's embarrassment, the clerk got on the loudspeaker and said, "Mrs. Bush is here and wants to buy her own book. Do we have any left?"

★   ★   ★

On January 22, President Bush jotted a note to Senator Bob Dole—once a political rival and now a good friend—thanking him for all his support the last four years. He ended the note with this observation: "Listen, I'm only a two-day expert but private life doesn't seem bad at all. Barbara can cook and I find I can walk the dogs OK."

A few weeks later, he wrote this note to columnist Philip Terzian with the *Providence Journal*, who had just written a very flattering editorial:

February 4, 1993

Dear Philip,

. . . I am now back in private life keeping my pledge to get active in the grandchild business. I am staying away from the head table, for the most part, and I am out of the interview business. Let history be the judge without my pushing and pulling . . .

I can't say [the election] didn't hurt, but now it's different. Barbara is way out ahead of me. She is writing away and even though she dropped a $3.00 jar of sauce and splattered it all across our tiny kitchenette she is proving once again to be a fine cook. It's far better than microwaving it. I am the dish man. I rinse the plates and put them in the washer. Almost simultaneously I load our coffee machine, and then we walk the dogs. And along the way we count our blessings.

GB

★   ★   ★

President Bush went to work every day in his new office in Houston, mainly to answer the mail that was coming in at the rate of seven hundred letters a day. He started planning his presidential library, to be built on the campus of Texas A&M University in College Station, Texas. He and his former national security adviser, Brent Scowcroft, started working on their joint book project about foreign policy, *A World Transformed*. (President Bush's draft of chapter 1 was five hundred pages. General Scowcroft's version of chapter 1 was longer. They hired someone to help.)

He became more active with the University of Texas MD Anderson Cancer Center, agreeing to join the Board of Visitors and eventually serving as chairman; and he became chairman of the Eisenhower Fellowships leadership program.

He and Mrs. Bush were building a house on an empty lot they had owned for many years. For now, they were staying in the house of a friend, just down the street. The neighbors were supportive and excited to welcome the Bushes home, except for one small problem: tourists. When a busload of them got out and tried to take photos of Mrs. Bush walking their dog, Millie, early one morning, everyone had had enough. Without a lot of coaxing, the Texas legislature passed a new law that said in part: Cities can "regulate and restrict access to streets, avenues, alleys, and boulevards in the municipality on which the dwelling of a former president of the United States is located." In other words, they put up a gate.

Except for those small hiccups, Mrs. Bush was loving some of their newfound freedom. She gave up her Secret Service detail (they would return a few years later, after 9/11) and was driving for the first time in twelve years. President Bush bought her a blue Mercury Sable station wagon to cruise around Houston and surprised her that summer with a dark blue Trans Am convertible in Kennebunkport. She loved it, and said she felt thirty years younger driving around town in what their son Marvin nicknamed the "Batmobile." There was one small problem:

Mrs. Bush couldn't see out the windows very well. I once was riding with her when we came to a stop sign and stopped. She got out of the car and looked both ways before getting back in and proceeding. Yes, it was terrifying.

The next year, they replaced the Trans Am with a small Chevrolet convertible with better visibility. And a few years later, President Bush bought her a Smart Car.

President Bush started working on his rather lengthy bucket list, doing things like attending baseball spring training with his oldest son, George W., then a co-owner of the Texas Rangers; fishing in Canada; and attending the Kentucky Derby.

He traveled a great deal, both at home and overseas, beginning to give what he called "white-collar crime" speeches. In other words, he received a speaker's fee.

But for the most part President Bush was adrift. He just wasn't sure what to do with himself.

Maybe for that reason, he decided being literally adrift was not a bad thing. He checked off another item on his bucket list when in early February he surprised Mrs. Bush with the news they were going on a cruise. They set sail from Miami on February 13 aboard the *Regal Princess*, which President Bush had seen advertised on TV. They only had to share the ship with sixteen hundred other passengers, all of whom—according to the Bushes—were just a little surprised to see the recently departed residents of the White House on their Caribbean cruise. They were so mobbed the captain invited them to eat their meals in his cabin. But it's possible the stark reality of their new life didn't really hit home until early one morning when, after working out and taking a steam bath, President Bush walked out of the sauna stark naked to find a fellow cruiser waiting to take his photo. Thankfully, the wannabe photographer asked permission; the former president said politely but firmly, "Hell, yes, I mind if you take my picture. Do you mind waiting?" (Mrs. Bush had a similar story, which involved buying "personal products" at the drugstore.)

President Bush told this story to friend and author George Plimpton, who interviewed President Bush about a year later for a piece for the *New York Times Magazine*. President Bush admitted to him it had been a tough year:

"[I miss] the decision-making, the actual involvement and trying to make things happen. I liked that. I liked it a lot. When it's gone, it takes a while to get over it. You sit there and there are no decisions; nothing to sign; nobody wants to know what you think on this, or that. It was just a cold-turkey shift."

But those of us who lived through that first year didn't have to read the Plimpton article to know he was having a hard time. Mrs. Bush wrote in her diary that she was amazed how little he complained, but she knew he was hurting. She especially noted how quiet he was.

All that hurt came pouring out in April when President Bush's dog Ranger died. He was devastated. Ranger had been one of the puppies born at the White House to Millie. Initially, they had given Ranger to Marvin, but he thoughtfully gave him back to his dad when he realized how attached he was to Ranger.

President Bush admitted, and Mrs. Bush confirmed, he cried more over Ranger than he did when he lost the election, and more than when his beloved mother died a few weeks after the election. His theory was that all his collected grief came pouring out when, on top of everything else, he lost his dog.

While on the cruise, President Bush, in an attempt to put aside his lost feeling and figure out what was next for him, wrote a memo to himself. I saw it for the first time while going through his "personal" files after he died. Here are some highlights from the five-page memo:

Memo on Life after the Presidency
I know I must begin to sort things out.

From the Love Boat here's my latest thinking:

a. *Make some money. BPB has signed up for a lot of money on her book. I want to make enough money so Bar can finish her life without changing her lifestyle. That means so she can keep both K'port and Houston. That she will not be burdened unduly if I have a long illness. I will make that money by giving some speeches . . .*

b. *I want to see the Library built and the school of Public Service up and running. The library should showcase our foreign policy success, but it is important that the following domestic areas be properly presented:*

> *Education*
> *Points of Light*
> *Environment Record*
> *Economy—spending caps*
> *Housing—ownership*

c. *I am very serious about the grandchild business. I want to see them grow. I want to be there, take them places, help them, lift them up. I want to help Jeb and George if they go ahead in politics.*

d. *Helping others. I want to do something worthwhile. Herbert Hoover, it seems, drove himself and did a lot. I want to select one or two areas and try to really help.*

e. *I want to stay fit and have fun doing that. Golf, but not on the pro-am name-dropping circuit. Tennis, for as long as my legs hold out. Hunting and yes plenty of fishing.*

Things not to do:

> *Get in the way of Pres. Clinton.*
>
> *Be a kingmaker or try to. That means turning down a lot of political invitations. It means trying to avoid joint letter signing with former Presidents on some requests.*
>
> *Cheapen the Presidency. That means avoiding money grabbing.*
>
> *Trying to influence how history will treat me . . . I want to avoid the many interviews, appearances, etc. to "set the record straight."*

★   ★   ★

I was watching all this unfold mostly from the sidelines, having moved to Houston to help Mrs. Bush with her memoirs. My job was to do research and fact-check, read and/or listen to her diaries (most of them were still on tape), and then edit what she wrote. I was a bit of a stepchild in the new Office of George Bush, as I worked on a card table crammed into President Bush's tiny office kitchen. Despite the cramped quarters, I didn't mind terribly as I looked out the window at Houston's picturesque Galleria skyline; and at least a couple of times a day, when he was in town, the former president wandered into his kitchen to make coffee or get a glass of milk.

It was how we became friends.

During the White House years, I was one of Mrs. Bush's deputy press secretaries—a fun, work-heavy, but low-on-the-totem-pole kind of job. I had never interacted with the president except in photo receiving lines at the annual Christmas party. I did remind him in one of our post–White House coffee sessions in the kitchen that we had met before, not only during the White House years but when I was a reporter at *USA Today*. He looked at me a little quizzically, and then I reminded him I was the reporter on the campaign trail who asked every single candidate in 1988 this question: If you were an animal, what kind of animal would you want to be? The question became infamous—and not in a good way. (It was my editor's idea.)

Then, of course, President Bush remembered, and I knew he was wondering how on earth I had ended up at a card table in his kitchen.

(For the record, he wanted to be a hunting dog. And although I've never been given credit for this, I do think it's possible Michael Dukakis lost the election that year because he wanted to be a fish: an Atlantic cod.)

On the other hand, I had gotten to know Mrs. Bush quite well on the campaign trail, since *USA Today* convinced both her and Kitty Dukakis to write a weekly column for the paper. I was their editor, a task that didn't thrill me at first but which I learned to love. After the election, I was shocked when I was offered a job in Mrs. Bush's press office. I wasn't sure whether I should take it until my father asked me what the hell was wrong with me. As usual, he was right. That began the trail that took me from *USA Today*, to the White House, to Houston, and then to Kennebunkport in the summer of 1993.

I went with the Bushes to Maine that summer so Mrs. Bush and I could continue working on the book. As nice as it was to escape Houston's heat and humidity, it was a tough summer.

Certainly, we would do great fun things like go out on President Bush's famous powerboat, *Fidelity*. He was rather shocked I had never been on a boat in the Atlantic Ocean, even when I told him I had grown up on a farm in Missouri. My family didn't even know people who owned boats, I explained. He taught me how to fish, which I never mastered.

But the Bushes were still hurting. Family friend and former staffer Chase Untermeyer remembers visiting and finding the former president really down. When George Plimpton asked him what he did in Maine that first summer, President Bush's answer was heartbreaking: "I just sat there and watched the tide come in and go out."

Mrs. Bush also would get down—probably more from worrying about her husband than anything else. Her aide, Peggy Swift,[1] and I had to call her best friend, Betsy Heminway, to come over one afternoon after Mrs. Bush locked herself in her bedroom after quarreling with a family member.

One day, when President Bush's beloved boat broke off its mooring and crashed on the rocks during a big storm, I jotted down in my sporadically kept journal exactly what he told us: "I lost the election, my mother died, my dog died, and my boat crashed. There's not much else left that can happen to me this year."

---

1. Now Peggy White, who lives in Chicago with her husband, Brian.

As for the staff,[2] we tried to be there when we were needed but also wanted to stay out of the way since we worked on Walker's Point. My and Peggy's office was a tiny guestroom; Michael, Rose, and Linda worked downstairs from where the housekeeper lived upstairs in the old caretaker's cottage. Sometimes it was hard to figure out where we should be when. (It didn't help that I was unhappy with where I was living—the upstairs of a small cottage owned by a woman who was a little crazy, made more so when she broke her arm and I literally was helping her in and out of her bra every day.)

We seriously thought about getting T-shirts made that said: "I survived the summer of 1993."

Years later, in 2000, President Bush put into writing more of his thoughts about that first year out of office. He wrote a piece called "10 Rules for Former Presidents" for his former speechwriter and good friend, author Christopher Buckley. Chris—or Christo, as President Bush called him—occasionally asked President Bush to write an essay for *Forbes FYI* magazine, a supplement to *Forbes*.

---

2. Besides Peggy Swift and me, that included President Bush's aide, Michael Dannenhauer; and Chief of Staff Rose Zamaria, who switched out after a few weeks with Linda Poepsel, head of President Bush's correspondence team.

1. *Get out of Dodge—fast. You're history on that cold January day. So be pleasant about it all. Smile a lot. Try not to wave to the huge inaugural crowd too much. They're there to see the new guy . . .*

2. *As you fly back home on Air Force One look around. Take a shower . . . Grab a few napkins and some notepads and Life Savers with the Presidential seal on them . . . Lie down on the bed in the President's cabin because 34E on the commercial airlines is quite different . . .*

3. *When you get off Air Force One wave from the top of the steps. A TV camera from the local station will probably be there. "How does it feel to be home?" [the reporter] will ask. "Great to be back!" And you look ahead and you try not to think what it used to be like just four or five hours before. You'll hurt a little but that will go away—sooner than you might think.*

4. *. . . Don't try to shape history by writing op-ed pieces all the time or by criticizing your successor. If you really want to make news and get back on TV you'll find the best way to do that is to criticize your successor . . . Don't! . . . If you really feel strongly about something, drop your successor a line but don't leak it to the press. The important thing is to quit worrying about your legacy. It's up to others to decide that.*

5. *When you're out walking your dog, try not to argue when you see the guy down the street who always insists on giving you his views on every issue. Oh, you've got to listen, but it is better to nod silently and not disagree when he says, "You should've invaded Cuba and gotten the CIA to knock off Saddam Hussein" . . . smile pleasantly and try to keep moving.*

6. *Play some golf but resist telling everyone what it was like to play with Jack [Nicklaus] or Arnie [Palmer] at the course near Camp David . . . And no one wants to know how many times you had the legends of sports to the White House. (They didn't really love you. They just wanted to see the White House.)*

7. *Be nice to all autograph seekers and tourists and people who inter-rupt your dinner. After all some of them probably voted for you, and those who didn't will swear they now wish they did.*

8. *Remember the five "stay" rules:*

   a) *Stay out of the way, out of Washington, out of the news, away from press conferences, off TV.*

   b) *Stay away from bashing the national press, even those that knocked your socks off when you were President.*

   c) *Stay away from most of those yellow pad think tank events—the ones where the conference proceedings are carefully written then printed, never to be read by anyone ever again. You might want to consider the occasional world peace seminar in Bermuda but be sure the organizers get you a tee time.*

   d) *Stay away from saying "here's the way I did it." You had your chance...*

   e) *Stay well. And when you get older, resist telling everyone about which body part hurts. Drink bulk stuff, exercise, stretch, keep younger people around you. Smile a lot. Feel young at heart.*

9. *Always count your blessings. Quietly remember the wonders of the White House. Never forget the many people that helped you get there or those that worked in your administration or the dedicated civil servants who treat the White House with such respect and dig-nity while making those who live there feel "at home." Remember the majesty of the Oval Office. And as the years go by, give thanks to God for your family, your true friends, and for having given you the chance to be President of the greatest country on the face of the earth.*

10. *Hug your grandkids. If you don't have any, get some. And if by chance you have a son or daughter who has [a] chance to be Presi-dent of the USA ask yourself, "Might this really come true? Only in America!"*

CHAPTER TWO

BACK IN THE SADDLE

When Mrs. Bush's book was finished in March 1994, I prepared to return to journalism and began exploring job possibilities. President Bush called me into his office one day to tell me that his chief of staff—a woman named Rose Zamaria, who had come with him from the White House—was retiring. Rose was a bit of a legend in Bush World—she had been around since President Bush's congressional days and was also a bit of a curmudgeon. Well, a lot of a curmudgeon.

She very proudly told the story about Lesley Stahl calling to ask President Bush to come on *60 Minutes*. When Rose said, "No way," Lesley pushed back: "Doesn't the president realize we have the largest TV audience every week?"

Rose's response: "Don't you realize he doesn't give a damn about that anymore?"

President Bush had no idea who could replace Rose and asked me to stay on a bit until he figured it out. He also admitted that it was Mrs. Bush's idea.

I told him I didn't know how to be a chief of staff. I had never been anyone's boss; I had never done a budget; I had never really been in charge of anything.

He replied that he just needed a "seat warmer" until he found a permanent replacement. His winning argument was it would mean another summer in Kennebunkport, so I agreed to stay until Labor Day and would do the best I could to keep the office running.

We never talked about it again. Well, not for twenty years we didn't.

By the time I became his chief of staff, President Bush's first-year malaise had worn off. Among other reasons, I think he had just gotten bored with being down. Now he was off and running into his post-presidency with almost an idea a day on what to do next. There was too much work to do to revisit old conversations.

(Years later—maybe about five years before he died—I teased him about that conversation. I told him I had lived in fear for twenty years that he would walk into my office one day and say, "Oh, Jean. I have found a chief of staff. You can get on with your life." He did not remember that my job began as a temporary arrangement; I am not sure he believed me.)

I was not terrified, but maybe mystified. I really had no idea what I was doing. Rose, God rest her soul, left me only one file, which was some old paperwork on presidential funerals; and the only advice she gave me was to make sure there was toilet paper in President Bush's bathroom.

What made me the most nervous in the beginning was that often when I ran a meeting or was part of a conference call, everyone assumed I knew what I was doing: "Okay, if that is what Jean thinks, that must be right." They should have taken my first title, "acting chief of staff," more literally.

Nevertheless, I had no choice but to jump in with both feet. I slowly began to realize that maybe the best way to really teach someone how to swim is to throw them into the deep end.

How deep was the water? At the end of 1994, Mrs. Bush was curious about how much speaking and traveling her husband had done just that year. She knew it had been a whirlwind, but she wanted proof. So the office compiled the statistics: He gave 111 speeches, campaigned for forty-eight different candidates for the midterm elections, visited twenty-two foreign countries—two of them twice—and set foot in at least half the states.

In between his travels, he hosted lunches and dinners for everyone from heads of state to old friends; became involved in the building of his presidential library; played golf and tennis and hunted; attended baseball and football games; welcomed visitors to his home and his office; made dozens of phone calls; and wrote hundreds of notes and letters. And he had ideas.

He was back.

I found a file of old memos that reminded me just how "back" he was. I should explain that long before BlackBerrys and then smartphones made long-distance communication easier, I often faxed President Bush long "this is what is happening" memos while he was traveling, or I would have a memo with attachments waiting for him the moment he landed, putting them either in the car so he could catch up on the way home from the airport or on his bed.

In one such note from 1995, I reported the following:

- General Scowcroft, Senator Bob Dole, Representative Newt Gingrich, President Ford, and General Colin Powell had all called to talk to him about Bosnia.[1]
- The National Security Council was sending someone to brief him on Bosnia.
- His lunch with the president of Angola was set.
- There would be a work session for him and General Scowcroft on their book during an upcoming trip to Washington, DC.
- He still needed a fourth for golf on December 18.
- The date was set for the annual office Christmas get-together.
- David Frost wanted to talk to him about an idea.
- The husband of one of his cousins had died.

---

1. President Clinton had decided the United States needed to intervene in the civil war that was ravaging the republics that once made up Yugoslavia.

- Marlin Fitzwater checked in.
- While he was gone, we had programmed his home phone for speed dialing. (In retrospect, this was a mistake on my part.)

Yes, he was busy. And for the most part, he loved it.

Politically, it had taken some coaxing to get him back into the game. He still thought of himself as the man who had lost and questioned the sanity of any candidate who asked for his help. But there was one area in which he could help a lot: raising money. He never liked doing it for himself but enjoyed doing it for others, especially for friends. So as he would say, he suited up.

Two candidates were of more interest than the others: his two oldest sons.

George W. was running for governor of Texas, Jeb for governor of Florida. Both were running against incumbents: Ann Richards was the popular governor of Texas who took to calling George W. "shrub" during the campaign; and in Florida, Jeb was running against Lawton Chiles, who seemed more vulnerable.

The day George W. told his parents that he was running, Mrs. Bush infamously told him he could not possibly beat Ann Richards.

The Bushes campaigned their hearts out for their sons, bouncing between Florida and Texas. President Bush especially focused on private fund-raising events, as his sons wanted to run for office outside of their father's very long shadow. Mrs. Bush did a lot more public events, often with her sons, and it was during this campaign that George W. began to tell audiences, "I have my daddy's eyes and my mother's mouth."

Having his sons running for governor played a big role in healing President Bush's wounds from 1992. He knew in his heart that if he had been reelected, they would still be on the political sidelines, waiting for their dad to exit the stage. His loss had opened the door for them. As always, he managed to find that silver lining.

As the election neared, George W. was surging in the polls, but Jeb ran into a big problem the week before the election: Approximately 750,000 Florida senior citizens received robocalls falsely claiming that Jeb Bush would cut Social Security. It later came out that the call was organized by Governor Chiles's supporters, for which he apologized and claimed no knowledge. But the election was over.

I was traveling with President Bush on a campaign swing for other candidates when Jeb's campaign manager, Sally Bradshaw, called to tell President Bush the bad news about the robocalls. We had just landed in Oklahoma City after doing five events in two days. This would be number six, his last. I watched him sitting on a folding chair backstage, waiting to be introduced into a large arena in Oklahoma City, and I worried there was absolutely no way he could go out there. He was devastated and exhausted. I had never seen him look that way and was convinced he had nothing left to give. My heart was breaking as I tried to figure out how to handle the situation.

Then his name was announced. He stood up and literally shook it off. He straightened his tie, stiffened his spine, and walked onstage to a roaring crowd and gave a wonderful speech for J. C. Watts, a candidate for Congress.

I was just beginning to appreciate what that man was made of.

With two sons running, the Bushes decided it was best to stay in Houston election night. They came to the office, where they could watch the returns on multiple TVs and, if necessary, we could quickly call a press conference. When it was confirmed that George W. had won and Jeb had lost—by the smallest margin in Florida election history—President Bush did a live press conference and then talked remotely with Tom Brokaw of NBC News. As he told the press that night, "The joy is in Texas but our hearts are in Florida."

Mrs. Bush headed home and to bed. President Bush went into his office and closed the door. He was behind that closed door forever, and the Secret Service began to question me if I should go in and check on him. I did not. I knew he was quietly licking his wounds.

It was a bittersweet night for the family: great joy for one son, and grief for another. George W. found out about his brother's loss as he rode the elevator on his way to declare his own victory. That wasn't easy, either.

But the story has a happy ending.

President Bush wrote this letter to George W. the morning he was inaugurated as governor in January 1995, which George W. shared in his book about his dad, *41: A Portrait of My Father.*

Dear George,

These cufflinks are my most treasured possession. They were given to me by Mum and Dad on June 9th, that day in 1943 when I got my Navy wings at Corpus Christi. I want you to have them now; for, in a sense, though you won your Air Force wings from flying those jets, you are again "getting your wings" as you take the oath of office as our Governor . . .

You have given us more than we ever could have deserved. You have sacrificed for us. You have given us your unwavering loyalty and devotion. Now it is your turn.

Devotedly,
Dad

And four years later, when George W. was reelected in a landslide, Jeb was elected and went on to serve two terms as governor. Jeb will always have a special place in the hearts of Florida residents for, among other accomplishments, leading and rebuilding the state through eight major hurricanes and four tropical storms during sixteen months in 2004 and 2005.

President Bush, of course, fretted about all those storms. It seemed every time he turned on CNN there was his son telling the people in Florida to evacuate. He constantly asked me for storm updates and my opinion on just how bad it was. Growing up on a farm where the weather always mattered, combined with the fact I briefly covered weather at *USA Today*, I already knew my stuff. But helping President Bush survive Florida's extraordinary and historical succession of hurricanes made me an expert. I could give the National Hurricane Center a run for their money.

In his last days of being governor, Jeb asked his dad to come and be the guest speaker at the lecture series the governor hosted for legislative and executive branch leaders. After a minute of speaking, President Bush began to weep and could not go on, his pride in his son was so deep.

President Bush would want me to add here that his pride in all five of his children—George W., Jeb, Neil, Marvin, and Doro—and his pride in their children, was deep. He wrote this in August 2001 for his friend Carl Cannon's book, *The Pursuit of Happiness in Times of War*:

I no longer pursue [happiness], for it is mine. Pride in my family guarantees that happiness. That one son is President of the United States might say it all; but it doesn't. Our Governor son in Florida is a part of this "happiness," because through him and the President I can still live and be a part of the vast political scene. But my happiness stems, too, from our other two sons and our only daughter, from all five spouses and from our 14 grandkids . . . I have found happiness, and it will be mine until the day I die.

CHAPTER THREE

A BUMPY RIDE TO THE WHITE HOUSE

There is a myth about the Bush family that when the five children were young, they sat around the dinner table and plotted the Bush family political takeover of the United States. Legend has it that George and Barbara Bush decided their four sons would move to four different states, run for governor or U.S. Senate, and then eventually at least one would run for president. They even used a map of the United States and a flowchart to track their progress.

None of that was true. Not even a little.

As Mrs. Bush often joked on the campaign trail for George W. and Jeb, she just hoped they would grow up, much less be a governor or a president.

So it was not by design that two sons became governors of their states and one became president of the United States. It was because they had, as their father called it, "the fire in the belly" to serve.

However, it would be a monumental understatement to say that President Bush was thrilled in the summer of 1999 when George W. made it official and announced he was running for president.

Let's just say his father was all-in.

Mrs. Bush worried about George W.'s twin teenage daughters, Jenna and Barbara. As the wife of a president and mother of five, no one knew better the tension and pressure on the family of the leader of the Free World. But once the decision was made, she was all-in, too.

The Bushes campaigned hard for their son, together or separately, doing numerous events between June 1999 and Election Day in November 2000.

However, there were hints on the campaign trail about the complications that might lie ahead if their son won.

For example, Karl Rove[1] called me during the campaign to say that President Bush absolutely had to stop calling Governor Bush "my boy" in his stump speech. It was never in his written remarks, but as he veered off his text to speak from his heart, he inevitably would become emotional and talk about "this boy of mine." What father wouldn't? But the media ridiculed the term and—given that the candidate was trying to convince voters he was the one who could make the tough decisions in times of national crises—well, "boy" didn't quite work.

When I told President Bush he needed to lose the "boy," he understood but was just a little hurt.

There were also the inevitable comparisons between father and son, usually not flattering to one or the other. President Bush had dealt with that issue back in 1998 during his sons' gubernatorial campaigns. Here are excerpts from a note he wrote them both:

---

1. Karl was George W.'s chief political adviser during his gubernatorial and presidential campaigns and served as a senior adviser and deputy chief of staff in the White House. President Bush first met Karl when he headed College Republicans while President Bush was chairman of the Republican National Committee from 1973 to 1974.

Dear George and Jeb,

... Your Mother tells me that both of you have mentioned to her your concerns about some of the political stories—the ones that seem to put me down and make me seem irrelevant—that contrast you favorably to a father who had no vision and who was but a place holder in the broader scheme of things...

Do not worry when you see the stories that compare you favorably to a Dad for whom English was a second language and for whom the word destiny meant nothing...

At some point both of you may want to say "Well, I don't agree with my Dad on that point" or "Frankly I think Dad was wrong on that." Do it. Chart your own course, not just on the issues but on defining yourselves. No one will ever question your love of family—your devotion to your parents... nothing can ever be written that will drive a wedge between us—nothing at all...

Go on out there and, as they say in the oil fields, "Show 'em a clean one."

This from your very proud and devoted,

Dad

The "shadow" issue always seemed to be hovering in 2000, even after George W. won enough primary votes to claim the nomination. As planning got underway for the Republican convention in Philadelphia, one of the big questions on the table was: Should President Bush speak? Typically, former presidents are invited to give remarks at their party's nominating conventions. President Bush had done so in 1996, when Senator Dole was nominated. But the campaign decided it would not work to have President Bush give remarks at the convention since one of their challenges, again, was keeping George W. out of his father's shadow.

President Bush not only readily agreed it was the right thing to do— he was relieved. He said all the "formers" hate the "trot the old guy out" night at the convention. But to really make this work, President Ford also should not speak. I was tasked with calling Ford's chief of staff, Penny Circle, to deliver the news. The Ford folks were great team players and thought it was best for the two former presidents to sit this one out. Instead, convention organizers honored the two former presidents with a video about their lives and accomplishments.

Although they did not appear onstage, President and Mrs. Bush worked tirelessly at the convention, attending delegation breakfasts and receptions, anchoring the family box every single night, and doing a ton of interviews. They were, bluntly put, the hottest ticket in town.

Unfortunately, their love for their son sometimes got the best of them—or maybe I should say—their tongues. After the convention, I sent this report to the staff in Houston:

"Less than 30 minutes after his arrival, George Bush made the now-infamous statement to Jamie Gangel,[2] who I love but is now banned from our office for life (or at least this year): 'In 30 days I'm going to tell the American people what I really think of Billy Clinton as a human being.' When he said it, I knew that life

---

2. Now of CNN but then a reporter for NBC's *Today* show.

as we knew it was over. Yes, it caused a huge firestorm. Gian-Carlo[3] and I were hounded by media and were afraid to leave our rooms. Karl Rove called and asked me what kind of dope I was smoking. Actually, that call came after the *Good Morning America* interview, which we scheduled to fix the *TODAY* show mess, during which Barbara Bush announced that Al Gore had no character, at which point President Bush turned to her and said, 'OK, you're now in a hell of a lot more trouble than I was yesterday.' Karen Hughes[4] called, too, after that interview and was calling at the request of the Governor who also wanted to know what we were smoking at our hotel.

"Don't tell the outside world, but the Bushes have been locked in the bathroom ever since. The people you might see occasionally on TV pretending to be the Bushes are not really them but some character actors I hired to play the part until November. Not only can I not trust them, but they can't trust themselves. The problem is the mail is running 2-1 in their favor...Maybe I should let them out now."

You could say these slips of the tongue foreshadowed things to come. In 2010, when CNN's Larry King asked Mrs. Bush what she thought of Sarah Palin, she answered: "I sat next to her once. I thought she was beautiful. I think she's very happy in Alaska. And I hope she stays there." In 2013, when *Today*'s Matt Lauer asked her if she supported Jeb running for president, she said: "There are other people out there that are very qualified, and we've had enough Bushes." For the record—no one campaigned harder for Governor Bush when he ran in 2016 than his mother.

---

3. Gian-Carlo Peressutti was President Bush's personal aide in 2000.

4. Karen was counselor to the president from 2001 to 2002 before returning to Texas for a few years. In 2005, President George W. Bush named her undersecretary of state for public diplomacy and public affairs.

★   ★   ★

The 2000 convention was a bit of an awakening for the entire Bush clan. There was some disappointment from the Bushes' grandchildren that on the last night of the convention, they would not be invited to rush onto the stage, as they did in 1988 and 1992 when their grandfather accepted the nomination. I reminded them that at their grandfather's conventions, his nieces and nephews were not invited up onstage, just his immediate family. This year they were the nieces and nephews; it made sense that only their cousins Jenna and Barbara would join their parents onstage. You could say it was an "aha" moment.

It wasn't just the family who had to get used to a few new realities. Some of President Bush's former White House staff envisioned brand-new opportunities for themselves, including jobs with big titles—such as Mr. Ambassador or Senior Adviser. They were excited at the possibility of going back into a Bush administration.

Again, I patiently explained that Governor Bush had his own team, his own friends, his own supporters. Yes, their help and support were appreciated, but there could be no promise of jobs or ambassadorships. Most understood; some did not.

Somewhere in here was when a former Bush White House staffer told me that I was getting the reputation as the Bush family consigliere, delivering news that was not always welcomed. Given that "consigliere" is a Mafia term, I wasn't thrilled with the designation, but as time went on, it became partially true. And so I would like to say for the record that I never left a horse's head in someone's bed.

The Bushes both admitted that during the 2000 election and then throughout their son's presidency, it was much harder to hear their son being criticized than themselves. I wrote this email to my siblings[5] on Labor Day, 2000:

---

5. A list of my siblings is in the Glossary of Names.

"I spent most of my weekend with George Bush. I will confess to all of you that I'm not sure I can handle another Bush election loss, but that's incredibly selfish of me. This is after all not about me. Anyway, all sorts of feelings from 1992 came creeping back this weekend and I'm doing my best to fight them but that was such a miserable time and I don't want any of us to go through that again. My heart just breaks for President Bush who is struggling so. I am worried to death about him. I came in yesterday morning knowing he would be in the office so the two of us just sat here for 4 hours pretending to work but mainly talking about the election. Then I went fishing with him for 3 hours in cold, wet, gray weather in rough seas. We caught one mackerel. We tossed and floated around the Atlantic casting one line after another, running around talking to other fishermen, crazy people all. I know many people would pay thousands of dollars for the privilege of fishing with George Bush, but I would have loved to have been home warm, dry, and watching TBS's movie marathon. But I truly feel my No. 1 job this fall is to support him in any way I can and if that means fishing for three hours in miserable weather, so be it…"

The debates, during both the primary season and the general election, were especially torturous affairs. Mrs. Bush decided not to watch and would needlepoint while President Bush listened through headphones. I watched several debates over the years with them and it was tough duty.

Like most Americans, my lasting memory of the 2000 campaign was election night. It was a night of incredible highs and lows. I had flown to Austin, Texas, with President and Mrs. Bush earlier on Election Day. They hung out with their son and Laura in the governor's mansion; I hung out with Karl and the campaign team at their headquarters.

During a big family dinner, one of the networks announced that George W. would lose Florida, and therefore the election. The family was devastated, and Jeb felt he had let his brother down. They all headed back to the governor's mansion.

What followed could be called a serious case of political whiplash.

We then got word that polls had not closed yet in the parts of Florida in the Central Time Zone, which leaned heavily Republican, so Florida was still in play.

Then the networks announced that George W. Bush had indeed won Florida and probably had won the election.

But Jeb was talking to his people in Florida, who were worried. His memory of that night: "The last county to complete the vote count was Miami Dade County. I spoke to my friend and numbers guy who said that most of the remaining votes were in Democrat precincts. But Gore called to concede, and George was ready to go outside where thousands were waiting. I tell him that he should wait, that the election is too close to call. He was, of course, upset. Then Gore called back to say he was not conceding."

Chaos ensued.

I was among the thousands waiting outside in the rain for whom we thought was the president-elect. I spent most of my time talking on the phone. What President Bush had not told me was that he had given out my cell phone number to several of his friends and told them to stay in touch with me to get up-to-date election results, and that I could even patch calls through to him. When Gore took back his concession, my phone started ringing: Brian Mulroney, the former prime minister of Canada; Drayton McLane, then owner of the Houston Astros; and Prince Bandar. John Major, the former British prime minister, called early the next morning. Whenever my phone rang, I would take a deep breath before saying hello, never sure who might be on the other end.

Around 3 a.m., that person would be the forty-first president of the United States. He wanted to know what was going on. By this time, I was back at election night headquarters with Karl and his team, who were frantically trying to figure out the same thing. I was surprised Pres-

ident Bush was calling me to get answers, as he was at the Texas governor's mansion with the candidate. "I don't know where anybody is," he
said to me. "I think everyone has gone to bed." I suggested he do the
same. He hesitated and thought about coming to the hotel. I convinced
him nothing would be resolved that night and he should go to bed.

The next morning we left for Houston, this time by motorcade
thanks to a driving rain. I had not slept at all and was hiding in the back
of the Secret Service car, hoping to nap the entire three-hour drive. The
two-car motorcade had driven about two blocks before it stopped, and
the message came back that President Bush wanted me to join them for
the ride home.

It would be among the more miserable three hours of the twenty-five
years that I was President Bush's chief of staff.

He was exhausted and frustrated. Mrs. Bush insisted on giving me
her seat next to her husband and moved to the third row so she could
stretch out and put her feet up. She furiously needlepointed away, telling
me, among other things, the bath towels in the governor's mansion were
in poor condition and Laura really needed to replace them. She never
mentioned the election.

President Bush started working the phones, calling George W., Jeb,
Karl, and Secretary Baker, who eventually would lead George W.'s
recount team in Florida. Jeb called his brother and his dad right after
he landed back in Florida and said he had just watched a Gore campaign
plane full of Democratic lawyers disembarking in Tallahassee. "They
are already ahead of us," the governor fretted. (Jeb soon would recuse
himself from having anything to do with the state's process of certifying
election results.)

The weather was horrible. President Bush was miserable. Mrs. Bush
was on another planet. I remember at one point wondering if anyone
would notice if I opened the car door and rolled out into a ditch, and
would they stop to pick me up?

When I got back to Houston, I went home instead of to the office and
wrote this email to the staff and volunteers:

"The Bushes and I got back from Austin a little while ago. Just wanted you to know they are alive and well but subdued...President Bush is dejected but trying hard not to be. Mrs. Bush is stoic. On the 3-hour drive back from Austin in the rain she told me things like, 'Jean, never buy towels that are smaller than 55 inches.' That sort of says a lot. President Bush banged away on his computer on a letter that no doubt could become chapters 1–5 of *All the Best: The Saga Continues*.[6]

"I cannot help but feel that God is testing the Bush family, the Gore family, and our country. I hope we all rise to the occasion.

"Two closing comments:

1. New York and Hillary deserve each other.[7]
2. The next time someone says to you, 'Why bother to vote? Our vote doesn't count,' cross them off your life list. I will. If they are that stupid—especially after this—they are not worthy of your time."

Ironically, just a few days after the election, on November 9, President and Mrs. Bush traveled to Washington to attend a black-tie dinner celebrating the two hundredth anniversary of the White House. When they had accepted the invitation a month or so earlier, Mrs. Bush worried that it would be a long night if George W. lost the election. I don't think she thought the current circumstances were much better. But off they went.

The Bushes said it was a lovely but odd evening. The Clintons could not have been nicer, although everyone knew they were rooting for Vice President Gore. The First Lady was in a great mood, ecstatic with her

---

6. Please see the glossary for a full explanation of *All the Best*. For the record: A later edition of the book actually did include this letter.

7. Hillary Clinton had won her bid to become a U.S. senator from New York. I am not proud of my ungracious comment and apologize to her and the state of New York. I was tired.

Senate win. Mrs. Bush was thrilled to see her dear friend Lady Bird Johnson, but she was there with her daughter Lynda Bird and her husband,
Senator Chuck Robb, who had lost his bid for reelection in Virginia.

Twenty years later, historian Michael Beschloss remembers the dinner well and shared with me this memory: "I saw President Bush in des-
ultory conversation with President Clinton around Lady Bird Johnson's
back—he caught me watching him and winked."

Mrs. Bush wrote in her diary the day after: "So there we were—a
winner (Hil), a loser (Chuck), and Mr. and Mrs. In-Between (us). It was
tense. Although I must add that the Clintons were very gracious."

The next few months were a roller coaster for the nation, but it's possible
no one found the ride bumpier than the Republican candidate's father.
Thankfully, right after the White House dinner, President Bush traveled to Spain for the opening of an MD Anderson cancer care facility in
Madrid. I was grateful he had something to do besides fret.

When he came home, we would do random things like attend mati-
nee movies to get out of the office and away from the television. I know
one movie we saw was *Best in Show*, which gave him ninety minutes of
comic relief. It had the added benefit of being a dog movie—perfect to
lift the spirits of a dog lover.

In early December, President Bush had hip replacement surgery at
the Mayo Clinic in Rochester, Minnesota. He called me from the recovery room to get a recount update and fell sound asleep and started snoring during my report.

A few days later, his doctor called to say that although it was too early
for President Bush to leave the hospital, the doctor thought he would be
better mentally if he was back in Houston. "He needs to come home,"
Dr. Bernie Morrey said with some concern.

Key to making this work was finding him a private plane—we did—
and home health care. The Bushes' wonderful internist in Houston, Dr.
Matthew Lenz, took care of the latter and was himself waiting for President Bush when they got home on a Saturday evening.

Just a few weeks later, on December 12, a Supreme Court ruling in the case of *Bush v. Gore* officially made George W. Bush the president-elect. I was watching NBC News and can still see their legal eagle reporter, Pete Williams, paging through the complicated ruling as fast as he could, trying to discern what it meant. Fairly quickly he announced it appeared that George W. Bush had won the case and therefore the election.

I quickly called the Bushes, and a very dejected President Bush answered the phone. They were watching another network, whose reporter had just said it appeared Vice President Gore had won. Not so fast, I yelled into the phone. Karl called the Bushes a short time later to confirm their son had won.

The next night, after Vice President Gore gave his concession speech, President Bush called and asked if I would get the vice president on the phone for him. I gently asked him if he thought he was the person Gore needed to talk to that night. His answer was simple: "Jean, I've been where Al Gore is. I know how he feels. I want to talk to him."

I suggested he think about it, and if he thought it was a good idea, to just call the White House switchboard. He loved the idea of cutting me—and my opinion—out as the middleman.

I then went back to my television, watching the vice president walk down the steps of the Old Executive Office Building,[8] and I could clearly see him pick up his phone as soon as he got in the car. I wondered if the caller had been President Bush. Surely not.

But a few minutes later President Bush called to report he had gotten Vice President Gore on the phone and had a very good chat. Then he said good night and hung up.

He wrote his friend Hugh Sidey[9] a few days later:

---

8. Located next to the White House, it is now the Eisenhower Executive Office Building. It was always called the OEOB.

9. You can find Hugh in the Glossary of Names. Already good friends, he and President Bush developed a pen pal relationship after President Bush left the White House. President Bush's letters to Hugh Sidey are almost his post–White House diary.

Dear Hugh,

The fat lady sang. The ordeal ended. And now a huge new chapter in the lives of the Bush family opens up. But let me finish my "election watch" series with this the 41st and final entry . . .

Right up until Gore spoke to the nation, I was not sure in my own mind what he would say, how he would say it. His speech was absolute perfection. He did it with grace and dignity and a genuineness that enthralled the nation. I know how difficult it was for him to do what he did.

As soon as I saw him on the TV leaving the OEOB, I called the White House switchboard and asked to be connected. I watched him get into his limo and but a few minutes later the phone rang and it was the Vice President. I congratulated him, just one sentence or two, just a few words. I suddenly felt for him, saw him as a man whose disappointment had to be overpowering. I knew he must be hurting. He was very gracious. He thanked me. The conversation was over in a flash, but I suddenly felt quite different about Al Gore. The anger was gone, the competitive juices stopped flowing . . . I thought of his long years of service and of his family. I thought back to my own feelings of years before when I lost, when I had to go out and accept my defeat. He did it better than I did, and his ordeal had to be tougher because the election was so close. True I had to actually give up the Presidency that he was now seeking, but still he had been in public life a long time and he and his family were shattered . . .

Barbara and I, alone here, climbed into bed to watch our son . . . I saw a couple of shots of George and Laura holding hands. I saw in his posture, in the way he walked, in his smile the same mannerisms and expressions we have known ever since he was a little boy.

[Texas Speaker of the House] Pete Laney, a good old boy from the Panhandle, gave a wonderful introduction emphasizing that George had worked in a bi-partisan manner to get things done for Texas. And then he goes: "The 43rd President of the United States, George W. Bush."

As the camera focused on George and Laura walking into the chamber, my body was literally wracked with uncontrollable sobs. It just happened. No warning, no thinking that this might be emotional for a mother or dad to get through—just an eruption from deep within me where my body literally shook. Barbara cried, too. We held hands . . .

We listened to our own son give thanks to God and tell our divided country what he planned to do . . .

May God give our son the strength he needs. May God protect the 43rd President of the United States of America.

Your friend, the proudest father in the whole wide world,
George

CHAPTER FOUR

TWO PRESIDENTS BUSH

Except for the moment his son took the oath of office and became the president of the United States, President Bush would tell you his favorite moment that weekend came the evening of Inauguration Day. The ceremony was over, the parade had passed, and a very tired President Bush was soaking in a hot bath upstairs in the White House residence.

A knock came on the door, and one of the White House butlers told him that the president would like for him to join him in the Oval Office.

President Bush got up, got dressed as quickly as his seventy-six-year-old achy body would allow, and raced downstairs. He could never really talk without crying a little about walking into that office and seeing his son sitting at the desk, already signing some papers. He did admit it was funny when Andy Card, already at work as chief of staff, said the name "Mr. President," and President Bush turned around prepared to answer when he realized Andy was talking to *the* president and not him.

That vignette might be the perfect segue to address one of the more amusing problems we had to address when George W. Bush became president.

Suddenly there were two people named President George Bush.

It had been confusing enough when there were two George

Bushes—really three, since Jeb's oldest son is George Bush as well. He got used to being called "George P.," or sometimes even just "P." And for the most part, people called George Bush No. 2 "George W." and then Governor. Problem solved.

Having two presidents with the same name had happened only one other time in history: When John Quincy Adams, the son of our second president, John Adams, became president on March 4, 1825.

President Bush loved wondering out loud about how John Adams and John Quincy Adams handled the situation. Did the second President Adams really like being called John Quincy Adams or did he feel forced to use his middle name because of his dad?

(Sadly, John Adams was not in good health when his son became president and did not attend his son's inauguration. He died a year later, on July 4, 1826, the same day as Thomas Jefferson. And with no television and no social media, I am thinking having two people named President Adams was not complicated.)

Both George Bushes were encouraged to use their middle initials. I am not sure how President George W. Bush felt about that, but President George H. W. Bush was not amused.

His full name was George Herbert Walker Bush. He was named for his maternal grandfather, whose children called their father Pop. Therefore, young George H. W. Bush acquired the nickname "Poppy" for the first eighteen years of his life. Mrs. Bush called him "Pop" until the day she died.

But by the time President Bush joined the Navy at age eighteen, then went to Yale, then moved to Texas, he had shed "Poppy" and simply became "George Bush." He didn't like having two middle names, especially after moving to Texas where few people did.

So as happy as he was to have a son named George Bush become president, he was most reluctant to start referring to himself as George H. W. Bush, a name he never loved.

To the rescue came Michigan congressman John Dingell, who, at the annual Alfalfa Club[1] dinner in Washington, DC, announced his solution to this problem: George H. W. Bush was the forty-first president of the United States, so therefore and henceforth he would be called "41." President George W. Bush was the forty-third president and would be "43."

And what do you call them when they are in the same room? Congressman Dingell wondered. He suggested "84."

The name "84" never caught on, but "41" and "43" solved the problem. The first President Bush loved being called "41," and suddenly there were T-shirts, baseball caps, golf balls, everything you can think of with "41" as the logo.

For the purposes of this book, now that we have come to the place in the story where "43" has taken office, we will call him the president; we will call "41" President Bush.

For the eight years their son was president, the Bushes loved making jokes about "when you're out, you're out," and even did a funny video to be shown at one of Mrs. Bush's Celebration of Readings—the annual fund-raisers she did every year in multiple cities for the Barbara Bush Foundation for Family Literacy—about the fact that they were the wrong Mr. and Mrs. George Bush.

The video might have been inspired by what happened shortly after George W. became the president-elect. Several years earlier, the Bushes had started the tradition of taking their entire family to Florida for the week between Christmas and New Year's, staying at their friend Will Farish's Gasparilla Inn in Boca Grande. Given the president-elect was part of the group this particular year, the entire family was reminded of how much tighter security would be for the foreseeable future.

Mrs. Bush was running late to a family lunch, and as she raced into

---

1. The Alfalfa Club is a prestigious Washington, DC, social club whose only reason for existence, according to their website, is to host a black-tie banquet on the last Saturday of January. It is named for the alfalfa plant, "whose roots travel deep to find refreshment."

the restaurant, a security guard stopped and ran a metal detector over her body. Another Secret Service agent stopped the guard, asking if he didn't realize who this was. He confessed he did not. Mrs. Bush asked the poor guard if he was wanding everyone like this. He assured her he was not, only people who "looked dangerous or like reporters." She loved telling that story, and always wondered which one he thought she was.

Besides dealing with name and sometimes identity confusion, there were a few other adjustments President Bush needed to make once his son became president. One major decision was to do few if any press interviews.

He had not been a newshound since leaving office, but when he felt like getting something off his chest or making a statement, he had done so.

For example, he very pointedly and publicly resigned from the National Rifle Association in 1995, after the NRA sent out a fund-raising letter he found offensive. The timing of the letter especially upset President Bush, as it was sent out not long after Timothy McVeigh and Terry Nichols orchestrated the truck bombing of the Federal Building in Oklahoma City, killing 168 people, including a Secret Service agent who had served on President Bush's detail. He wrote in part:

I was outraged when, even in the wake of the Oklahoma City tragedy, Mr. Wayne La Pierre, Executive Vice President of NRA, defended his attack on federal agents as "jack-booted thugs." To attack Secret Service Agents or ATF[2] people or any government law enforcement people as "wearing Nazi bucket helmets and black storm trooper uniforms" wanting to "attack law abiding citizens" is a vicious slander on good people.

Al Whicher, who served on my USSS detail when I was Vice President and President, was killed in Oklahoma City. He was no Nazi. He was a kind man, a loving parent, a man dedicated to serving his country—and serve it well he did.

---

2. Then known as the Bureau of Alcohol, Tobacco and Firearms.

★   ★   ★

But now, with his son in the White House, President Bush knew every single thing he said would be analyzed and dissected through the lens of what his son said and thought. The best thing would be not to say much at all.

For the most part, he was happy with this decision. But there were times he felt muzzled.

A perfect example would come a few years later, when in 2004 the *Washington Post* partnered with the History Channel to do a documentary on presidential leadership, with Bob Woodward as host. They of course wanted to interview all the former presidents, all of whom but one had said yes.

Pat Butler, then vice president of the *Post* company, sent me an impassioned email asking President Bush to change his mind. He also enlisted people like General Scowcroft and Secretary Baker to talk him into it, and he sent a report of the interview Woodward had with President Ford, which had gone very well.

"The program is about presidential leadership, and as the sample questions below that we sent to President Ford make clear, our purpose here is not to engage in ambush journalism, but rather to engage in a thoughtful discussion of leadership with the four men who have exercised it at the highest level," Butler wrote. "His interview will in no way be edited or construed to appear to be offering advice to his son or second-guessing him. That's not the point of this program."

I discussed his email with President Bush, encouraging him to say yes. I did not want him to be left out. After giving it a lot of thought, he decided to put his answer in writing, so I could share it with Pat. Here are some excerpts:

Dear Jean,

Please assure Pat that my decision has nothing to do with him or Bob Woodward—nothing at all . . . Rather, I have decided to keep a low profile as long as President Bush is in office. I do not want anything I say, no matter how innocuous, [to] in any way be used to show a division between father and son . . . Tell Pat I am a History Channel watcher. That makes this decision even more difficult.—GB

But despite things like acquiring a new nickname and occasional hic-cups, the Bushes' world really was "life as usual," even if their son was president of the United States.

President Bush loved telling the story about the first time the president came to Walker's Point to visit his parents as—well, the president. After an early-morning run, the president came back to the house to col-lapse on the couch in his parents' bedroom so he could visit with them while they read in bed.

Mrs. Bush looked up and sternly told the president: "George, get your feet off my coffee table."

To which President Bush said: "For God's sake, Bar. He is the presi-dent of the United States. You can't talk to him like that."

"I'm still his mother," came the reply. The feet came down.

My main memory of the president's first visit to Maine was a tiny issue that occurred when father and son went fishing for the first time.

President Bush 41 had invited his fishing buddy Billy Busch—an interesting, rather salty character from New Jersey—to go with them. I was enjoying some quiet time in the office when I got a frantic phone call from someone in the White House press office. The photographers and TV cameras trailing *Fidelity* could not use any of their photos because right in the middle of every frame was Billy, wearing a T-shirt with the F word emblazoned on the front. Yes, that F word—the one that most newspapers and TV broadcasts still avoid using. (He was protesting something, but I cannot remember what it was. He was not protesting the president.) I was informed this was my issue to resolve. So I asked the Secret Service to radio the agents on the boat and ask them to tell Billy to take off that shirt or stay out of sight. He took off the shirt.

Funny how urgent that problem seemed at the time. Sadly, it would be just a few weeks before we learned what the word "urgent" really meant.

President and Mrs. Bush began September 11, 2001, in Washington, DC. They had arrived a few days earlier to attend the annual meeting of

C-Change, an umbrella nonprofit cancer group that they founded in 1994 and chaired. After spending the night at the White House, they were wheels up at 8:30 a.m. on a private plane to give speeches in St. Paul, Minnesota. I stayed behind to attend a meeting of C-Change's board of directors.

The first plane hit the World Trade Center at 8:45 a.m. When the second plane hit at 9:02 a.m., the nation realized this was no accident. As soon as I could, I called the Secret Service in Kennebunkport, where we were then headquartered, to find out the Bushes' location. One of the supervisors told me they were safe and on the ground, but he could not tell me where since I was on an unsecure line. For purposes of national security, their location was a secret. I immediately imagined they were in West Virginia, in one of the not-so-secret underground bunkers that had been built during the Cold War as a place where the nation's leaders could go in the event of a nuclear war.

The agent said the Bushes were anxious to know where I was, and I asked him to assure them I was safe at the Renaissance Hotel in Washington. The city was under martial law. I had tried to leave the hotel to go be with a friend, but National Guard troops were on the street telling people unless you were medical personnel trying to get to a hospital or parents with young children at home, you needed to stay put. The hotel was able to guarantee our rooms since no new customers would be coming to town anytime soon.

That evening most of the hotel's guests gathered in the lobby bar, watching big-screen TVs the hotel had kindly brought in. No one wanted to be in their room alone. We were waiting for the president to address the nation when my cell phone rang. We were all startled as cell phone service that day in Washington had been spotty at best. It was hard to make or receive calls. The whole room seemed to be watching as I said hello.

It was President Bush. And despite the overwhelming tragedy of the day, the conversation that followed would forever be one of my favorites with him. I remember it so well, I am certain this reconstruction is almost word for word:

"Jean, where are you? Bar and I are worried to death about you."

I told him where I was, that I was fine, and I was so grateful to hear from him. I told him I knew he could not tell me where he was as his location was confidential.

"Really? We are at the Hampton Inn outside Milwaukee, Wisconsin. I don't think it's so secret. We just ate dinner across the street at Outback Steakhouse. We were glued to the television all day and then realized we were starving. People seemed a little surprised when Bar and I walked in. I must say it was nice. They gave us a standing ovation and told us they were thinking about the president."

I was a tad shocked at this news. So much for the bunkers in West Virginia. When I told him I thought they had been taken to a place a little more secure, he replied, "Well, Jean, I don't think anybody would expect to find us at a Hampton Inn in Milwaukee. We feel pretty safe."

He told me he had talked to the president, who was calm and focused on what to do next. He was curious when I would be back in Maine, and I told him I had no idea since all flights were canceled. The president had given their plane permission to fly the next day and take them home. I told him I was not getting that kind of service.

I was able to start my drive back to Maine the next day in a rental car, giving two of my fellow C-Change members a ride to Philadelphia on my way. My plan was to drive the entire ten hours that day, but as I approached New York City and saw the black spiraling smoke where the World Trade Center had been, I began sobbing. Two of the Bushes' best friends, Spike and Betsy Heminway, lived just outside New York, in Greenwich, Connecticut. I called and asked if I could spend the night with them. When I got there, Spike gave me a glass of pure vodka and called the Bushes to say they were keeping me for the night.

The Bushes did not know that day the person they should have been worried about was Marvin. He was in New York City on a subway under Wall Street when the planes hit. Like many thousands of others, he came up out of the subway and was told to just start walking, which he did, seventy blocks back to his hotel. Although he was not in harm's way by the time they found this out, it shook them to know how close he was to Ground Zero.

On September 14, the president called for a National Day of Prayer and sent Air Force planes to pick up all the former presidents so they could attend. When the presidents are together, protocol dictates they sit in the order in which they served. Therefore, the lineup in the cathedral should have been the president and First Lady, the Clintons, the Bushes 41, the Carters, and the Fords. (President Reagan had retired from public life after being diagnosed with Alzheimer's in 1994.)

On the way to the airport that morning, President Bush called to tell me he would really like to sit next to his son and could I run "that idea up the flagpole." I called Joe Hagin, one of President Bush's former staffers and now a deputy White House chief of staff, to pass on the request. Joe promised to try to make it happen.

At the end of the day, it was President Clinton's decision on whether to move down the totem pole and allow the Bushes to sit next to their son and daughter-in-law. I was told the answer was an immediate "of course." Was that the beginning of the friendship that eventually would be called the "Odd Couple"? Maybe.

One of the most memorable photos from that church service would be when the president returned to his seat after his stirring remarks to the nation and his proud father reached out to squeeze his hand.

In the days following 9/11, most of the former presidents gave interviews about their feelings on that day and about the challenge ahead for the president. President Bush did not feel comfortable doing so, once again wanting to stay out of his son's way. Yet, he was frustrated. He also had thoughts and feelings he wanted to share with the country he once led and still loved.

I talked about the dilemma with Karen Hughes, then director of White House Communications. We agreed to keep an eye out for an opportunity for President Bush to make a public statement that could help and not complicate the president's monumental task at hand.

In the meantime, I was hounded by the media, wondering why President Bush was so quiet. Why was he not speaking? When would he speak? Did I know what he was thinking? Tom Brokaw, the anchor of *NBC Nightly News*, called me every single day at the exact same time, requesting to have the first interview. Another persistent caller was a producer for ABC's Diane Sawyer.

About a week after 9/11, President Bush was scheduled to fly on a private plane back to Houston for an event. But then he had an idea.

No one was flying in America. The planes were empty. People were terrified of being hijacked. The airlines were losing millions of dollars, as were other industries who depended on business and tourism travel. President Bush decided he would take a Continental Airlines[3] flight from Boston to Houston, to demonstrate to the country it was safe to fly. He told me to pitch the idea to Tom Brokaw that if he were to meet him at Logan Airport in Boston, he would do an interview right before he boarded his flight.

The White House loved the idea. Brokaw conducted the interview at Logan, with the plane sitting right behind President Bush. NBC put a camera crew on the plane and followed him to Texas.

President Bush was happy he finally got to tell America that like them, his heart was broken; but that together we could and would recover from the horror of 9/11. And for him, his first step was getting on the plane to Texas.

After 9/11 President Bush watched anxiously but with pride as his son dealt with a crisis like no other at that point in our history. It was during this time period that the curiosity about President Bush the Father's relationship with President Bush the Son truly grew to astronomical proportions. I've been asked for years, both during President Bush 43's presidency and since, about what they talked about and what they disagreed on, and how they really felt about each other.

My answer to the first question is: I have no idea. If I was in President

---

3. Continental Airlines merged with United Airlines in 2010.

Bush's office when his son the president called, I got up and left the room. Their discussion was none of my business. Sometimes President Bush would wave me to stay, but I always left. Quite frankly, it was a brilliant decision on my part, but a source of huge disappointment to the media and historians. I truly knew nothing. And for that, I have been grateful.

Did I know what their disagreements were? Sometimes. Am I going to tell you now? No. But of course they disagreed. Do you know any father and son who do not? Any presidents who do not?

One incident in particular had the media worked up into a frenzy of trying to analyze the father-son relationship. Shortly before the president ordered the invasion of Iraq in 2003, General Scowcroft wrote an op-ed piece for the *Wall Street Journal*, recommending to the White House that they not invade.

A rumor immediately began making the rounds that this was really President Bush's opinion—some claimed he even wrote it—and he used one of his best friends as a conduit to get the message to his son.

Not true. This piece was all General Scowcroft.

Did President Bush know it was going to be published? Yes. General Scowcroft did not want him to be blindsided, so he called and not only gave him a heads-up, but also asked if he was okay with him writing the piece. President Bush assured his friend he had a right to express his opinion, especially given that at the time General Scowcroft was one of the opinion shapers in Washington, DC. He had a right for his voice to be heard.

Was the current president happy about the piece? No, of course not. It was advice that was in direct disagreement with him. He called and gave me an earful about it—I was happy to give him a chance to vent, which he did now and then. On another occasion, when a book about the Bush family—filled with a lot of half-truths and downright falsehoods—was published, the president called and asked if it was true I had fully cooperated with the book and in fact I had encouraged family members to spill their guts. (The answer was no, I had not, although for some reason a cousin had told the president the opposite.)

Again, the president needed to vent, and again, I was happy to let him do so as I held the phone at arm's length.

When he hung up, White House chief of staff Andy Card called to ask if I was okay. "I guess you heard what the president said to me," I said to Andy.

Andy's reply: "Jean, the entire West Wing heard what the president said to you."

Did he ever vent to his father? Of course I would not know the answer to that since I left the room. But I think I was the designated ventee. Truthfully, it was an honor. These sessions were never personal, and I sort of liked knowing now and then what was on the president's mind.

As to the second question—how did the two Presidents Bush really feel about each other?—my answer to that would be to share with you another phone call story and another letter.

At some point while George W. was president, his mom had a series of medical issues that were never fully diagnosed and that eventually disappeared as quickly as they came. But we were worried about her for a while. She was imagining things that were not happening, she would lose her balance quite easily, and she was in a mood.

After one particularly troubling day, I decided I needed to let the Bush children know something was up with their mom. Their dad was not being particularly helpful, as he was in denial that anything was wrong. Neil lived across the street from his parents and was typically in the loop on their health issues, but he was on a long overseas trip, and I didn't think it could wait. So I called Marvin.

Not long after I hung up with Marvin, our receptionist buzzed and said the president was on the phone.

Marvin had, of course, called his oldest brother. The president was calling to get his own report on their mother, and to tell me that he was the oldest child and if I had concerns about either of his parents, I should call him. I told him I could not do that as long as he was president. I did not feel comfortable calling the Oval Office to say, "Your mom is acting sort of funny."

Two Presidents Bush 55

He disabused me of that notion. "I might be president but I am George and Barbara Bush's son first." I am not sure why, but that call deeply touched my heart. He had the worries of the world on his shoulders, but his love for his parents was unconditional. I knew that, but it was still very sweet to hear from the Oval Office.

As for how the father felt about his son?

I will let him tell you by sharing a few excerpts from a letter he wrote to the president on April 9, 2003:

Dear George,

... This letter is about your leadership and the way you have conducted yourself as you face an accumulation of problems that no American President in the last 150 years has faced.

You have borne the burden with no complaining, no posturing. You have led with conviction and determination ...

The other day I started to tell a group of very close friends how I felt about you and your service to our country ... I shamefully choked up, the tears running down my aging cheeks. I was embarrassed, but then I realized that I shouldn't worry if people see this visible manifestation of a father's concern, a father's love ...

> *Devotedly,*
> *Dad*
> *AKA George Bush #41*

CHAPTER FIVE

GETTING YOUR PASSPORT STAMPED

Just because they were the parents of the president of the United States did not mean the Bushes' manic schedule of travel and speeches and charity events and get-togethers changed much. They were busier than ever, including for President Bush a great deal of foreign travel.

Except for the long flights, he loved traveling abroad. The respect for him around the world was deep, given that he had overseen the end of the Cold War, masterminded the reunification of Germany, and put together a historic coalition of nations to drive Saddam Hussein out of Kuwait in Operation Desert Storm.

In addition, for the first few years after he left the White House, many of President Bush's head-of-state peers were still in office. So when he traveled to an international capital, a good friend often was awaiting his arrival.

Michael Dannenhauer, his first post–White House personal aide, remembers that in the years immediately following 1992: "President Bush was treated as if he was still a Head of State. No matter where we went the world leaders still wanted to meet with him while he was in their country. Presidents, Prime Ministers, Kings & Queens—even dictators. I think the world honestly couldn't believe he had lost the election."

A couple of quick stories prove Michael might have been right.

In December 1994, while visiting Japan, President Bush mentioned he would love to meet with Emperor Akihito. Michael remembers the moment well: "President Bush mentioned to one of his Japanese 'minders' that he wondered if the Emperor was in town and if he might drop by to see him. Well, you would have thought he had asked to go to the moon and back in one afternoon. We were basically told, in a giggling kind of way, 'No one sees the Emperor. His schedule is set months and months in advance.' Well, a couple hours or even less later, the 'minder' sheepishly came back to me to say the Emperor would LOVE to see President Bush, so off to the Imperial Palace we went!"

When Israeli prime minister Yitzhak Rabin[1] was assassinated in November 1995, President Clinton asked the former presidents to accompany him to the funeral, which President Bush and President Jimmy Carter did. President Bush confessed when he returned that he was almost embarrassed by how many heads of state attending the funeral asked to meet with him, adding that he felt like he was holding rogue bilateral meetings.

He wrote Hugh Sidey:

At the funeral I had a chance to greet many Heads of State with whom I had dealt. It was a wonderful reunion for me even though the occasion was very sad. Helmut Kohl sought me out . . . John Major gave me the warmest of greetings . . . I sat next to Turkey's charming Prime Minister Ciller . . . [Hosni] Mubarak renewed his invitation to visit Egypt . . . I had a very nice visit with the King Hussein of Jordan.

---

1. I am fairly certain Rabin's death was the first of many I had to tell President Bush about. He was in the air when it became news, and I asked the Secret Service to call me the minute he landed. It was one of the least favorite parts of my job.

From Europe to the Middle East, to China, to Vietnam, to Singapore, to Pakistan, to Australia, to South America, to Africa, to Mexico and Canada, there was not a corner of the world that President Bush did not visit after leaving office.

His popularity was such that numerous countries awarded him their highest honor—their equivalent of the United States' Medal of Freedom: Germany, Kuwait, Albania, Bahrain, Qatar, United Arab Emirates, Hungary, Poland, Saudi Arabia, Italy, Kazakhstan, Dominican Republic, the Czech Republic, and Nicaragua—who gave him their highest honor twice, by two different presidents.

Queen Elizabeth bestowed upon him the "Most Honourable Order of the Bath-Knight Grand Cross," which made President Bush a knight. (Mrs. Bush was only mildly amused when he asked her to call him "Sir George." Shortly after he was knighted, he went down to the kitchen early one morning to get a cup of coffee. Mrs. Bush had left this handwritten note on the coffeepot: "Fix it yourself, Sir George!!")

Of course not everyone loved, respected, and honored him. While Kuwait shortly after leaving office, American and Kuwaiti intelligence uncovered a plot by Saddam Hussein to assassinate President Bush. A 175-pound car bomb was discovered as the weapon meant to kill him while he enjoyed a hero's welcome to the country he had liberated from Iraq during Desert Storm. President Clinton later ordered a bombing raid, targeting the Iraqi Intelligence Service headquarters where the plot had been hatched.

And then there was President Bush's rather harrowing journey from Damascus, Syria, to Beirut, Lebanon, during a tour of the Middle East in the spring of 1996. Intelligence sources warned the Secret Service that there was chatter that President Bush's plane or helicopter might be targeted by ground-to-air missiles when he flew into Lebanese airspace. The Secret Service urged President Bush to cancel that leg of his trip, but President Bush did not want to disappoint Lebanese prime minister Rafic Hariri, as a visit by a former American president would be historic. He liked Hariri a great deal, and felt he deserved a show of support from the United States.

President Bush mentioned his dilemma while meeting with Syria's president Hafez al-Assad,[2] who offered to give President Bush his own security forces to protect him while driving, not flying, to Beirut—eighty-five miles through mountains inhabited mainly by terrorists. Michael Dannenhauer remembers the journey well:

"So off we went by car, through the most mountainous road. Like cloak and dagger. I was in a separate car and had no idea what car President Bush was in. At the front and back of our little motorcade were two SUVs with turret-like machine guns mounted on their roofs. At the top of this mountain range, at the border, we STOPPED and had to switch to a different set of cars! During the transition, President Bush of course agreed to take photos with Assad's security detail. The Secret Service were not particularly thrilled."

Although I was back in Houston, I was aware of what was happening, as the Secret Service were keeping me in the loop. (At one point they were hoping I could talk him out of going to Beirut; I tried but failed.) I was such a wreck that I finally went to church and prayed. There wasn't much else I could do.

Ironically, Hariri was assassinated in 2005 by a suicide bomber with presumed ties to Syria.

So what happened in all these meetings with heads of state? Having witnessed one or two, and having read all of President Bush's letters to Hugh Sidey, I found that most of them followed a similar pattern: an exchange of pleasantries, an update on the family, and always a long discussion of current events. Often advice and opinion were sought, which was given.

President Bush was discreet then, and I will be discreet now.

Before and after his trips, President Bush often would brief his close friends and former teammates James Baker and Brent Scowcroft.

And sometimes the president and current secretary of state, especially if that president was also a son.

---

2. This was the father of the current president, Bashar Hafez al-Assad.

But except for this small group, perhaps the only other people to whom President Bush occasionally entrusted the details of these meetings were his former associates at the CIA. Like all former presidents, President Bush was offered—and he accepted—daily intelligence briefings. But his relationship with the agency he once headed was a special one.

So perhaps personal aide Gian-Carlo Peressutti should not have been surprised by this incident during a visit with Russian president Boris Yeltsin. He sent me these notes from his journal of the trip:

"President Bush was received by President Yeltsin in their equivalent of the Oval Office, and there was a massive amount of media covering the meeting. I remember standing in a room off the one where they were meeting when one of our agents came running in and told me I needed to go into the meeting room and sit behind President Bush. I told him he was crazy. Actually, I said something else.

"Seconds later a huge Russian came running in and started yelling at me. That's when, with legs of Jell-O, I crept into the formal meeting room and took a seat behind 41 hoping the seat cushion would swallow me up and I'd vanish inconspicuously...

"When we were in the car with the doors closed, President Bush turned to me and said, 'When you get back to your room, I want you to immediately write down every single thing you remember about that meeting. From what was said, to how Boris acted and moved, to your thoughts on his state of mind.' What a guy, I thought. My boss knew how historic what I just experienced was and he wanted me to have my own record of the encounter for posterity. Well, not quite. Later on, having done what President Bush asked, he came into my room with his own handwritten series of pages and handed them to me. 'You know why I asked you to do this, right?' He could tell by the look on my face that I was now not quite sure. He continued, 'Our briefers back at home will be very interested in every detail of that meeting, no matter how small or inconsequential they may seem.' Ah. Now I got it. And just like that I had become a spy for the United States of America."

★   ★   ★

Although most of President Bush's international travel was private, he also represented the United States numerous times at official events, including:

- The inaugurations of President Ernesto Zedillo of Mexico in 1994; President Felipe Calderón of Mexico in 2006; and President Aníbal Cavaco Silva of Portugal in 2006.
- The reopening of the American embassy in Berlin in 2008, the first time the embassy had been in Berlin since World War II.
- The opening of the 2004 Summer Olympics in Athens, Greece,[3] as head of the U.S. delegation.

I did not often travel overseas with President Bush, but I did go to the Olympics in Athens with the Bushes in 2004, which turned out to be a bigger adventure than we could have imagined.

The Bushes were frequent visitors to Greece. Not long after he left office, President Bush accepted an invitation from Greek businessman John Latsis to use his yacht, the *Alexander* (and later, the *Turama*), for a cruise around the Aegean Sea. President Bush's first instinct was to say no, but when he realized he was no longer a public servant and could say yes, he did so with gratitude and excitement.

The Greek Cruise, as it came to be known, was an almost annual occurrence. I managed to sneak aboard about once every two or three years, and there really is only one word to describe them: glorious.

But back to the 2004 Olympics. The annual cruise was timed that year to coincide with the Olympics. The official delegation included the twin daughters of the president of the United States, Jenna and Barbara Bush, and a handful of other Americans, including tennis star Chris Evert and Greek American Alex Spanos, the owner of the San Diego Chargers. The rest of us were just lucky to tag along.

---

3. President Bush also attended the Opening Ceremonies of the 2008 Summer Olympics in Beijing, as honorary captain of the U.S. Olympic Team.

There was just one major hiccup: Security was extremely tight in Athens, as intelligence reports showed that numerous terrorist groups had designs on disrupting the Olympics. Adding to the strain was that these were the first Olympics since 9/11. The threat was so severe that several Secret Service agents who took the trip left behind letters for their families in case they didn't come home. (I didn't find that out until after we did indeed come home.)

President Bush's aide at that time, Tom Frechette, worked closely with the Secret Service advance team, talking with them daily from Greece. They felt the threat was so severe that President Bush absolutely should not come. (Tom remembers the F word was used a lot.) President Bush walked into Tom's office during one of these calls, so he gave President Bush the phone. He told the agents he understood the dangers but that he must represent the United States at the Games.

The president of the United States called his father before we left to say that after the Opening Ceremonies, he needed to get out of Athens with his mother and his daughters as quickly as possible. He insisted we could not stay for any part of the Games themselves. This was a crushing blow to all of us, but especially to a sportsman like President Bush.

When our boat pulled into Athens, I had never seen so many machine guns as those carried by the Greek soldiers lining our pier. And I had never seen the Bushes' agents carrying machine guns, either. We had a special ops team assigned to us, and no boat was allowed within so many feet. As Tom remembers, it was as if a war zone surrounded our boat.

Nevertheless, President and Mrs. Bush carried out their head-of-delegation duties with great enthusiasm, including speaking to a gathering of the American team. They posed for photos with every single athlete and attended a welcoming reception hosted by the Greek prime minister for all the VIPs.

Not surprisingly, while attending this reception, President Bush had an idea.

He and Mrs. Bush had already planned to host a cocktail party on board the *Turama*, with the help of their Greek hosts, for friends who were in town for the Olympics. President Bush came back to the boat after the reception to tell us he had invited more people. Suddenly, everyone from Prince Albert to the president of Albania (and five other heads of state) and NBC's Tom Brokaw and Katie Couric were coming.

Somehow it all worked and a grand time was had by all. Some guests did overstay their welcome and it fell to me to tell Prince Albert it was time to go.

But the real drama was our attending the Opening Ceremonies.

Security decided that the American delegation would not sit in the special seating reserved for the other VIPs, as there was intel that the terrorists had possibly planted explosives in the stadium as it was being built. We would sit high up in the stadium, in what we Americans would call the "cheap seats."

And we would not stay until the very end but would leave rather abruptly and spontaneously. The idea was to keep anyone plotting anything nefarious off their game. The Secret Service emphasized to me and the other staffers on the trip—Tom Frechette; Laura Pears, whom we called the "cruise director," as she organized the cruise every year; and Mrs. Bush's aide, Michele Whalen—that when they said leave, we had five minutes to get the Bush family and friends out of the stadium and onto the bus. If not, the motorcade with the Bushes would leave us behind.

When we got to the stadium, the Greek security tried to prevent the head of President Bush's Secret Service detail, Andy Almblad, from entering the stadium because he was carrying a gun. When the security tried to push Andy aside, President Bush firmly grabbed Andy's arm and said, "He goes where I go," and pulled him through the gate. No one tried to stop him.

The look on people's faces when we arrived at our seats was amusing. There were no VIPs anywhere near us, and suddenly the former president and First Lady of the United States came and sat down in their midst.

When the agents said, "Let's go," I had never moved so fast in my life. If you blinked, you missed us leaving.

Despite the plan—and the presidential directive—not to attend any of the Games themselves, President Bush could not help himself. The agents checked the schedule for something happening out of the limelight, and it was finally decided that the USA women's softball team's first game would be safe. Again, the looks on the faces of the teams and the few spectators were priceless when President and Mrs. Bush and their entourage settled into their seats in a nearly empty pavilion. The surprise factor made it more fun than attending some of the marquee events. (Okay, a track-and-field event would have been nice.)

Here is part of the note I wrote to the staff and volunteers when I got home:

"We pulled into Athens about 3 p.m. Thursday. That was quite the sight as the harbor was filled with boats of all sizes including the *Queen Mary II*. It would have been nice to sneak into town but we were surrounded by gunboats…much to the Secret Service's dismay, 41 stood on the top deck of the boat in plain sight. Like all of us, he wanted to see all the pageantry. He waved at everyone, from all the passengers on the *Queen Mary* to all the men carrying guns to protect us. Even some of them waved back.

"Due to security concerns we were held hostage on the boat…no Acropolis tour for us…We all went to the Opening Ceremonies, which were spectacular. I never thought George Bush would sit in his seat for four hours, but he did. From 8 p.m. until midnight, he never budged…We screamed our lungs out for the Americans. The embassy would not let us wave flags—'we need to be low key,' they told us. I know the team saw us and heard us as they all turned and waved and waved. I know this will sound odd, but we felt this huge responsibility to make our team feel loved and welcomed.

"As I mentioned our security was huge…we were living in an armed camp. This was not totally bad because Greek men, dressed in black, carrying big black guns is quite a sight to behold...even Barbara Bush was sneaking a peek now and then. When we sailed out of port Saturday evening, the Greeks all lined up and saluted 41. The women made fools of themselves, almost hanging off the boat waving good-bye to them."

Two years later I took another trip with President Bush where, just like in Athens, security concerns dictated much of our schedule.

In January 2006, President Bush flew to Pakistan as part of his role as UN special envoy for the Southeast Asian earthquake, which had struck the region the previous October. The United Nations, when they asked him to take on this task, assured him all he had to do was write a few letters asking for disaster relief funds. President Bush's response was, "Nonsense." He insisted on visiting the region and learning firsthand what needed to be done.

Pakistan was not the safest country to visit at that time, and to get there, we needed to fly over a lot of countries that did not love us. Part of that issue was resolved by using a private aircraft that was not American owned. This allowed us to fly directly over Afghanistan and Iran, which in an American plane would not have been possible. All our noses, including President Bush's, were pressed against the plane windows, watching the landscape and wondering what the people below would think if they knew who was flying above.

When we landed in Islamabad, the idea of motorcading to the residence of the American ambassador, Ryan Crocker, was nixed. It was not safe. Instead, we were given bulletproof vests and loaded onto helicopters, where I think everyone but President Bush, Tom Frechette, and I hung out the open doors with a machine gun pointed at the ground below. The helos flew a zigzag pattern over the city, again to throw off anyone who thought they knew who we were and where we were going.

Thankfully, the visit went well. A few years later, the Marriott Hotel where we had met with rescue workers and UN officials was blown up in a terrorist attack—a stark reminder of the risk President Bush had taken.

He would tell you his risk was nothing compared to what we saw. Visiting the refugee camp filled with thousands of people whose lives had been reduced to a tent pitched in the mud and the clothes on their backs was truly humbling.

Five years later, when Osama bin Laden was killed by American Special Forces in his house near the Islamabad Airport, Tom Frechette and I convinced ourselves we had flown over that very house. In our minds, the house looked eerily familiar. We briefly flirted with the idea of spreading the rumor that we were the ones who had spotted bin Laden on his rooftop waving a gun at us, which began the road to his being captured. We then decided the story was too outrageous; plus, we knew President Bush would blow the whistle on us.

Maybe we should get back to President Bush's other foreign travels...

Occasionally, he was called upon by the sitting president to attend a funeral on behalf of the United States. It was a duty quite familiar to him since, as vice president, he attended so many funerals that Secretary Baker gave him the mantra: "You die, I fly." He didn't attend that many, but there were a few:

- As previously mentioned, Prime Minister Rabin of Israel in 1995.
- King Hussein of Jordan in 1999, accompanying President Clinton and former presidents Ford and Carter.
- Pope John Paul II in 2005, part of the delegation headed by President George W. Bush and First Lady Laura Bush, along with former president Clinton.
- President Yeltsin in 2007, accompanied by former president Clinton.

President Bush confessed to me more than once that he guiltily enjoyed the camaraderie of these funerals, seeing old friends and making new ones. He wrote in a letter to his children after King Hussein's funeral:

Have I now re-established my own name-dropping credentials? I could go and on. The truth is I really enjoyed seeing all these people, but it did make me realize that I still do miss the part of my job that had me interacting with all these folks.

It is oh so different for me now. No agenda, no authority have I. It was simply a chance to greet friends.

In addition to President Bush's own travels, many current and former heads of state came to Houston, Kennebunkport, or his presidential library in College Station, Texas, to pay their respects.[4]

All the visits were exciting, but some were more memorable than others.

For example, President Hamid Karzai of Afghanistan came to Kennebunkport to seek President Bush's advice. If I knew what advice he sought, I could not tell you—it was a highly classified trip organized by the CIA. (When I tried to pry information out of President Bush after the visit was over, I remember he told me something like, "Karzai just needed someone to talk to.")

The secretiveness of the Karzai visit presented a very large dilemma: One of President Bush's habits when current or former heads of state visited him in Maine was to buy the flag of the visitor's country and hang it from the flagpole at Walker's Point. There was a flag store in nearby Wells, Maine, which the former president kept quite busy and maybe even kept in business. (He always flew the U.S., Maine, and Texas flags; if the governor was in residence, he also flew the state flag of Florida.)

This was a lovely idea unless the visit was supposed to be secret. Among other issues, the Afghan leader was on the Top 5 Hit List in the world. So when President Bush raised the Afghanistan flag to

---

4. My editor says there are too many to list!

welcome President Karzai, everyone from the staff to the Secret Service to the CIA had a complete nervous breakdown. President Bush, despite his great respect for classified information, would not be deterred. His argument: No one in Maine would recognize the Afghan flag. The flag flew. Everyone lived.

My favorite flag raising, though, was when President Vladimir Putin came to Walker's Point in July 2007 to meet with the president of the United States. President Bush asked the Russian advance team to help him raise their flag. They were shocked and honored that the Russian flag would fly at all, much less the fact they would help raise it with the president who had ended the Cold War.

The Putin visit created almost a Hall of Fame of behind-the-scenes stories that, unfortunately, almost never get told. We won't make that mistake here.

It all began in April of that year when a horrific spring storm pounded the Maine coastline. Waves crashed into the living room and dining room at Walker's Point, destroying most of the furniture and carpet.

So imagine my nervousness when a few weeks later, on a day when the Bushes were out of the country, someone from the National Security Council at the White House called to see if the president could invite Vladimir Putin to an important meeting at Walker's Point in July. I told the caller the Bushes couldn't be reached, and by the way, the downstairs part of the house had been hit hard by a storm and might not be ready for such a visit in just a few months.

A few minutes later our receptionist told me the president of the United States wanted to talk to me. In a strong voice and using stronger words, he said he needed for his parents to sign off on this visit right now. Secretary of State Condi Rice was literally sitting outside Putin's office in Moscow, and the president wanted her to issue the invitation.

I knew the president's father would say, "Of course." I knew the president's mother would be nervous, given the condition of the house. As he should have, the president made the call in his parents' absence and the invitation was issued.

But I'm the one who told Mrs. Bush.

Her reaction was to immediately order new furniture from a factory store in North Carolina, and to cover every single piece—every chair, every couch, every love seat—with the exact same lovely Ralph Lauren floral pattern.[5] There just wasn't enough time to think through mixing and matching and color patterns. It just needed to be done.

The furniture arrived at Walker's Point a few weeks before the Putin visit when everyone but me, the summer intern Ty Hobbs, and the household staff were in Greece. The peace and quiet had been heavenly. Until the furniture truck arrived and could not fit through the entrance gate into the Point. The truck driver didn't seem all that perturbed. Despite the threatening storm clouds—and desperate pleas for mercy from me—he calmly started unloading Barbara Bush's brand-new matching living room furniture on Ocean Avenue. He said this was not his problem.

Ty and I started working the phones, calling everyone we knew who owned a truck. In fifteen minutes an armada came racing down Ocean Avenue—friends had called friends who called neighbors. I think most of the town came to the rescue. Betsy Heminway directed traffic around the odd sight of furniture sitting on the road, while Ken Raynor—the golf pro at Cape Arundel Golf Club—organized loading the furniture onto pickup trucks, including the one owned by the Bushes' trainer, Heath Pierce, who walked out of a meeting or a workout session to answer the SOS.

Just as the first raindrop fell, the last truck was unloaded at the house.

Directed by the Bushes' longtime housekeeper, Paula Rendon, and her daughter, Alicia, we managed to put the living room back together. What a glorious surprise for Mrs. Bush to come home to a

---

5. Kristan King Nevins, Mrs. Bush's personal aide at the time, remembers that Ralph Lauren himself had to get involved to track down every available swatch of the pattern, as it had been discontinued. She now lives in Washington, DC, with her husband, Kyle, and their three children.

furnished living room. The thank-you cocktail party the Bushes threw for the rescuers was a joyous celebration.

A few weeks before the Putin visit, the White House and Kremlin advance teams arrived at Walker's Point for a preliminary walk-through. Thankfully, Joe Hagin was head of the White House team. My job was to escort the large group around Walker's Point and keep my mouth shut.

I almost made it.

It was a torturous meeting that went on for hours. The Russians obsessed about every rock along the jagged Atlantic Coast, every lobster pot bobbing in the ocean, and every house along Ocean Avenue. They wanted snipers behind every boulder and bush and an aircraft carrier off the coast. They wanted the Bushes' neighbors to be moved out of their houses. Joe patiently and professionally talked them down from most of their demands.

The very last discussion was the shortest. The plan for when Putin arrived was for the two presidents to get on *Fidelity* and go fishing. As we stood on the pier from where they would depart, the Russians simply said something like, "Okay, great."

Tired, frustrated, and likely hungry, I could not help myself. From the back of the group, I said: "Let me get this straight. After all your concerns today over every single blade of grass on Walker's Point, you have zero questions or concerns about the fact that these two world leaders are going to get on a boat with three 300-horsepower engines and driven in the often-choppy Atlantic Ocean by an eighty-three-year-old madman who can and will outdistance every single boat the Secret Service has in about five minutes flat?"

The Russians frantically started talking and speaking to each other in Russian. Joe Hagin gave me a withering look. Oops.

Did they go fishing? Yes. Did anyone die? No. Obviously my concerns were overwrought. However, Joe does remember that as *Fidelity* roared out of sight with the two heads of state on board, more than one onlooker muttered, "Holy shit."

It was odd to consider the things we worried about in advance of the visit—"we" being me and the Bushes' two aides, Jim Appleby and Kristan King Nevins. Things like the fact that the entire Russian advance team went to see the movie *Die Hard 3* one night. We immediately began obsessing that the "bad guys" in that movie were Russians (none of us had seen it), and we feared they would cancel the whole visit, they would be so outraged. As it turned out, at least according to the Russians, the "bad guys" were French, which we all agreed made sense.

This is what I told my diary about the visit:

"No one had more fun than 41. He was like a kid who was having friends over to visit. He drove Condi to the golf course; he took the Russian advance team out on the boat; he took Joe Hagin on the boat;[6] he took Tony Snow[7] on the boat...He took Putin on the boat twice."

That night, after a very exclusive dinner at Walker's Point, President Bush even wandered down to Kennebunkport's River Club, where the Bushes' daughter Doro Bush Koch was hosting a dinner for all the other delegation members. Both the American and the Russian teams were thrilled when he strolled in, just in time to catch the entertainment that he had arranged: his nephew Hap Ellis and his brother Bucky Bush, strumming their guitars and singing their sometimes rather odd collection of ballads. Bucky closed the night singing about a man who

---

6. Joe recently told me he took two Russians with him on his ride: Dmitry Peskov, currently Putin's head of communications and spokesman; and Anton Vayno, Putin's current chief of staff. Joe had to warn them to hold tight as the boat took off.

7. Then White House press secretary. Tony was already dealing with colon cancer then; he died a year later.

fell in love with a mermaid but couldn't quite figure out how to make
love to her. As I noted in my diary:

"I think this was an important moment in American-Russian relations. How can you possibly hate a people who sing about mer-
maids? After it was over, I was kissed by Russians I had never
met before."

The next day, after the talks had concluded, President and Mrs. Bush
crashed the press conference held by the two presidents on the front lawn
of Walker's Point. I was at the back of the large group of press, just to
be available to troubleshoot any problems. Okay, I wasn't really needed
but I wanted to watch. I wasn't the only one. Suddenly, here came the
Bushes, President Bush wearing sunglasses in order to be incognito; and
Mrs. Bush, who had become quite the shutterbug, sidling over to join
the crush of photographers in the White House press pool, pretending to
be one of them. Once the press spotted them, they all turned around to
take photos of the president's parents, who seemed unaware of the commotion their presence had caused.

The day they all left, Mrs. Bush summoned everyone on the Point
(except the Secret Service) to the house on Walker's Point called the
Bungalow, the longtime home of President Bush's mother, Dorothy
Walker Bush, and now Doro's summer cottage. It was where Putin and
members of his team stayed during the visit. The condition of the house
was, simply put, awful. The Russians had left scattered throughout the
house and the patio half-eaten smoked fish, cigarette butts, and a variety
of other trash. Ants were everywhere. The smell was terrible. Everyone
rolled up their sleeves, including President and Mrs. Bush, and started
cleaning. I think even the agents pitched in.

Despite the mess, the visit had gone well. And thanks to President
Bush 41, who summoned us to the pier right before *Fidelity* arrived from
the fishing trip, Jim, Kristan, and I even managed to get a photo taken
with President Putin. Just a few years ago, a cable repairman noticed this

photo on the wall of my home office. He looked at Putin, looked at me, and asked, "Who the hell are you?"

Perhaps one of the more unusual visitors President Bush had was when one of the sons of Libyan dictator Muammar Gaddafi, Saif, came in November 2008. (This time I was the notetaker.) At the time, he was considered someone "the United States could deal with," which was why Secretary of State Condoleezza Rice asked President Bush if he would meet with him on his tour of the country. Among the questions the son asked President Bush was: "Did the United States orchestrate Iraq's invasion of Kuwait in 1990 so the Americans could go in and kill Saddam Hussein?" President Bush assured him the United States did not do such things.

In many ways, President Bush served as an informal special envoy from the United States to the rest of the world, very quietly spreading goodwill while listening carefully to what international leaders were thinking.

But he would not approve of that assessment. He would worry that it was "Carter-esque." Despite his friendship with President Carter, President Bush had been disappointed when he learned President Carter had lobbied members of the United Nations Security Council against supporting Desert Storm back in 1990. President Bush was determined to stay out of the way and out of the business of the sitting president and not have his own foreign policy agenda.

Nevertheless, the stories of President Bush's interaction with foreign visitors and friends during the twenty-five years of his post-presidency are truly endless.

He counted among his best friends—besides Brian Mulroney and John Major—Helmut Kohl of Germany, Mikhail Gorbachev, Carlos Menem of Argentina, and Carlos Salinas of Mexico.

President Bush might have left the world stage, but he never lost interest in what was happening in the world. As he wrote Hugh Sidey in 1994, on his way to Albania:

Why are you going to Albania? That's what our friends asked me, that's what Portugal's wonderful Prime Minister Anibal Cavaco Silva asked me—why Albania? I went because I wanted to see what happens to a country when it moves out of the darkest of the dark totalitarian ages into freedom.

Coincidentally, a valet parker at one of President Bush's favorite Tex-Mex restaurants in Houston was from Albania. The first time we arrived for lunch when this young man was on duty, he almost fainted when President Bush got out of the car. Many photos and autographs later, he wept as he thanked President Bush for, first, ending the Cold War; and second, for visiting his homeland.

The respect given him around the world perhaps was best characterized by Brian Mulroney in his eulogy at President Bush's state funeral at the National Cathedral in Washington, DC:

"No occupant of the Oval Office was more courageous, more principled and more honorable than George Herbert Walker Bush... There is a word for this: it is called 'leadership'—and let me tell you that when George Bush was President of the United States of America, every single head of government in the world knew they were dealing with a true gentleman, a genuine leader—one who was distinguished, resolute and brave."

CHAPTER SIX

THE ODD COUPLE

While he was winging his way around the world, President Bush also was in the process of making a new friend: William Jefferson Clinton.

The friendship between President Bush and President Clinton remains one of the great political mysteries in our country. Still today I am asked, "Was it real, or for show?"

You decide.

When Pope John Paul II died in April 2005, the president wanted to invite the former presidents to join the delegation he and First Lady Laura Bush would be leading to the funeral. White House chief of staff Andy Card called me to float the idea, and President Bush sent back the advice that maybe the president should fill Air Force One up with prominent Catholics instead.

A day later, President Bush changed his mind. He had met the pope numerous times and credited him for helping end the Cold War. Plus, he also decided his son had been right: The best way for America to show respect for John Paul II would be for all the presidents to attend.

I called Andy and asked if it was too late. He assured me it was not but hung up to call the other presidents.

President Clinton's chief of staff, Laura Graham, called me soon after, to give me a heads-up that her boss's doctor did not want President Clinton making the trip. He had just undergone heart surgery and should not be traveling. But he told Laura he wanted to call President Bush and get his opinion on whether he could go. Laura asked me to ask President Bush to discourage her boss from traveling.

I raced into President Bush's office to tell him what was coming, just minutes before the call came in. As he picked up the phone, he assured me "I have this."

This is the part of the conversation I heard:

"Hi, Bill. Yes, I am going..."

"Yes, I think you can go..."

"Does your doctor know there is a medical unit on board the plane? They will take good care of you. I bet George would give you his bed."

I am frantically waving my hands, writing him a note, telling him this was *not* his assignment.

"It would be fun for you to go, Bill. Good. You're in."

I immediately got a phone call from Laura. "What the hell happened?" she yelled.

Well, they were two friends who wanted to make this trip together. They really didn't care what anyone else thought.

Maybe we should go back to the beginning.

The first hint of a growing friendship between the two was November 18, 2004, the day the William J. Clinton Library and Museum was dedicated in Little Rock, Arkansas. President Bush's remarks got a lot of attention that day. Here are a few excerpts:

Of course, it also has to be said that Bill Clinton was one of the most gifted American political figures in modern times. Trust me: I learned this the hard way . . . Simply put, he was a natural. He made it look too easy—and, oh, how I hated him for that.

Another gripe: Bill Clinton enjoyed debates far too much for my taste. To be candid, I hated debates. When I checked my watch at the Richmond [Virginia] debate, it's true: I was wondering when Ross Perot would stop and when I could get the heck out of there. But it was also clear that Bill was in his element that night . . .

After you leave the White House a number of things happen to you. First of all, the crowds of protestors get smaller—disappointing, really—and when you play golf, no one seems to give you short putts anymore. But one of the great blessings is the way one-time political adversaries have the tendency to become friends, and I feel such is certainly the case between Bill Clinton and me.

There is an inescapable bond that binds together all who have lived in the White House. Though we hail from different backgrounds, and ideologies, we are singularly, uniquely, even eternally bound together by our common devotion and service to this country.

It might be said the table had been set.

Just a few weeks later—the day after Christmas—a tsunami in the Indian Ocean came ashore in parts of South and Southeast Asia with one-hundred-foot waves, killing an estimated 228,000 people in fourteen countries and devastating the coastlines. The world had never really seen a natural disaster of this enormity. Hardest hit were Indonesia, Thailand, Sri Lanka, and India.

Barely aware of the growing disaster on the other side of the world, I was enjoying a wonderful New Year's weekend in Santa Fe, New Mexico, with a group of friends. Then I had a voice mail from Karl Rove, who said he needed to talk to me about an idea the president had regarding his dad, Bill Clinton, and the South Asia tsunami.

I remember telling my friend and fellow staffer Laura Pears that I feared our lives were about to turn upside down.

The idea was for the two former presidents to encourage the private sector to get behind the effort to rescue the affected areas. The U.S. government would do as much as possible, including sending Navy ships and personnel to help with rescue operations, and USAID[1] staff and funding, to start the long road back to recovery.

But this needed to be an all-hands-on-deck effort. The nonprofit sector was already on board. Organizations such as Americares, the Red Cross, Doctors Without Borders, and Catholic Relief Services already had boots on the ground, but they couldn't do their job without a huge infusion of cash from the private sector.

The two former presidents readily said yes and flew to Washington to meet with the president and get their marching orders. The first order of

---

1. The United States Agency for International Development, created by President Kennedy in 1961, provides humanitarian aid around the globe. Our USAID point of contact was Mark Ward, who would guide us through a number of humanitarian aid projects and become a good friend. President Bush called him "Mr. Disaster."

business was to do a series of public service announcements and media interviews to get the word out about how everyone could help.

The idea was not for them to set up a new foundation but to encourage the American people to give to already existing programs and organizations.

Because it was impossible to track the donations made because of their getting involved, we'll never know how much money they raised, but the nonprofit groups estimated tens of millions of dollars. Despite our best efforts to encourage people *not* to send the two of them money, people and groups did so anyway. Their reasoning: They trusted the presidents to figure out how to use it wisely. So we quickly set up a fund, housed in the Greater Houston Community Foundation, and ended up with more than $12 million. America wanted to help.

Up until now, everything between the two former presidents had been quite cordial, but then the president asked the two of them if they would mind traveling to the region to represent the United States and the concerns of the American people.

Again, the answer was "Of course."

They embarked on the five-day trip in February 2005 as two political opponents who had decided to put their differences aside for the greater good.

They came home the Odd Couple.

As President Bush wrote Hugh Sidey on our way home: "I thought I knew him; but until this trip I did not really know him."

So what happened? Maybe that can best be answered with a single word: "life."

It began shortly after takeoff when President Clinton, out of respect for President Bush, who was twenty-two years his senior, insisted that President Bush take the only bed and bedroom on board the Air Force plane for the overnight trip to Thailand. President Bush put up a weak argument and then gratefully gave in. (I would like to add that President Bush's aide, Tom Frechette, and myself did our part by staying up all night with President Clinton and his staff playing the card game "Oh

Hell." He did finally lie on the floor on a blanket and got a few hours' sleep.)

We did not know it then, but President Bush was in the early stages of a form of Parkinson's disease. He was still mobile, but slow and unsteady on his feet. Throughout the trip, President Clinton graciously waited for him and helped him up and down stairs, in and out of boats, planes, helicopters, and cars. Especially since the staff needed to stay out of the photos, it fell to President Clinton to give him his arm, which he did without being asked.

For his part, President Bush treated the man who denied him a second term with great respect and kindness. And sometimes like a son. At times he scolded him, especially when President Clinton was running late or when President Bush worried he was maybe talking too much.

At a state dinner hosted by the prime minister of Sri Lanka, President Bush felt we had overstayed our welcome, especially given the enormous problems facing the prime minister. But President Clinton was chatting away, and when I urged his staff to pull him out because President Bush thought they should graciously depart, they explained he did not like to be pulled from events. He decided when to leave.

When I delivered this news to President Bush, he said, "I'll take care of that." He waded into the crowd, grabbed President Clinton's arm, and said, "Bill, time to go."

"Yes, sir," was President Clinton's answer, and they left.

One morning in Thailand, I was waiting on the front porch of our hotel for President Clinton to come out and get in the motorcade. President Bush was already sitting in their car, reading a book. When President Clinton came out and saw that, he muttered under his breath, "Oh, shit." He tried hard to be on time after that.

The two of them had long visits about world affairs, caught up on mutual friends and heads of state they knew, and enjoyed each other's company.

President Clinton told me years later he was so touched by how accepting and kind President Bush was to him. After all, given their political history, it could have been a very awkward journey. Mrs. Bush would come to believe that her husband was in many ways the father Bill Clinton never had.

As for President Bush, despite their history, he had a soft spot in his heart for President Clinton and genuinely enjoyed his company. He knew a lot about everything. As he got older, President Bush used to tease President Clinton that he enjoyed his company because he, President Bush, had run out of things to say and he never had to worry about that around President Clinton, who was most capable of doing all the talking.

It wasn't long before we were calling President Clinton "42," which he loved, and some of the Bush siblings were calling him "our brother from another mother."

And while they were becoming friends, they also were doing great work. On the tsunami relief trip, they not only met with heads of state, but they also hugged and listened to as many victims as possible. In Sri Lanka, they visited schoolchildren sitting in the dirt because their school was gone. Near Banda Aceh in Indonesia, they visited a small village and literally wept with the survivors—700 people out of a population of 6,500—standing amid the rubble that once was their hometown. Only the mosque survived. The two presidents knelt in the dirt and visited with a fourteen-year-old boy who was now the oldest in his family.

I had never seen such devastation. President Bush told me he had seen a lot in his lifetime, and until the tsunami, the worst he had seen were the Palestinian refugee camps in Lebanon. But this was worse.

With the $12 million that was sent to them directly, the presidents worked with the American embassies in each country, USAID, and nonprofit groups to help finance fishing boats in Thailand; schools, houses, and places of worship in Indonesia; playgrounds and a pediatric hospital wing in Sri Lanka; and houses in India and the Maldives.

Everywhere they went, they were treated like rock stars. Mostly, people could not believe they came. In the Maldives, a young woman came up to me and grabbed my hand and said, "No one else came. Just you."

One of the few press who traveled with us was Tony Freemantle of the *Houston Chronicle*. His memory of the trip fifteen years later: "I was an outsider on that trip—gratefully invited to tag along as the hometown reporter. But I instead was lucky enough to observe up close a profound lesson in what America can do for a world in crisis if political differences can be put aside and allow friendship and compromise to guide us."

The Odd Couple's budding friendship likely cemented during their trip to Pope John Paul II's funeral in April. As it turns out, they were the only two former presidents who went: President Ford was unable to travel for health reasons, and President Carter had a scheduling conflict.

Despite the solemnity of the occasion, it was somewhat of an adventure for the two formers. While the sitting president held bilateral meetings and worked, they met old friends over dinner and drinks.

I was not on the trip, so I asked traveling aide Tom Frechette to share part of the story:

"Although it was midnight Rome time, the delegation went straight from the airport to the Vatican to pay their respects to the pope, who was lying in state. The president invited his dad and President Clinton to ride in the presidential limo with him to the Vatican. When we came out of St. Peter's, the president and the First Lady were headed to the American ambassador's residence, where they would spend the night; we were headed to a hotel. The president asked his dad and President Clinton if they needed a ride. They assured him they did not; their own motorcade was nearby. The president wasn't thrilled with the idea of leaving his dad and another former president standing in St. Peter's Square at such a late hour. But they insisted again, so the huge presidential motorcade sped away. And when they were gone, there wasn't a car in sight. The square was empty.

"Except for the presidents, we all panicked and started running about looking for our motorcade. The two presidents just continued chatting and started taking photos with members of another delegation who had just arrived at the Vatican and were quite surprised to see George Bush and Bill Clinton standing there. What delegation, you might ask? The Iranians.

"Thankfully, the cars were found just outside the Vatican gates, since the president's motorcade had filled the square. I guess the presidents were right not to panic."

A few months later, when Hurricane Katrina devastated parts of the Gulf Coast and flooded the city of New Orleans, the president once again called on the Bush-Clinton team to help raise money in the private sector. President Bush and I flew to New York City to meet with President Clinton and his staff, and because the two presidents wanted to be more proactive this time around, they decided to set up the Bush-Clinton Katrina Fund.

They immediately did a round of interviews and public service announcements to get the word out that they were raising money, then traveled to Houston over Labor Day weekend to meet with the thousands of people who had been bused there from New Orleans to escape the floodwaters. President and Mrs. Bush and President Clinton roamed the floor of a huge arena that is part of the Houston Texans football stadium complex, where people were sleeping on cots. Once again, they touched as many people as they possibly could—sometimes hugging; sometimes crying; sometimes praying. (Senator Hillary Clinton went to another building to visit another group of evacuees, along with a friend she brought with her—the brand-new senator from Illinois, Barack Obama.)

In the next year, the two presidents traveled to New Orleans numerous times, including giving the Tulane commencement address and sitting down together to do an interview with Louisiana native Ellen DeGeneres. They were a team.

And they raised money—$130.6 million. At the request of the president, they immediately gave grants to higher education totaling $30 million to help colleges reopen; and another $25 million to churches for the same purpose.

They also provided a total of $40 million in grant money for the governors of Louisiana, Mississippi, and Alabama, to be used to help "people who were falling through the cracks."

After the initial grants were given out, nearly $80 million remained. The decision was made that each president would come up with a plan to spend $40 million, with each reserving the right to veto the other's ideas.

By this time I had hired a woman named Lynn Schlemeyer to manage our disaster relief projects for us. She had emailed me the weekend Katrina came ashore to see if we needed help; she stayed for five years.

To figure out how to best allocate his $40 million, President Bush checked in with the governors of each state and tasked Lynn with calling the mayors of some of the other hardest-hit cities. It was fascinating to see how different the answers were, from the mayor of Waveland, Mississippi, who needed $2 million so they could get a FEMA[2] matching grant to rebuild their sewer system; to the governor of Alabama, who asked us to help shrimpers get their boats back into the water.

For years I unsuccessfully encouraged several academic groups to do a case study on how the two presidents approached this project. It was fascinating to watch their totally different philosophies. President Bush wanted to give his $40 million away in big chunks—$1 million or more. For example: He gave $5 million to help rebuild libraries in the region.

President Clinton's projects were more numerous but smaller in scale, including buying new choir robes for a church in New Orleans.

It made for a perfect partnership in many ways. Between the two of them, they were taking care of all things big and small.

When Hurricane Ike hit the Texas Gulf Coast in September 2008, they suited up again to raise money and even spent a day in Galveston, Texas, helping clean debris off the beach.

Thankfully, the next few hurricane seasons were a little quieter, allowing the two presidents to step back from their disaster work. President

---

2. Federal Emergency Management Agency.

Clinton did partner with President George W. Bush, at the request of President Obama, when a devastating earthquake hit Haiti in 2010.

But then Hurricane Harvey ripped apart President Bush's hometown in August 2017, with a record-setting forty inches of rain falling in forty-eight hours. Floodwaters poured into every part of Houston, including downtown; and if your home did not flood, it's likely something leaked—such as the Bushes' roof.

The fourth-largest city in America was paralyzed.

By this time President Bush was ninety-three years old and very frail. He had been on the brink of dying numerous times in the previous few years but always managed to come back. He just wasn't ready to go yet.

We were in Maine when Harvey hit, but our hearts were in Houston. It was right before Labor Day weekend, and President Bush gave me that look that I knew meant he had an idea. "We have to go to work, Jean."

The first call, of course, was to the other Texas president, George W. Bush. He was all-in. It was decided everyone needed to be "all-in," so calls went out to Presidents Obama, Clinton, and Carter to join them. The answer was an immediate and resounding yes.

They recorded a public service announcement that began airing immediately; billboards featuring the five of them popped up everywhere; and the NFL heavily promoted the fund throughout its opening weekend. In the end they would raise $42 million, not only for Harvey relief but also for Puerto Rico and the U.S. Virgin Islands, where Hurricane Maria had come through shortly after Harvey; and for Florida, hit hard by Hurricane Irma.

It was an incredible joint effort as all the presidents brought to the table their social media networks and friends who provided pro bono support and work.

In the middle of all this, the George H. W. Bush Presidential Library Foundation was getting ready to celebrate the twentieth anniversary of the library's opening. The idea was to put up a tent and have a good old-fashioned Texas barbecue with President Bush's friend Larry Gatlin providing some music.

With so much heartbreak in Texas, President Bush decided it was not the time to celebrate something that had happened twenty years before. But rather than cancel the event, scheduled for October 21, he thought maybe we could turn it into a Harvey fund-raiser. I called the head of the library foundation, David Jones, and he loved the idea. He and his team went to work to plan something a little bigger.

I called President George W. Bush's chief of staff, Freddy Ford, and he said of course the forty-third president would join his parents for this event.

I then sent a casual email to the chiefs of staff to the other three presidents and said something like this: "We are going to do this fund-raiser at Texas A&M on October 21. Larry Gatlin is going to sing and maybe we can raise some money. We are not asking you to come, but if you just happen to be in the neighborhood, we would love to have you."

President Obama's chief of staff called and said, "He's coming."

Then President Clinton's chief of staff called and said, "He's supposed to be in Europe but he'll come home early."

Then President Carter's chief of staff called and said, "Well, if everybody else is coming of course he's coming!"

Then, out of the blue, Lady Gaga called and said she was coming. No, she is not a former president, but we didn't say no.

So onstage were five former presidents, Lady Gaga, Alabama, the Gatlin brothers, Lyle Lovett, Sam Moore, Lee Greenwood, Yolanda Adams, and so many others.

And it all just sort of happened.

When I told the Bushes all the former presidents were coming, Mrs. Bush's first reaction was: I guess we need to feed them.

That might be a good idea.

The dinner was for the presidents only, and two other high-profile Americans who wanted to come for the evening: James Baker and former vice president Dick Cheney. I confess I told them they could crash the dinner only if they leaked all that was said to me and to me only.

They readily agreed.

Their report was disappointing. They said the conversation was a lot about family, golf, their summers. Not much conversation about the current president.

Unfortunately, I did have to briefly slip into the role of the consigliere. President Clinton was deep into conversation with Secretary Baker, oblivious to the fact that everyone else was seated and ready to eat.

I might add here that I was under enormous pressure to keep the presidents on time since we were going live on several networks and social media platforms at 7 p.m.

Taking a deep breath, I told President Clinton I loved him, but for heaven's sake he had to quit talking and sit down. He gave me a hug and sat down.

We arrived at the arena where the show was to be held with just barely enough time to do a photo op with all the entertainers—our only way of really thanking them. When Lady Gaga was leaving the room, I boldly tried to introduce myself, but she was sobbing with emotion. "I'm sorry," she stammered. "I am too overwhelmed to talk." Yes, it was a moment.

Somewhere in the middle of all this, President Bush told me he wasn't sure who Lady Gaga was but he found her quite charming.

To close the loop on the Odd Couple: President Clinton came to Maine every summer to visit, play golf, hang out. There was only one small problem with his Maine visits: President Clinton was *not* a fan of fast rides on *Fidelity*. President Bush eventually forgave him for that, too.

And when he was anywhere near Houston, President Clinton would drop in. I remember once when he had another scare with his heart, his aide called to whisper in my ear that on the way home from the hospital, President Clinton told him he was exhausted and did not want to take any phone calls unless 41 called. He would talk only to him.

I was in the car with President Bush when the aide's call came in, and President Bush immediately said, "I wanted to call him but wasn't sure I should." Now he knew that 42 assumed and was kind of hoping he would indeed call.

In the summer of 2018, after Mrs. Bush had died in April, 42 came for a long lunch with President Bush. He told story after story after story as President Bush listened, nodded, and smiled. While he talked, he signed copies for all of us of the book he had written with James Patterson, *The President Is Missing*.

I walked President Clinton to his car as he was leaving, and he broke down. He could see that his friend was beginning to slip away. He made me promise to call him for one last visit if I thought the time was near. It was a promise I was to break, although not intentionally. They would not see each other again, but maybe that was best. It was a sweet last visit.

When I saw President Clinton at the funeral, he collapsed sobbing into my arms. Then Secretary Clinton started crying, and then Chelsea. The four of us stood in the middle of the side aisle at the National Cathedral, just hugging.

We had come a long way since 1992.

Although never as close as the Odd Couple, President Bush and President Obama also became good friends over the years. You could say the beginning was almost an accident.

In the summer of 2009—just a few months after President Obama had been sworn in as president—his senior adviser and longtime friend, Valerie Jarrett, reached out to me to see if President Bush could attend a ceremony at the White House commemorating the twentieth anniversary of the signing of the Americans with Disabilities Act. Unfortunately, a schedule conflict prevented a disappointed President Bush from attending. In the back-and-forth emails between us, Valerie wrote: "President Obama is looking for an opportunity to do something with President Bush. Would you please keep that in mind?"

It seemed like such a genuine offer that I mentioned it to President Bush. He said most likely the president was just being nice. But one Friday night when I probably was too tired to be working, I decided—without permission—to email Valerie and tell her that President Bush would be hosting a big twentieth-anniversary celebration of Points of

Light at his presidential library that fall, in case that would be something that would interest the president. I was more or less thinking out loud, rolling the dice, running a flag up the flagpole—pick your idiom.

Imagine my surprise when a few days later Valerie emailed me back and said, "President Obama is delighted to accept President Bush's invitation to come to his library."

Oops. The president of the United States had just graciously accepted an invitation that had never been issued.

The next step was obvious: Tell President Bush. I read him the email exchange and waited for him to be hopefully only just a little annoyed with me for getting way out ahead of him and everybody else. I had definitely misstepped.

He was thrilled. He immediately declared it the best mistake ever and called the president of Texas A&M and let him know the president was coming to town. In the meantime, I let Michelle Nunn, the president and CEO of Points of Light, know the major breaking news. I decided the whole affair was my version of "I have an idea."

The visit was a huge success. When President Obama left the auditorium to return to the airport, President and Mrs. Bush stayed behind to speak to the crowd and shake as many hands as possible. I was watching offstage, just so happy we had pulled it off, when a White House advance person came running up to say President Obama wanted President Bush to ride with him to the airport. I told him "No can do" and pointed out that President Bush was still onstage. He nodded and ran off, but then came back: "President Obama is not leaving without him." So Jim Appleby walked out onstage, interrupted President Bush's spontaneous speech, and whispered what was going on. President Bush announced to the crowd: "I'm so sorry, but President Obama needs for me to drive him to the airport."

Just about a year later, President Obama called President Bush and told him he would like to give him the Medal of Freedom, our country's highest civilian honor. President Bush was deeply touched. In bestowing the award a few months later, President Obama cited President Bush's long résumé of public service and commended him for ending the Cold War, among other accomplishments. But the words that touched President Bush the most were these: "His humility and decency reflects the very best of the American spirit."

Going forward, Valerie would call or email me occasionally, asking if President Bush was "coming to town" anytime soon. If so, would he come over for a cup of coffee? President Bush took the president up on that a time or two, but not always when he was in town. "Jean, I don't want to bother the president," he would tell me when I reminded him of the standing invitation.

In March 2012, when President Bush read in the paper that President Obama was coming to Houston for an election-year fund-raiser, he felt he should return the president's hospitality and invite him for a visit at the house or office.

In my email exchange with Valerie, she said the president would love to see President Bush, but as we started comparing schedules, we saw it was complicated. By the time the president landed, President and Mrs. Bush would be on their way to the Houston Livestock Show and Rodeo, where their great friend Reba McEntire was to perform that night. It looked like a visit would not work out after all.

Then Valerie emailed back: "POTUS is thinking he might want to go the rodeo with 41."

As Yogi Berra would say: It was déjà vu all over again.

In my slight panic I emailed my sisters:

"Huh? Are you kidding me? I didn't INVITE THE PRESIDENT OF THE UNITED STATES TO THE RODEO. Gulp. how the hell did that happen? POTUS GOING TO THE RODEO WOULD BE A REALLY BIG DEAL. And in an election year, it's not what 41 should be doing. We should be taking Mitt Romney[3] to the rodeo for God's

---

3. President Bush was a huge fan and friend of Governor Romney, who went on to become the Republican nominee that year.

sake. This all happened yesterday and I haven't seen 41 yet to tell him. Gulp and double gulp. This is funny, right?????? oh god."

I told Valerie my concerns, both politically and logistically. Taking a sitting president to the Houston Rodeo with seventy thousand screaming fans in the Houston Texans football stadium would be a security nightmare. She got it immediately. But her boss did not. He would like to go.

So with a deep breath, I told President Bush the next day that somehow I had managed to do it again: Kind of, sort of, somehow I had invited the president of the United States to the rodeo on his behalf.

And once again, President Bush was thrilled. "This will be great fun," he declared. "Barack will love the rodeo."

When I reminded him it was an election year and he was already openly supporting Governor Romney, he hesitated for a moment, then had what he thought was the perfect solution.

"Let's see if Mitt can come to the rodeo next week. Problem solved." (The rodeo is a three-week event.)

Thankfully, none of this came to pass. The White House advance team, with great encouragement from the Secret Service, shut it down.

But President Bush was to get a second chance to be hospitable.

In April 2014, President Obama was coming to Houston to do a large fund-raiser for the Democratic Party, and President Bush announced he was going to meet him at the airport upon arrival. When I expressed surprise, he said when the president comes to town, you meet him at the airport. I pointed out that he had never greeted President Clinton or his own son at the airport. (I should note that when the forty-third president came to town he would always come see his parents or they would go see him, making an airport handshake obviously a little silly.)

President Bush was insistent. He finally admitted that he was annoyed at some of the press President Obama had been receiving of late—press that he felt the president did not deserve or need. (Sadly, six years later, I don't remember what the bad press was.) He felt showing up at the airport would be a good way to show his support. Besides, he argued, Air Force One was landing at George Bush Intercontinental Airport. Shouldn't he go to welcome him to his airport?

So waiting at the bottom of the stairs in his wheelchair and wearing a pair of his now-signature, very colorful striped socks was the forty-first president to welcome the forty-fourth president to Houston. The White House advance team had a hard time getting the president and First Lady in the motorcade and off to their event. They were enjoying their reunion.

The last visit between the two of them was in November 2018, when President Obama was in town to speak at the twenty-fifth anniversary of Secretary Baker's public policy institute at Rice University. As early as that summer, President Obama's post–White House chief of staff, Anita Breckenridge, had given me a heads-up that President Obama was coming to Houston in late fall and wanted to get President Bush on his schedule. I didn't have the heart to tell her that President Bush's health had been in steep decline since Mrs. Bush's death in April, and we weren't sure President Bush would still be alive in November. I simply assured her that he of course would have time to see him.

The day of the visit, President Bush was not feeling well at all, which was making him even more frail than usual. I told him I felt strongly that we should cancel the visit with President Obama. He insisted we let it go forward. "I would like to see Barack," he told me. He might have been ninety-four years old and frail, but he still knew how to get his way.

I asked Anita's permission to include the Bushes' son Neil in the visit, to help carry the conversation, and presidential historian Jon Meacham, who was in town for the same event and also was coming over to say hello. When President Obama arrived, I warned him of President Bush's frailty and that we felt his time was near. He took a deep breath and went to the living room where President Bush was waiting. After about a thirty-minute visit, during which President Bush mainly listened and smiled, President Obama asked for the room. He wanted to spend a moment alone with his friend.

A few minutes later, I realized Jon had crept back down the hallway and was trying to eavesdrop at the door. I gave him the devil, to which he argued, "I am a historian and this is history." He reluctantly backed away, but he had heard enough to know why President Obama wanted some time alone: He wanted to thank President Bush for his service to his country—service that had begun, Obama graciously noted, in World War II. "We all took a lot of flak," President Obama told President Bush, "but you took it for real."

President Bush died four days later.

CHAPTER SEVEN

A POINT OF LIGHT

In addition to big deeds and big efforts, President Bush also was the master of small acts of kindness. Just as he had asked me when he was dying if I was okay, he always seemed to have the other guy in mind.

When going through my endless files to write this book, I found this memo he had written to longtime staffer Don Rhodes:[1]

I gave my driver's license to a guy in Oman. It is 0018435. He had a big collection of licenses, etc. I doubt I will ever need it but save this number in case I do. Or request another one if you think I may need the license. Say "lost in the sands of Oman."—GB

It's such a random story but helps paint the bigger picture of a man with a huge and giving heart. He literally would give you the shirt off his back—or, in this case, his driver's license.

---

1. Don is a legend in Bush World. We will talk about him a lot more in chapter 11.

Historian and writer Mark Updegrove[2] wrote this about President Bush in 2013, calling him "our most revered former president": "Bush was never one to grandstand, but was more apt to reveal himself through small, quiet gestures that made a deeper impression. It's what made him both a great statesman and a good friend."

One habit I loved was his always offering people a ride. After every meeting, meal, event, occurrence, if he was walking out with a group of people, he asked if they needed a way home.

The problem was they sometimes said yes. Case in point: After we landed late at night from our tsunami trip, he asked the question of all who got off the plane. Much to my dismay, *Houston Chronicle* reporter Tony Freemantle said yes. I think I gave him a look, but off they went. Tony, now a good friend, has never forgotten that a former president took him home and that along the way, he asked Tony's permission to call his daughter Doro. He did not want to be rude.

At the 2000 Republican convention in Philadelphia, it became a huge problem as President Bush asked that question of very random people as we left the convention center every night. We had a three-car motorcade—the Bushes' car, the Secret Service car, and the staff car. A lot of people said yes, including, one night, General Colin Powell. We kept squeezing people in to the point you could barely close the door.

For the 2004 convention in New York City, I was ready. I got a bus.

Once when I was in the hospital, he called to see if I needed him to come pick me up when I was discharged. I already had that covered—my friend and former East Wing staffer Ann Brock was taking me home. But it was these kinds of sweet gestures that you never forgot.

He was just as prolific at offering up beds. President Bush considered everyone he met a friend and felt the need to invite them to spend the night if they were going to be in town. Most people said no, but some

---

2. He also is the president and CEO of the LBJ Library. He and his wife, Amy, became good friends of the Bushes.

people said yes. Especially in Kennebunkport, Mrs. Bush used to keep track of how many overnight guests they had between May when they arrived and October when they left.

It was always more than one hundred. Even when you took out the huge Bush family, the numbers were impressive.

I found a fax President Bush had written in 1994 from overseas, responding to a memo I had sent telling him Václav Havel, the president of the Czech Republic, wanted to "stop by Walker's Point." President Bush wrote back:

An enthusiastic "yes" for Vaclav Havel. Please ask him for two nights if we are free . . . he can bring a couple of people with him if he wants. I am delighted he wants to come. Barbara, my wife, is showing restrained enthusiasm.

(President Havel did not spend the night but did go out on *Fidelity*.)

One night in Maine the Bushes were sound asleep when they realized a child they did not know was on the couch in their bedroom watching TV. When they inquired just who he was, it turned out he was a friend of a grandson, who was in another room watching a baseball game. But this child wanted to watch something else, and he remembered there was a TV in the master bedroom.

I don't think that happened again, but a common occurrence was for President Bush to look down the long dining room table, which could seat thirty if everyone squeezed, and see people he did not know. They were usually friends of grandchildren, but one child identified herself as a friend of a friend of a granddaughter, neither of whom were at the dinner table.

"My mom forgot to pick me up," came the explanation.

All of us who lived in Maine during the summer had an overabundance of houseguests. One of mine gave me a tea towel that said, "Friends of friends may not invite friends." I did enforce that rule in my house. Mrs. Bush gave up.

I learned a lot watching President Bush deal with events of the day—common or otherwise—and figure out a way he could help. He was such a man of action, rarely taking the time to think about pluses or minuses, should we or shouldn't we. He just did.

Here are some of my favorite "random acts of kindness" stories.

In 2001, while attending an Amy Grant and Vince Gill Christmas concert in Houston, President Bush raised his hand when the singers asked the audience to support an organization called Compassion International, which raised money for children around the world. The specific ask at the concert was to give a certain amount of money to sponsor a child, whom you then would occasionally write. What followed was a three-year pen pal relationship with President Bush's new friend Timothy, who lived in the Philippines. He never told Timothy who he was, and signed his letters by his alias, George Walker. The program thought it best to do it that way, as did the Secret Service. In his first letter he told Timothy:

I want to be your new pen pal. I am an old man, 77 years old, but I love kids; and though we have not met, I love you already. I live in Texas. I will write you from time to time. Good luck.

He did admit to Timothy in one letter that he "got to go to the White House once in a while." Timothy once wrote back to him, "I hope you won't get tired of writing to me."

Timothy was told who George Walker was after he graduated from the Compassion program. I am not sure how the media found out about the friendship when President Bush died—actually, I think Compassion International leaked a few letters—but they were shocked. President Bush's spokesman, Jim McGrath, admitted to reporters he also was unaware of the friendship, but he was not surprised. "He spent his entire life reaching out and trying to help lift the lives of others, both in and—as we see here—out of elected office," Jim told *Time*.

As for Timothy—now married with a child—he told the media it really didn't sink in who President Bush was until he died. He told the British newspaper the *Daily Telegraph* that the letters and support from President Bush changed his life forever. In addition to notes, he said President Bush mailed him notebooks, pens, and pencils and encouraged Timothy to send him sketches, which he did. "If given a chance, I would like to personally thank his family for what they did for my life," he told the reporter.

One of my favorite "just do it" examples came in 2003 when the space shuttle *Columbia* blew up while reentering earth's atmosphere, killing the seven astronauts on board. We issued a statement the day it happened but President Bush did not feel words were enough. After a few days had passed, he and Mrs. Bush went to NASA, located just south of Houston. I sent this email to the staff about the visit:

"I have never been prouder than today to work for No. 41. We insisted NO press, which shocked NASA. I think they are so used to VIPs doing this kind of thing for the press. We worked all the mission control rooms, the room where the engineers are huddled trying to figure out what happened; GB and BPB talked to the astronauts on the International Space Station (who apparently are pretty shook up); they shook every hand; lots of hugs, etc. GB only cried once, but I think it meant a lot to these NASA folks that he cried. It made me proud to be an American to be there and to see all those people, grim but determined and carrying on. In Mission Control, the big screen you see on TV all the time is still stuck exactly where they lost contact with the space shuttle. That's about the only time I almost lost it. I couldn't take my eyes off it. You see the shuttle's flight path, then nothing. Like it fell out of the sky, which of course it did."

In April 2004, I wrote this email to my sisters:

"A Houston firefighter was killed this weekend, in a fire that has now been determined to be arson. The funeral was yesterday. President Bush could not go to the funeral but went to the church about 30 minutes early to privately meet with the family and firefighters…He comes back to the office from this meeting to announce that he has invited the 13-year-old son of the firefighter to go to the Astros game with him last night. It's a little complicated, he says, but I'm sure you all can work it out. Well, it was complicated because this family lives in Sealy, a tiny town about 60 miles due west of Houston. We were all in a state of shock he had invited this child on the spot and his mother was going to let him go to a game on the day of his father's funeral with a stranger. I'm sure she had no idea what to say other than, 'Sure.' On top of everything else, it was Justin's birthday.

"In the end, Laura Pears and I volunteered to go to the game as well so we could drive him home after the game. His family arranged to stay in town long enough to drop him off…

"Before the game, 41 took him to BOTH locker rooms. He met all the Astros and Giants, except for Barry Bonds who never came out and said hi to him. (This may be unfair but I like thinking he purposely snubbed him.[3]) The kid got so much loot that

---

3. I am a St. Louis Cardinals fan, and we do not like Barry Bonds. In 2001, he hit seventy-three home runs, breaking the previous seasonal record set by Cardinal Mark McGwire.

Laura and I had to help him carry it all to the car and then in the house (which is another story). He got signed bats, baseballs, jerseys etc. Even the umpires gave him stuff. Even the Secret Service gave him stuff.

"He and 41 talked through the whole game. You would think they had known each other for years. Laura and I could barely control ourselves, we felt like weeping through the whole game. Watching 41 with this stranger who had just lost his dad was almost too much to bear. Laura and I felt guilty because the child never ate dinner—cotton candy, cracker jacks, and cookies only. When we encouraged him to at least eat a hot dog, GB of course said he could eat whatever he wanted and to leave him alone.

"The game was incredible. Roger Clemens' debut here in Houston. He struck out Barry Bonds twice and pitched a one-hitter through seven innings. He even got a base hit. It was awesome to watch and I'm glad I got to see it. A great baseball moment. The Astros had lost their first two [games of the season], so it was almost magical for Clemens to come in and do this. Even for a Cardinal fan, it was hard not to appreciate the magic of the moment.

"So we leave at the end of 7. First, GB takes Justin back to the Astros locker room so he could visit with Clemens. Finally, we get him in the car and drive him home. We run into the biggest old Texas thunderstorm—torrential rain, ferocious lightning and thunder. We didn't care. We were just grateful to play a small part in the most difficult yet memorable day of this child's life.

"When we got to the house it was filled with family and friends who had been watching the game. They welcomed Justin home like a conquering hero."

One summer during this same time period I randomly told the Bushes that I had several neighbors on my street in Kennebunkport who were newcomers to town. They all were having a hard time meeting people. As much as they loved the area, they were finding it hard to be accepted. I wasn't the least surprised, since I had noticed for years that as much as I loved New Englanders, there was this certain attitude that if your ancestors didn't come off the *Mayflower*, you were an outsider. They were completely unaware they were cliquish. The fact I worked for the Bushes had helped me a great deal—people were too afraid *not* to accept me.

I told the Bushes about my neighbors' dilemma in casual conversation. The first thing I knew, they were planning a party for all the new people who had moved to town and were going to include a smattering of the "old people" as well, so maybe they would get the hint. We sent our summer intern out to knock on doors and collect names, all of whom were a tad surprised.

Did it work? Of course.

Probably the most touching random act of kindness was in 2013, when President Bush shaved his head in support of a Secret Service agent's child who had leukemia and was bald from chemotherapy. Except for a few agents, President Bush's entire security detail had shaved their heads to support their comrade, so President Bush shaved his with the help of his personal aide, Coleman Lapointe—who then shaved his own head. President Bush failed to warn his wife he was going bald for a while. She was not pleased. But happily for President Bush, she blamed me and not him. I tried to tell her the first I knew of his plan was when I heard a buzzing in the office kitchen and was shocked to discover a bald President Bush surrounded by his hair. By the end of the day, the photo had gone viral and was even featured on the big billboard in New York's Times Square. His gesture had touched the heart of the nation. (I should note that although President Bush was eighty-nine years old at the time, his hair grew back a little thicker and even a little darker.)

Prejudice of any kind deeply disturbed President and Mrs. Bush. Over the years he and I had numerous discussions about the fact that neither one of us knew what it felt like to be the subject of discrimination or bullying. He was frustrated that more progress had not been made.

So if he saw an opening to make a difference, he took it.

In the year after 9/11, he asked me to find a Muslim event he could attend. He was greatly disturbed by the anti-Muslim sentiment festering in the country and he wanted to show their community he supported them. I found a local Muslim group that was about to host its annual dinner. Cold-calling them and asking if President Bush could "drop by" their dinner would be in my top ten favorite phone calls I got to make on his behalf. It also was one of many times I got the standard: "You are who calling about what?"

Not long before the Bushes died, they both became concerned by what they saw as growing anti-Semitism in the United States. They had stopped accepting awards of any kind, but when a Jewish group wanted to honor President Bush, he shocked me by saying yes. But he had one condition: The event had to be held in a synagogue in front of the press.

He had a point he wanted to make.

In the spring of 2015, President Bush welcomed to his office a group of Black ministers and Houston police officers, organized by Jim McGrath and the president of the police union, Ray Hunt. The meeting was held in the aftermath of Michael Brown's shooting in Ferguson, Missouri, and tension was high nationwide between Blacks and police. In Houston, the police and ministers had been working together for a number of years, thanks to a program called Thumbs Up, founded by Houston Police Department auxiliary chaplain Floyd Lewis. But Hunt told Jim the meeting at the office with the former president gave them the encouragement they needed to try even harder.

That same year President and Mrs. Bush hosted a "sneak peek" party for the soon-to-be released movie *Selma*. They filled a theater in Houston with friends, local leaders, and really anyone who would fit, to watch Martin Luther King, John Lewis, and so many other brave souls walk across that bridge.

I should explain that throwing movie parties was one of President

Bush's favorite things to do, and we did several every year, in both Houston and Maine. The tradition had started in 2005 with Disney, who—in an attempt to create some buzz—asked President Bush to host a watch party for the golf movie *The Greatest Game Ever Played*. In return, Disney would use the Bushes' party as part of the movie's publicity. Over the next few years, the Bushes must have hosted twenty such parties, inviting friends, doctors, corporate executives, waiters at their favorite restaurants, barbers, manicurists, the janitorial staff at the office building—just about anyone who touched their lives.

My favorite movie party of all time was the one they gave for Disney's *Glory Road* in 2006. The movie told the true story of the first all-Black men's basketball team[4] to reach and win the NCAA championship game, facing horrific racism and discrimination every step of the way. President Bush's idea was to invite all the area men's and women's college basketball teams—whose players were predominantly Black—reaching all the way to Texas A&M, which was ninety miles away. The movie premiere was in the middle of the college basketball season, so we picked a night when few games were played, but we also were aware we would run into issues with practice sessions.

Well, no one practiced that night. They *all* came. We had to keep moving the watch party to a bigger theater, which was okay because Disney loved the idea and offered to pay for all the food and drink. (They typically paid for popcorn and soft drinks only.) I am not sure they made enough on the movie when it was released to pay for all the hot dogs consumed that night.

The Bushes spent a long time taking team photos, during which I remember thinking I had never seen the six-foot-two President Bush look—well, short. President Bush invited Houston Rockets superstar Clyde "the Glide" Drexler to join him and talk to the four hundred–some college basketballers who came to the party.

---

4. The team came from Texas Western College, now known as the University of Texas at El Paso (UTEP). They beat Kentucky in the championship game.

Toward the end of the movie you could hear a pin drop in the theater as the audience appreciated the importance of the history being made.

Along with just "doing," the Bushes were also tireless fund-raisers for charity. I think they managed to attend a lunch or dinner for just about every nonprofit group in Houston. One spring—the prime season for nonprofit events in Houston—President Bush asked me to call one of the organizations that wanted him to come speak and explain he was out of new speech material. He fretted that everyone in Houston had already heard all his jokes. The group did not seem concerned about that issue, so President Bush said yes, and he told me the morning after that his jokes still got a laugh.

For the causes nearest and dearest to their hearts, they worked hard until they were ninety. However, as they got older, I think it began to wear a little bit when we tried to use every single major event in their lives to raise money. I guiltily remember telling President Bush, when a group of us pitched him the idea of using his eightieth birthday as a fund-raiser for the George H. W. Bush Presidential Library Foundation, the George Bush School of Government and Public Service, Points of Light, and MD Anderson, that it would be the last fund-raiser of its kind.

But then we raised a staggering $56 million. The response to attend the main event was so huge—even Mikhail Gorbachev came—we had to use the Houston Astros' Minute Maid Park for the concert part of the celebration.

It was going to be hard to stop.

As Mrs. Bush once said, "I'm afraid our friends will never talk to us again," since it was their friends who were always asked to dig deep into their pockets.

At one point there were four annual Celebration of Reading events for the Barbara Bush Foundation for Family Literacy—the mothership event being in Houston, but then we added Florida, Dallas, and Washington, DC. President Bush once asked me, a tad grumpily, "When do we do Dubuque, Iowa?"

But given their devotion to the causes important to them, it was hard for the Bushes to say no. As modest as they were, they knew they had the celebrity to raise the kind of money needed to do good work.

The last such event was Mrs. Bush's ninetieth birthday party, for which we raised $17 million for the Barbara Bush Foundation for Family Literacy. It was a whirlwind of activities for three days, and although hugely successful, I knew we could never ask this of them again.

Despite their willingness to help a large spectrum of causes and organizations, there were several about which the Bushes felt so strongly that they did more than just raise money or, as President Bush used to call it, "wave the flag." For Mrs. Bush, it was, of course, literacy, and she was devoted to her foundation literally until the end, asking me just two days before she died about our search for a new president and CEO. She was still worried that thirty-six million Americans could not read or write.

After leaving the White House, she also became ambassador-at-large for the international relief organization Americares, which had been founded by the Bushes' good friend Bob Macauley. Over the years, she (and sometimes President Bush) went on numerous relief missions.

President Bush focused on volunteerism and public service, about which we'll talk more in a bit.

Their great mutual passion was fighting cancer.

After they lost their daughter Robin, age three, to leukemia in 1953, they helped raise money and were active in cancer charities. But when they left Washington for the last time and officially entered retirement, they decided it was time they gave it their all.

President Bush became a more active member of the MD Anderson Center Board of Visitors, serving as chairman from 2001 to 2003. He was proud of his hometown hospital, consistently ranked as one of the world's most respected cancer centers. Through numerous events the Bushes helped organize, hosted, and attended—and through more than one parachute jump—MD Anderson estimates the Bushes helped raise nearly $90 million for cancer research.

To honor the Bushes, MD Anderson dedicated the Robin Bush Child and Adolescent Clinic in 2004, on President Bush's eightieth birthday. Later the institution established the George and Barbara Bush Endowment for Innovative Cancer Research.

But the Bushes still weren't done.

In 1997 a group of cancer leaders asked to meet with the Bushes. Led by John Seffrin, president of the American Cancer Society, they told them there was a multitude of problems in the cancer community, including a lack of communication and cooperation between all the major players. The Bushes were surprised to learn many of these "players" had never even met.

The end result was the establishment of C-Change (originally called National Dialogue on Cancer), which President and Mrs. Bush chaired. It brought together for the first time cancer activists representing the medical, government, nonprofit, and private sectors. The idea was for them to share information and resources, address disparities in cancer care and information, and establish prevention as a national priority.

Later, after specifically challenging a group of corporate CEOs involved with C-Change to make fighting cancer part of their mission, the CEO Roundtable on Cancer was established to do just that. They have expanded their work into China, where the leaders report some success in convincing the Chinese to quit smoking.

It wasn't easy. At the first meeting, hosted by the Bushes at the library, one leading cancer doctor got up and walked out of the room because he so disagreed with what some of the others were proposing. President Bush quietly but firmly asked the room, with the support of his vice-chair, Senator Dianne Feinstein, to please check their egos at the door.

One of the president's cancer mentors, Dr. Andrew von Eschenbach—then head of the prostate cancer program at MD Anderson[5]—remembers

---

5. Andy, now president of Samaritan Health, went on to become the commissioner of the Food and Drug Administration and director of the National Cancer Institute, both under President George W. Bush.

thinking that he now saw clearly how President Bush won Desert Storm. "I think he understood that day what I had been telling him, that we desperately needed to create a coalition of people with different agendas but with a common enemy, just like he did in the Gulf War."

The Bushes dutifully attended all of C-Change's annual meetings, which wasn't easy, either. The keynote speakers were typically doctors, researchers, cancer experts. Frankly, the Bushes and I often had no idea what they were saying.

When the Bushes retired as chairpersons in 2010, President Bush admitted as much in his farewell remarks. "And yes, it's true, we sometimes weren't sure what the heck the speaker was talking about," he told them. "My favorite was the woman who got up and declared I was the father of the genome. I don't even know what a genome is. But I am proud to claim it."[6]

The group was surprised by this confession. After all, President Bush was famous for furiously scribbling notes during all these meetings, while Mrs. Bush needlepointed. Many C-Change members had marveled to me over the years at his notetaking and often hinted they would love to see those notes. I pretended not to hear them.

It was a ruse.

What he actually was doing was playing a game he called BS Bingo, which he took quite seriously. He explained the rules in an email to family and friends in 2003, asking their help in coming up with twenty-five words to put on a bingo card:

---

6. He was more or less teasing. In 1989 President Bush signed the legislation that funded major genome research, which was a game changer in the science community.

I think I have stumbled across a great way to make money. I am going to apply for a patent on the new game, "Bull Shit Bingo." . . . On the bingo card I will place 25 terms that are over-used, terms or words that often crop up in speeches. Words that are used to impress, words or terms that have become clichés and that frankly the listener is tired of. A few examples: cut to the chase; symbiotic; 24/7; synergy; interdisciplinary . . .

Once the 25 words have been selected I will have them printed on the cards. The cards will be sold to the Aspen Institute, the CFR, the Davos conference,[7] athletic banquets, roasts. I see the UN General Assembly as a major buyer. The market should be huge for this game.

People that go to conferences and listen to long speeches will be encouraged to try to get 5 up and down, or 5 across. When they do, they will stand right there in the audience and yell "Bull Shit" . . . This could help guard against future excesses.

---

7. All well-known annual conferences. CFR stands for Council on Foreign Relations.

When President Bush told the C-Change members about his bingo game, they were at first shocked. "So yes, when some of you thought I was furiously taking notes, I actually was keeping score," he admitted.

However, his confession was incomplete. What he did *not* tell them was that he also was constantly scanning the room during these daylong meetings looking for people who had fallen asleep. This tradition he started in the White House, where every year at his annual cabinet dinner he would give out awards to those who fell asleep during important meetings. Perhaps the best way to describe the award is to share this letter he wrote to President Clinton in 2008:

Dear Bill,

My heart went out to you when I saw you trying to keep your eyes open during an MLK Day sermon.

I could indeed "feel your pain." I have been there myself, more than once I might add, and it physically hurt as I tried to keep my eyes open. I don't remember if I ever told you about the prestigious Scowcroft Award, given during my White House days to the person that fell most soundly asleep during a meeting. Points were added for "recovery":

A standard recovery gambit was to awake from a sound sleep and start by nodding one's head in agreement to something just said in the meeting, something you had not heard at all. Writing something on a pad, anything at all, scored points. Good recoveries were awarded lots of points in determining the Scowcroft winner.

I remember when [Dick] Cheney won the award one time. We presented it to him at a nice dinner in the Rose Garden. Modest fellow that he is, he proclaimed himself unworthy, though his solid sleep in the Cabinet meeting had been witnessed by all assembled.

Scowcroft, of course, was hopeless. He could sleep in any meeting at any time of day. Always pleasant when he woke up, he was a leader without peers in both the sleep field and the recovery field.

Such was his leadership that the award was named for him.[8] He never fully appreciated that. Anyway having been a Scowcroft award recipient myself I send you now my total understanding and my warmest personal regards. As I heard that minister droning on I made a challenge for the trophy myself.

Your friend,
George

After President Bush died I rediscovered two handwritten notes he had passed me during a C-Change meeting. (Sadly, I wasn't smart enough to keep any of the bingo cards.) The first was about the then president of MD Anderson:

Jean, We have a Scowcroft winner. John Mendelsohn.

A classic sleep.

---

8. In General Scowcroft's defense, he was famous for working eighteen-hour days, often going home at dinnertime to feed his disabled wife and then returning to the White House to toil late into the night.

No recovery yet but it should be good.

Oops, he's up but watch and learn.

I am oddly proud of the second note:

9:16 a.m.

We have a winner. Jean Becker has just won the Private Sector Scowcroft Award.

Solid sleep for 3½ minutes.

Recovery—good. Looked right at the speaker Gordon Binder as though she heard him.

Then eyes closed again—briefly 'til applause for Binder again awakened her.

Again recovery—gets up and gets papers.

Summary: Brilliant.

Despite the bingo cards and needlepointing, both Bushes did pay close attention to what was being said and weren't afraid to ask questions or give recommendations—not on the question of how cancer could be cured, but how the group could work closely together.

President Bush was indeed listening attentively the day the prevention conversation centered on diet, and he took it quite personally when he was chided for refusing to eat broccoli, which he truly hated. "Why are they giving me such a hard time?" he complained to Dr. von Eschenbach. "I am seventy-five years old and jumping out of airplanes, how the hell can I get much better?"

He felt vindicated when Andy told him that thanks to the genome project, doctors now know that certain people have a gene variation that causes them to hate the taste of broccoli and it even makes them sick. I was never sure I believed that.

How much impact did President and Mrs. Bush have in the world of cancer? That's an impossible question for me to answer, so I asked Dr. von Eschenbach to give it a try:

"Can a person change a culture that has been ingrained for decades? Can a person have the courage to tell 'the establishment' that they are wrong and there is a better way? Can a person have the wisdom to know the right way? The answer is yes if that person is George Herbert Walker Bush. His public legacy in transforming the culture of cancer research and care will endure as our community continues to emulate his courage to say no to the old ways and the wisdom to know the better way."

Founding C-Change member and founding director of the CEO Roundtable, Dr. Martin Murphy, credits President Bush for never letting any of them give up on their goals. Not long before he died, he wrote these words of encouragement to Dr. Murphy, who was trying to make China stop smoking:

My last piece of advice to you is to never ever let anyone use the word "impossible." In my 94 years I've heard that word a lot. Man will never land on the moon. Smoking will never be curtailed in China. A black man will never be President. The Chicago Cubs will never win the World Series. Everything IS possible . . . and

you will prove it again when your mission is accomplished. It will
not happen in my lifetime, or maybe not even in yours, but I truly
believe from the bottom of my heart that victory will ultimately be
yours. For that I thank you very much.

President Bush's other passion was the idea that every single person, whatever their circumstances, needed to find a way to get involved in their communities, to give something back. No matter the subject of any given speech, he found a way to include his life's mantra: "Any definition of a successful life must include serving others."

He felt so strongly about it, he founded an organization to encourage the whole world to do just that: Points of Light.

President Bush first uttered those words in his acceptance speech at the 1988 Republican convention, when he described the United States as "a nation of communities...a brilliant diversity spread like stars, like a thousand points of light in a broad and peaceful sky."

Years later, Senator Alan Simpson told me that he and Secretary Baker hit the campaign trail with President Bush right after the convention, and sitting with him in a holding room before a big campaign rally, they tried to talk him out of the whole "Points of Light" idea, which he had included in his speech for that day. "We both didn't see it going anywhere," Senator Simpson told me. "We just didn't think it would win him any votes. He was very irritated with us and went right ahead."

President Bush spoke about it again in his inaugural address on January 20, 1989:

I have spoken of a Thousand Points of Light, of all the community
organizations that are spread like stars throughout the Nation,
doing good. We will work hand in hand, encouraging, sometimes

leading, sometimes being led, rewarding . . . The old ideas are new again because they're not old, they are timeless: duty, sacrifice, commitment, and a patriotism that finds its expression in taking part and pitching in.

It didn't take long for President Bush to put his words into action. Even before taking office, he announced the creation of the White House Office of National Service, with longtime family friend Gregg Petersmeyer in charge. A year later, he established the Points of Light Foundation, an independent, nonpartisan foundation, asking some of the most distinguished leaders in America to be on the founding board.[9]

"He fully employed the bully pulpit, speaking constantly about the importance of people simply finding ways to step forward to help one another," Petersmeyer remembers. "He knew how important it was to have this idea become a bigger part of the cultural values of American society."

Even before he established the foundation, President Bush established the Daily Point of Light (DPOL) award, where he formally recognized someone five days a week from the White House for their volunteer work. He signed the letters of congratulations until he died, a duty his son Neil, chairman of Points of Light, has assumed. President and Mrs. Obama hosted an event at the White House in July 2013 to honor the five thousandth Daily Point of Light, which now number more than 6,500.

President Bush felt a real connection to the DPOLs, asking that they

---

9. Some of the early leaders included: philanthropist Ray Chambers, the foundation's founding chairman; former governors Tom Kean of New Jersey and George Romney of Michigan—the latter considered by President Bush to be his mentor in all things volunteerism; civil rights activist Vernon Jordan; Disney's head, Michael Eisner; actor Louis Gossett Jr.; Spelman College president Johnnetta Cole; and nonprofit leader Frances Hesselbein.

be among those who greeted Air Force One when it landed in a city. When his presidential library was dedicated in 1997, DPOLs from the surrounding states were invited to be in the crowd of family, friends, and dignitaries. After an exhausting few days of events, when we thought everyone had gone home and the Bushes were finally getting a chance to rest, I heard a commotion outside their apartment on the library grounds. When I went out to investigate, it was a rowdy group of DPOLs hoping to get a glimpse of their hero. I told them he was exhausted and just could not come out. But he overheard the conversation and of course he came, waving to them from his second-floor balcony. You would have thought Elvis was in the building.

When he died, DPOLs from the Washington, DC, area were among the groups invited to watch Air Force One depart Joint Base Andrews, carrying President Bush's body back to Texas; and in Houston, DPOLs were invited to watch the plane land.

"I think of Points of Light as the soul of America," President Bush once wrote. "They are ordinary people who reach beyond themselves to touch the lives of those in need, bringing hope and opportunity, care and friendship. By giving so generously of themselves, these remarkable individuals show us not only what is best in our heritage but what all of us are called to become."

President Bush didn't quit when he left office, continuing to support Points of Light in any way he could—attending conferences, raising money, and, once in a while, jumping out of a plane.

In 1997, President Bush became the first president to agree to help convene a historic national summit on volunteerism. The end result was the Presidents' Summit for America's Future, held in Philadelphia in 1997 and attended by almost all the living presidents. Chaired by General Colin Powell,[10] participants included Vice President Al Gore, 25

---

10. The summit set in motion the establishment of the America's Promise Alliance, led by Colin Powell, which has become the largest alliance in America dedicated to helping children and young people meet their full potential.

governors, 92 mayors, 122 business leaders, 7 cabinet members, everyone from Oprah to LL Cool J, and 50 state and 145 community delegations, totaling 2,500 citizens.

I confess that I was grumpy about this summit before it began, only because 1997 was proving to be a bit much. It was the year of President Bush's first civilian parachute jump; we had cooperated with and attended a summit on his presidency held at Hofstra University; and we were racing to the finish line on building his presidential library, due to open in November with a cast of about twenty-five thousand.

Did we really need a summit on volunteerism?

And how foolish I felt sitting on the lawn of Independence Hall, watching the historic moment featuring Presidents Ford, Carter, Bush, and Clinton—with Nancy Reagan representing her husband—standing together for a cause so important to my boss.

The phrase "Points of Light" had become such a part of President Bush's DNA that four of his six eulogists used the term in their speeches.

Did President Bush make a difference when it came to volunteerism?

The current president and CEO of Points of Light, Natalye Paquin, says absolutely:

"We still believe in the power of people. And now as a global, nonpartisan organization spanning thirty-seven countries, his spirit sustains our mission. Though some of the ways people are engaged are different now than they were in 1990, we still believe every person has the opportunity to serve others, and we continue to support and recognize them every day."

Over the years, what impressed me more than big events and big efforts was the fact that both President Bush and Mrs. Bush not only talked the talk but walked the walk when it came to volunteerism. They weren't afraid to get their hands dirty:

- The day before the Philly summit started, teams of volunteers were dispatched around the city for various projects. The Bushes insisted they help and were assigned to cleaning up a vacant lot. (Mrs. Bush and I both admitted we had never seen so many used condoms in our lives.) Coincidentally, the Oak Ridge Boys were in town and found out about the project, and they showed up to help as well.

- When Alan and Ann Simpson spent Thanksgiving with the Bushes in 2001, the four of them decided it made no sense to sit around and look at one another. They went to Houston's George R. Brown Convention Center to help serve lunch to the homeless.

- Six months after Hurricane Ike, in April 2009, President Bush and Secretary Baker volunteered to participate in Shell Oil's annual beach cleanup day, in which hundreds of Shell employees spread out along Texas's Gulf Coast beaches to pick up trash, driftwood, and whatever else might be found. (That particular year a lot "else" was found as Ike continued to return to land what it had swept out to sea.) By then President Bush was very uneven on his feet, but he insisted he pick up trash. So Jim McGrath held on to his belt to keep him upright, while at the same time trying to stay out of the photos.

- Mrs. Bush tirelessly read to children, both in schools and in hospitals, as long as she could, sometimes taking her husband along. They both were big on hospital visits, comforting friends and strangers alike.

I'd like to end this chapter by sharing one of the stranger stories, sent by email to Jim McGrath just a few days after President Bush died. None of us had ever heard this story, told by a woman named Susan Willis:

"Politics were the last thing on my mind January 10, 2010, standing in the top-floor hospice room of MD Anderson Cancer Center in Houston... My only sister, Michelle, we called her Lili, the oldest in our family, lay dying on the bed literally in the middle of us...

"Lili's [death] would be the third death [in our family] in about twenty-four months. Our surviving family members were drowning in loss. The effort it took not to crater just can't be articulated. All of us just one crack away from avalanche.

"A commotion caught Mike's eye[11] . . . four Secret Service men arrived in the main hallway of the hospice floor. Mike stepped into the hall to investigate. One of the agents came over to grab Mike's hand. Turns out they worked a security detail together when President Bill Clinton was in Houston. They had an easy camaraderie as most guys in law enforcement do . . .

"Out of nowhere and much taller than expected strode in former President George H. W. Bush, the forty-first president of the United States, just going like holy hell. He literally came in like gangbusters.

"Right next door was former U.S. Secretary of Commerce Robert Mosbacher, a powerful man who was a longtime friend with President Bush from their early careers. He also was dying of cancer. His time was drawing near . . .

"Noting his agent had seen a friend, the president popped his head over to say hello. We all shook his hand and made introductions. He inquired about my sister, regal and kind in his gentle questioning . . . Interested, curious, with a quick wit and ready smile; I liked him right away . . . He could tell from my crumpled face the weight of her dying was crippling me. President Bush could detect we were raw. His concern showed on his face.

"He popped over to visit [Mr. Mosbacher], then unexpectedly returned to our room to talk further about all kinds of stuff. Eight years later I still remember what he said. Twenty-five years from now I'll still remember what he said . . .

"He told the story of going to see a movie with his lovely wife Barbara.

"'Barbara and I went to see that new movie, the one with Matt Damon. There's rugby and it's about South Africa. *Invictus*, was it?' he

---

11. Susan's brother Mike, who was a Houston police officer.

asked, looking to his men for clarification. They nodded. 'The one with Nelson Mandela,' he paused. 'Yes, Mr. President.'...

"The crinkle in his cheeks and glistening eyes would make you think he's one of Santa's elves instead [of] the former leader of the free world. We hung on every word, and he knew it. I had no idea he was such a charming storyteller. After telling us about the movie, the darndest thing came out of his mouth.

"'Yes, he was okay. I liked him, Mandela. But Winnie? She was a witch.'

"Then we laughed. No. Guffawed. We couldn't help it.

"His face beamed brighter because he cheered us up. He smiled because we smiled.

"'Well, they're telling me I have to go. So I better be off. I hope you all are okay.' He turned to every single one of us in the room shaking hands, giving condolences. Each of us had his full attention and time. 'I'm sorry, so sorry you are dealing with this,' he said as he grabbed my hand to shake it and gave me the sweetest look... then he said a very earnest, 'God bless you.'...

"The last sound I heard was his cane's click-clicking over the white tile floor. And he was gone.

"Our room returned to quiet... it's impossible to describe our collective new disposition. I think of it like we got a positive blast of ions or rained on by a meteor, maybe. An energetic radiation of light, for sure.

"I credit President Bush [with] being the life preserver keeping me from fully drowning that day. A moment I desperately needed. As the sun set that evening, Lili was declared gone. Machines were stopped. Personal effects collected. We hugged. We cried...

"Driving away from the hospital, I was alone with my thoughts. Worst day ever. The only bright moment was meeting a star."

Or you could say, a Point of Light.

CHAPTER EIGHT

"I HAVE AN IDEA"

By now you likely have noticed that "idea" might have been the most-used word in President Bush's vocabulary.

Big ones, little ones, complicated ones, wistful ones. In a way they made up the tapestry of his very big life.

And while I was his chief of staff, his ideas pretty well ruled my life, too.

For the most part, his ideas are *the* reason why I loved my job for twenty-five years. They made all our lives sing—and yes, very full. Sometimes too full.

In 2002, when I was filling out one of those very annoying email chains, this one with the theme "getting to know you better," two of the questions were:

"7a. FAVORITE SOUND? Rain on the roof when I'm in bed and sleeping and can stay there.

"7b. LEAST FAVORITE SOUND? President Bush when he says, 'Jean, I have an idea.'"

He especially loved ideas that were also surprises, especially for his wife. I was never sure how Mrs. Bush felt about all the things he sprang on her. For the most part she was a good sport and went along, but . . .

I had been chief of staff for barely a year when I got my feet wet in the surprise business. The Bushes' fiftieth wedding anniversary was January 6, 1995, and President Bush decided to throw a big party at the Grand Ole Opry in Nashville.

Without telling his wife.

He conspired with Donna Sterban, who is married to Richard Sterban of the Oak Ridge Boys, and together we started planning a grand event with major country stars performing and Bush family and friends and several celebrities in the audience. I confess it made me nervous that Mrs. Bush had *no* idea.

At some point in late 1994, Mrs. Bush confided in me she knew her husband was planning something for their anniversary, and she hoped she knew what it was: to go back to the Cloister resort on Sea Island, Georgia, where they had spent their honeymoon all those years ago. "I hope he's not planning some big event," she told me. She had in mind something a little more romantic.

Did she suspect something? Probably.

I of course ran to President Bush with this unsettling development. By this time, it was too late to call off the Grand Ole Opry event. Hundreds of people already had their plane tickets and hotel reservations. A host of performers had agreed to participate, from Vince Gill and Amy Grant to the Oak Ridge Boys, Ricky Skaggs, Lee Greenwood, and so many others.

President Bush had an idea.

The party was to be on a Sunday night, so he planned a long weekend first at the Cloisters, putting a note under their Christmas tree announcing he was taking her on this romantic getaway. We'll never know just how he planned to spring the big party at the Grand Ole Opry: Mrs. Bush found out about it in the newspaper in the "People" column. She laughed that they would publish something so absurd.

The good news was that a grand time was had by all. Mrs. Bush loved the night. And more than $100,000 was raised for the Barbara

Bush Foundation for Family Literacy, the George H. W. Bush Presidential Library Foundation, and the MusiCares Foundation.

Ten years later, before President Bush could even think about organizing a surprise party, the president and First Lady of the United States offered to give his parents their sixtieth wedding anniversary party with a sparkling black-tie dinner at the White House. Whew.

They celebrated their seventieth holding hands in their den in Houston, watching their favorite TV shows. And their seventy-first, seventy-second, and seventy-third. For a while they held the record for having the longest marriage of a president and First Lady, until President and Mrs. Carter celebrated their seventy-fourth anniversary in July 2020.

Then there was Mrs. Bush's seventy-fifth birthday, on June 8, 2000.

President Bush, of course, planned a surprise party.

He personally wrote all the invited guests, this letter going to Al and Ann Simpson:

May 4, 2000

Dear Alan and Ann,

This is a Save the Date letter—an advance peek at a great event which lies just over the horizon.

There will be a surprise birthday party on June 10, 2000.

The birthday girl is BARBARA PIERCE BUSH.

Barbara Pierce Bush, aka Silver Fox or Former First Lady will be 75. The actual date of birth was June 8, 1925, but the party will be on Saturday June 10th.

The place—Kennebunkport, Maine. A block of rooms has been reserved at the Nonantum Hotel. OK, it ain't the Ritz but it is nice. A list of other hotels is attached. All our immediate family will hopefully attend, but a handful of Bar's close friends must come, too. That's you!

Program—Informal Supper at the informal River Club. After dinner, some entertainment—skits, singers, clowns, men jumping out of cakes, jugglers. Speeches needling the Silver Fox—laughter, tears, joy, and wonder.

SURPRISE is the key word here. SH-SH-SH-SH!!! If you are a definite "Yes" or "No"—let me know now. If you are a "maybe" just circle the date for now.

All the best from her husband and Bar's kids who want this to be very special for her. Your coming will help make it so!

George Bush

This is easy—Please fill out this form checking the proper boxes. Mail to address shown below, Attention Gian-Carlo Peressutti.[1]

*RSVP from:*_____

*Dear Mr. President*_____

*Dear George*_____

*Hey You*_____

---

1. Gian-Carlo was President Bush's aide at the time.

Yes, I will be there_____

No, I cannot make it, so there!_____

Sorry I cannot make it_____

I'm a "maybe"___ So is_____ (my spouse, my girlfriend, my boyfriend)

I know who Barbara Bush is but I need more information before I can decide._____

After weeks of planning, the party came within twenty-four hours of being a surprise. It was spoiled when Senator Simpson called Walker's Point the day before the party to announce that, sadly, they could not attend. At some point during the lengthy conversation, he suddenly realized Mrs. Bush was the one who had answered the phone! (She eventually forgave him, but it was a gaffe she would tease him about for the rest of her life.)

Nevertheless, she pretended to be surprised, and once again it was a rousing success.

President Bush and I did have one of our bigger fights during the planning of this party. The River Club could hold only about one hundred people, which meant we had to be very discerning in choosing whom to invite. President Bush's first draft of the guest list included most of his West Wing staffers, but *none* of Mrs. Bush's East Wing staff. As a former East Winger, I was most offended. Plus, it was just wrong.

I walked out on him and went home, refusing to answer my phone. Finally, Mrs. Bush's aide at the time, Kara Babers,[2] came and knocked on

---

2. Now Kara Sanders, who lives in Houston with her husband, Dax, and their two daughters.

my door, begging me to come back as President Bush was distraught. So I grew up and went back to work.

For the record: The East Wing was invited.

One of President Bush's favorite outlets for his constant flow of ideas was his presidential library. He loved putting together "leadership forums," and inviting his friends to come talk with the Aggie students and members of the community. The events were quite popular and almost always overflowed the library's six-hundred-seat auditorium.

What was sometimes confounding was the lack of any kind of theme for these forums. It was as if President Bush woke up one day and decided to invite this rather disconnected group of people to appear together at the library.

Actually, that was how it usually did happen. And they almost always came.

Here is just one example of one of his very diverse panels: Tom Selleck, Diane Sawyer, astronaut Steven Lindsey, and Las Vegas hotelier Steve Wynn. The conversation was fascinating if maybe a little disconnected.

One day he did pick a theme: successful women. Wonderful! I encouraged him. Then he invited tennis player Chris Evert; actress Teri Hatcher; astronaut Eileen Collins; and President George W. Bush's White House counsel, Harriet Miers.

The panel discussion was interesting; but the dinner afterward was truly fascinating, to watch these incredible women find common ground with each other. And they did: their love for President Bush.

He also believed strongly in being nonpartisan, which sadly seems like an archaic idea in today's political climate. For example, Nancy Pelosi, Ted Kennedy, Mitt Romney, and John McCain all gave major addresses at the library at President Bush's invitation.

And like most of his ideas—it all worked. The students loved these random leadership sessions, and I do think they learned a thing or two. Certainly, the A&M community loved them. Never in its history had so many famous people come to campus.

Slowly but surely I began to understand just how he had put together the international coalition for Desert Storm, or how he had convinced a very reluctant President François Mitterrand of France and Prime Minister Margaret Thatcher of Great Britain to go along with German unification. The man knew how to bring people together.

Although almost all of President Bush's ideas affected my life in one way or another, there was one that was quite personal.

At some point in 2011, Mitt Romney came to Houston to tell President Bush that he had decided to run again for president. I sat in on their discussion, which at some point turned to religion. President Bush asked Governor Romney if he thought being a Mormon would be as controversial as it had been when he ran the first time in 2008. At that time, Governor Romney had come to President Bush's library to give his "I am a Mormon" speech, much as President Kennedy had given his "I am a Catholic" speech in 1960.

Governor Romney felt strongly that it would not, especially since America had elected the first African American president in 2008. He said that every glass ceiling that is broken puts cracks in the ones that remain.

At some point during this discussion, but apropos of nothing really, President Bush asked Governor Romney the following question:

"Mitt, are you aware that Jean's little brother is on the short list to become the next pope?"

I almost fell off my chair.

First, the facts: I am Catholic. And my little brother, the Reverend Edward Becker (Eddie to his sisters), is a Catholic priest. And at that time, like thousands of priests, he was studying in Rome.

I should also add that President and Mrs. Bush felt close to Eddie. Our mother had died in 1983, the year Eddie graduated from high school; and our dad died six weeks before 9/11 in 2001. So Eddie typically spent his summer vacation time in Maine with me, and as a result, saw them quite often. He had been whale watching with President Bush on *Fidelity*, been invited numerous times to Taco Sunday,[3] and had even prayed with them a time or two.

They were fascinated by his career arc—Eddie had practiced law for nearly ten years before he went to seminary and was ordained in 2005 just a few months shy of age forty.

No wonder I was surprised to find out he was on the short list to become pope. Eddie had just been a priest for five years and didn't even have his own parish yet.

Governor Romney seemed surprised, too.

I tried to change the subject but President Bush persisted:

"Yes, he's studying in Rome. We are very proud of him."

A few days later, President Bush made the exact same comment to a larger group of people at a Points of Light luncheon. Again, I smiled, made a joke, and changed the subject.

But in the car after lunch I told President Bush he absolutely had to quit telling people this, since (1) there likely would never be an American pope; and (2) even if there would be, it would not be my little brother.

His reply:

"Jean, I am trying to start a buzz."

I told him that the Catholic Church didn't do "buzz."

"I feel you are being very negative about this. I am going to continue my campaign."

End of conversation.

I sent Eddie an email with this amusing bit of news, and he was of course flattered. However, there was a huge "but" in his email back to me: It was one thing to tell Mitt Romney and a bunch of Points of Light

---

3. Taco Sunday refers to the Tex-Mex lunch the Bushes hosted every Sunday for whatever family was in residence at Walker's Point and, if there was room, whoever else might be in town. In early and late summer, the staff often got to fill the empty seats.

people, but please, please, dear sister, do not let him say this to a cardinal or a bishop. That could be embarrassing.

I was not too worried about this happening, since President Bush was an Episcopalian.

If there was ever any doubt God has a sense of humor, what happened next would prove that theory wrong. For, sure enough, a few weeks after all this transpired, I was having lunch with President Bush, sitting out on the patio of a local club, when we both noticed a group of people obviously headed our way.

"Jean, who are those people coming over?"

I discreetly glanced over and realized it was Cardinal Daniel DiNardo, the new archbishop of the Diocese of Galveston-Houston, whom President Bush had not yet met.

"Great, I have been wanting to meet him. Remind me what I should call him."

I told him to call him "Your Eminence," and then, at the last minute, I implored him not to bring up Eddie.

"Jean, this is our big chance to get this buzz going. Isn't he one of the voters?! This is perfect."

I made him swear, and he grumpily agreed. The president and the cardinal had a lovely visit and at the very end, President Bush said:

"Your Eminence, did you know my chief of staff is a double-dip Catholic?"

President Bush loved the term "double dip," whose meaning was largely known just to him. He went on to explain that I was not only Catholic, but my brother was a priest, studying in *Rome*.

Cardinal DiNardo nodded politely, asked me where Eddie was stationed, and then moved on.

President Bush was quite proud of himself. The seed had been sown. And I think he was teasing me a bit.

Before we talk about some of his *big* ideas, I would love to share one of my favorites among his spontaneous thoughts.

President and Mrs. Bush were always quite grateful when they were in town for Astros home games, especially since owner Drayton McLane would seat them with him right behind home plate. The fans always loved when they came to the games, and especially cheered if they showed up on the "kiss cam."

One fine spring day when Mrs. Bush was traveling, President Bush decided he would like to go to the game, but he would not let us call Drayton. Unhappy with the Astros' low attendance thus far in the new season, he decided he wanted to do something about it. So he invited the staff and their families; the Secret Service and their families; and some other random people—for example, CBS sportscaster Jim Nantz happened to be in town with his daughter Caroline—and off we went to the game, sitting in the upper level in left field. President Bush gave the closest concession stand his credit card and told his fifty guests or so to buy whatever they wanted.

His idea was at some point to surprise Drayton with who that mystery group was way out in left field; unfortunately, the scoreboard camera found us first.

It just so happened that the only other group anywhere near us was a children's choir visiting from Uganda. Go figure. Someone in their group realized that a former president of the United States was sitting nearby, so suddenly, during a rather exciting inning of baseball, they started singing to him. Apparently, the rest of the ballpark—including Drayton—was curious as to why those folks out in left field were singing instead of cheering. Before long, here he came, charging up the stairs and giving President Bush the devil for sitting so far away.

I might have been the only person who recognized the person trailing behind Drayton: St. Louis Cardinals superstar and Hall of Famer Lou Brock. Brock was my childhood hero and my favorite Cardinal ever. He just happened to be in Houston for a Hall of Fame weekend.

At some point I managed to blurt out to Brock that I loved him. That was a conversation stopper. Jim Nantz decided to test my sincerity and demanded to know if I was such a Lou Brock fan, what number he had worn on his uniform.

Really? Number 20. Every Cardinals fan knew that.

Jim looked shocked; President Bush smiled broadly—he was quite proud that I knew the answer. And Lou Brock? He was a little surprised not only to find a former president but a fan of his in Section 405 of Minute Maid Park. He gave me a huge hug. For me, a dream come true.

It was a great night, and as always, a great idea.

If I had to pick the biggest ideas President Bush had during his post-presidency, the two that immediately come to mind would be his decision to start, as Mrs. Bush put it, jumping out of perfectly good airplanes; and his decision to return to Chichijima, where he had been shot down during World War II.

In fact, the two ideas were related. President Bush would not like me saying this, but both were about getting closure, a term he considered overused. It even made a bingo card now and then.

Early in 1997 President Bush told me he had been thinking about something for a very long time—doing another parachute jump. His one and only jump had been on September 2, 1944, when his plane was hit during a bombing run over the Pacific island of Chichijima.

In some ways, he remembered the jump as if it were yesterday. Neither of his crew members had survived, and he confessed to author James Bradley[4] that he had thought of them almost every single day of his life since that fateful day.

In the rush of leaving a plane that was on fire and worrying about whether his crew, John Delaney and Ted White, had gotten out of the back of the plane, the jump had not been perfectly executed. He described it in a letter he wrote to his parents the day after, from the USS *Finback*, the submarine that had plucked him out of the water:

---

4. James Bradley wrote the best-selling book *Flags of Our Fathers*, the story of the men, including his father, who raised the flag over Iwo Jima during World War II. When he interviewed President Bush, he was working on his next book, *Flyboys*, about the nine American pilots shot down over Chichijima.

I will have to skip all the details of the attack as they would not pass the censorship, but the fact remains that we got hit . . . As I left the plane my head struck the tail. I now have a cut head and bruised eye but it is far from serious. After jumping, I must have pulled the ripcord too soon for when I was floating down, I looked up at the canopy and several of the panels were all ripped out. Just as I got floating down, I saw the plane strike the water. In the meantime, I noticed there was a life raft down in the water. Not until later did I discover that it was mine that was supposed to be attached to my lifejacket. I had forgotten to hook it on, and when I left the plane it had come loose and had fallen into the water.

As President Bush explained it to me, he needed a do-over. He had been a scared twenty-year-old when he jumped the first time. And now, at age seventy-two, he wanted to jump again.

My first question was "Does Mrs. Bush know?"

No, but he assured me she would be supportive. (And for the most part, she was.)

Second, did he have a suggestion on how we go about making this happen without simply calling the local parachute club and telling them he was headed over?

Of course he had an idea about that, probably best told by sharing excerpts from this letter he wrote his five children. The letter was written over six weeks, so it is more or less his diary of the jump:

February 11, 1997

Dear Kids,

Okay, so you might think I have lost it.

I plan to make a parachute jump. So there!

Yesterday I went to the International Parachute Association's annual meeting here in Houston. Asked to describe my [war] experience, I told them how terrified I was, how I pulled the rip cord and released my chest straps too early, and how I had sunk fairly deep when I hit the water.

As I recounted those errors, however, something happened. For some reason, I went back to a thought I had way in the back of my mind. It has been there, sleeping like Rip van Winkle, alive but not alive. Now it was quite clear.

I want to make one more parachute jump!

I was excited, but thought I better sleep on it—to give it a little time. This morning, however, I was more determined than ever, so I asked Chris Needels to come over. He brought Lt. Col. Danny Greene[5] and two other association people. They arrived bearing the kind of chute I would use and began by explaining the safety features involved. That seemed appropriate.

---

5. Danny was then a member of the Golden Knights, the Army's elite parachute jumping team. Chris was a former Golden Knight, now retired from the Army and running the United States Parachute Association. He had served in President Bush's White House as national security director of counterterrorism.

"Piece of cake," thinks me.

The next move is up to them, but not entirely—for when I go home tonight I'll tell your Mom about this. She will not like it, but in the final analysis I will convince her (1) that it is safe and (2) that this is something I have to do, must do.

February 12th

So far, so good. Last night at home, sitting in the den, I casually told your Mom, "Bar, I'm going to make a parachute jump."

"You're crazy," came the reply. She meant it, but she didn't sound angry.

I was firm. "This is something I must do."

"Sure, you must do it. Sure!" She could have well said, "Yeah, right!" That's what people say these days when they mean you're wrong.

Having clearly established my position, I changed the subject. "Another glass of Chardonnay, Bar? How'd the construction go today?"[6] Smart, for she answered both questions and never came back to the parachute jump.

---

6. The Bushes were having some work done on their house.

February 27th

I attend a Desert Storm reunion party in Northern Virginia hosted by Prince Bandar. It is in honor of his father, Prince Sultan, who is the number three man in the Saudi hierarchy.

As the dinner crowd readies to leave, Colin Powell,[7] with an amused look on his face, pulls me aside and asks: "Are you planning to jump from a plane? It's the talk of the Pentagon."

When I told him it was true, his only reaction was "Really?" Colin, too good a friend and far too polite to call me nuts, only smiled. I think I detected a shake of the head.

February 28th

I called Colin.

This time he is armed with examples where men far younger than I had landed hard and were badly hurt.

Colin reports that the Pentagon can hardly believe this; and he confesses that Denny Reimer, the top General in the Army, had called him.[8]

---

7. General Powell had retired from the Army and from being chairman of the Joint Chiefs in 1993.

8. President Bush wanted to jump with the Golden Knights, thus the involvement of the Army. He insisted on paying all the costs so his idea would not cost the taxpayers any money.

I assure Colin that I will fully understand if Reimer vetoes this and ask him to have Reimer call me directly—promising to be light of heart.

So Colin goes into the fray not convinced of my sanity, certainly not a strong ally (understatement), but willing on his own to report back to Reimer that this is for real.

Has this shaken my determination? No it has not, but I will now make further inquiry. I do not want to do anything dumb, but I must complete my mission.

Why has this now become an obsession? I have everything in life, far more than I deserve. I want to finish my life as God would have it. I have never been happier, but I want to do this jump.

Chris Needels calls. "All systems are go. General Reimer has agreed to permit the jump to go forward. No military plane, but the Knights can jump with the President at Yuma."[9]

I was so elated and caught off-guard that I'm afraid I made a ribald comment to Jean Becker. I told her that, if any press ends up covering the event, we should be sure not to give them the name of my laundry man. Should'na dunnit. Wasn't prudent. Wasn't nice. I'm a little ashamed.

Why did I do this? It goes back to my carrier days. We pilots would joke like this when we had a night landing or a rolling deck. "Only my laundry man will ever know!" we used to say. It helped to ease the tension.

Then I start to think that so much of this relates back to my pilot days—back to that dreadful day, September 2, 1944. I was scared then. Will I be scared again? I know I will not panic, but I expect to feel a touch of fright when I first look down from 12,500 feet— ready to jump.

I have a goal. I will achieve it. I will do it right.

---

9. The Army base in Yuma, Arizona.

*Notification day for the kids. I first break the news to Marvin.
"Are you kidding, Dad?" then becoming very supportive. "I can
understand. I can see why you want to do this. Go for it!" He will
talk to his Mother—to help put her at ease. I tell the Governor of
Texas. Like Marv, there was the momentary "Are you kidding?"
followed by enthusiasm. He was great about it, though he did add:
"Don't tell anyone about your 18-year-old girlfriend."*

*Next was Jeb. He fully understood. Never one for idle chatter, Jeb
says what he means and then hangs up. "Fine, Dad, but don't
change your sexual preference." I put him down as positive.*

*Neil was abroad when I tried to reach him, but he was instantly
supportive when told of the jump.*

*Finally I called Doro, who gasped upon hearing the news. I asked
her not to tell anyone. She said, "You must be kidding. Do you
think I'd tell anyone about this?" I felt Doro was ready to support
me—tentative but okay.*

*I went with your Mother to the jump area. Then, wearing my
Desert Storm boots, I was off to a final plane-side briefing and into
my white Elvis suit (with white helmet and white gloves—the King
would have approved) before boarding. We were off . . .*

*Nearing the exit zone, I was told to stand and back up towards the
rear of the plane. My instructors kept saying, "Back up a little more,
sir, a little more." It was only then that I felt a twinge of fear—not
panic, but rather a halting feeling in the leg, groin, and gut.*

Finally, it was time.

"Are you ready to sky dive?"

"Ready to go!"

Before I knew it, I was plummeting face down towards the desert at 120 mph, shoulders arched, pelvis out.

When I pulled the rip cord at 5000 feet, the jolt was far greater than I expected. Looking up, I saw the multi-colored canopy fully deployed. I grabbed the handles over my head for steering. I checked the altimeter on my left wrist, amazed at the slow and gentle descent. I practiced my turns and the flare.

I was at peace. Gone was the noise from the free fall. I was alone, floating gently towards earth, reveling in the freedom, enjoying the view. It was a marvelous sensation . . .

Pulling down hard on the two shrouds gently softened the descent. I didn't hit hard, but a gust of wind seemed to pull me back. By then, my chute had been swarmed by the Golden Knights.

I was down. It had gone well. I had lived a dream.

Bar hugged me and smiled. All was well with the world . . .

Devotedly,
Dad

So you might think President Bush would have checked this off his bucket list and moved on. He would jump six more times, often to help raise money for a good cause.

Somewhere along the way, the Golden Knights convinced him to do tandem jumps, which did not thrill President Bush but he did give in. Being tethered to another person as you floated down wasn't quite the same.

When he decided to jump one last time, on his ninetieth birthday, I was aghast. The man was, after all, in a wheelchair.

Mrs. Bush was furious. He was going to jump in Kennebunkport, on the grounds of their summer church, St. Ann's. She said half in jest, but not entirely: "Well, if it goes wrong, we'll just carry him inside and have the funeral."

Behind President Bush's back I called his oldest son and suggested he talk to his dad. The forty-third president asked me what my biggest fear was. It was, of course, that he would die. His reply: "Jean, let him do it. It will help him feel younger."

He also pointed out that if the worst happened, that would be a glorious way to go out. Let him do what he wants to do. He promised to talk to his mother.

And that was that.

The forecast for the day of the jump, June 12, 2014, was terrible. There was great discussion the day before about if the jump should be canceled. Mrs. Bush certainly was pushing for that. The decision was made—largely by President Bush—it was all systems go—and I was dispatched to the house to let Mrs. Bush know. (Yes, my role as consigliere was still alive and well.)

As I gave her the news, she looked out the window and saw President Bush coming up the driveway along with the former Golden Knight Mike Elliott, who had done the last several jumps with him. Now that I had broken the news, the plan was for them to sweep in and convince her all would be well.

She told me he had her permission, but she had no interest in talking to any of them at that moment. When I went out and shooed them off, they didn't seem all that upset.

He did indeed take that last jump. He landed hard. Really hard. But he was fine. And joyful.

The year before, President Bush liked to tease me (I think he was teasing) that he planned to jump on his ninety-fifth birthday. By this time he was very frail. I told him I would not help in any way, including calling and lining up his jumping partner, Mike Elliott. He said he had his ways to make it happen. And yes, I am sure he could have. He died six months short of his ninety-fifth birthday, so we'll never know for sure.

Bright and early on January 2, 2002, President Bush sat down in my office and told me he had an idea, something he had been thinking about over the holidays.

I was terrified.

It was our first day back in the office since Christmas Eve, and my plan had been to drink some coffee, dig out, get organized, take down the Christmas decorations—a slow but steady start to the new year.

Then President Bush casually announced that he had decided he needed to go back to Chichijima. It was something he had been thinking about and it was something he needed to do. He needed closure.

So I drank a pot of coffee, broke the news to the Secret Service (it was at times like this I wished I had a helmet cam), and got to work.

It didn't take long to discover the biggest problem: getting there.

The Japanese island of Chichijima is seven hundred miles south of Tokyo. It's a volcanic, rugged island with no airport. The only commercial transportation was a thirty-three-hour boat ride from Tokyo.

The obvious solution was to call the U.S. Navy, which I did. After all, President Bush was a Navy pilot when he was shot down. Their response was at first enthusiastic, and given that the United States has a large Navy presence in the Pacific, they said it would not be that hard to find a ship scheduled for training exercises in the neighborhood.

But eventually the Navy nixed the idea, and President Bush agreed. The feeling was, given who was president, it might not look right, and some people might think it was a misuse of taxpayers' money. I heartily disagreed, as I knew the Navy would have taken over this mission from me. But the decision was final.

As luck would have it, the United States ambassador to Japan was President Bush's good friend Howard Baker.[10] When the Navy backed out, President Bush picked up the phone and called to ask him what he thought.

He could not have been more excited and threw himself into the project.

At the end of the day, ironically, it was the Japanese government and its navy who got us to Chichijima. They were delighted to play host to the former president who wanted to revisit the place where he was shot down by them while bombing them.

This was another trip I decided I needed to take. Traveling with us was journalist Paula Zahn, then of CNN, who was going to do a documentary on the trip; and author James Bradley. Rather than rely on my memory of this extraordinary trip, I will share excerpts of a letter I wrote to the staff and my family when I returned.

June 26, 2002

I've tried but failed several times to put into words a description of our journey to Chichi Jima[11] last week. Time is up. First, your patience has been wearing thin (but did

---

10. Mr. Baker's long résumé included representing Tennessee in the U.S. Senate, from 1967 to 1985, where he played a starring role in the Watergate hearings and was Senate majority leader from 1981 to 1985. He served as President Reagan's chief of staff from 1987 to 1988.

11. This is how President Bush always spelled Chichijima, so I did, too. I like his version better.

we have to get nasty about it?), and the boss is on his way home (early, I might add) from a 3-day fishing trip to Canada, so life as we know it is about ready to end for the foreseeable future.

So I'll quit obsessing about this and just write, as long as you promise to forgive what promises to be a rambler. I think my problem is that this was not my journey. It was President Bush's. So I feel odd writing about it. But I also know I was very blessed to be the "fly on the wall" of this trip, and since President Bush is unlikely to blow on about it, it's up to me to do so.

Let's start with some disconnected but hopefully insightful random thoughts:

1. Chichi Jima is probably one of the most beautiful places on earth most people will never see.
2. The first-class section of our JAL[12] flight home is nicer than most houses I've lived in. I was probably the only one on the plane who was devastated when the 13-hour flight was over because I didn't want to vacate my "pod."
3. Those of us who never fought in a war will never understand what it must be like, no matter how many books we read, movies we watch, or stories we hear.
4. It's possible No. 41 is an even more remarkable person than we realized.

Ok, back to the beginning.

---

12. Japan Airlines.

President Bush, Paula Zahn, and I left Walker's Point at 5:45 a.m. on Sunday, June 16th, flying by private plane first to Anchorage where we refueled then on to Tokyo. 13 time zones, 5 bottles of water, several bad episodes of 41 snoring loudly, and two bad movies later, we landed in Tokyo almost to the minute of our scheduled "wheels down" time of 12 noon Monday. There was a rather emotional welcoming ceremony where Japanese and American sailors stood at attention while President Bush told the group of Japanese and American dignitaries why he was making this journey; that he needed to go back to the spot where at age 20 he almost died but didn't for reasons he still wonders about. He talked about his love and affection for Japan and how he had no bitterness in his heart, only friendship and respect. We then immediately left for Iwo Jima, another two-hour plane ride where we were to spend the night.

There we met up with James Bradley, author of the best-selling *Flags of Our Fathers*, about the six men who raised the American flag there, on Mount Suribachi, including his own father. Iwo Jima is a dreadful place, hot and humid and covered with black sand and soil, all created by a dormant but not dead volcano. There is still wreckage of American landing boats on the black beaches, where 6,800 Americans died trying to capture this tiny, ugly island, all for the sake of an airstrip where we ourselves landed. Having James along as the tour guide made the visit all that more emotional and interesting, since he has done extensive research on what happened there...A very emotional President Bush raised another flag on the top of Mount Suribachi, and I think even the Japanese with us were wiping away tears...

We got up the next morning and headed to Chichi Jima, a 90-minute helicopter ride, courtesy of the Japanese Navy...I seemed to be the only nervous person aboard. I thought that any minute we might land in some combat zone and I would be expected to jump off the helicopter and start shooting. Obviously and gratefully, this did not happen.

President Bush had a special seat near one of the few windows on the helicopter, so he could see clearly as we arrived on the island. The pilot followed the same flight path 41 had flown on September 2, 1944 (President Bush remembers it exactly and I had e-mailed it to the American embassy in Tokyo several weeks ago): He flew in from the south, flew over most of the island where his plane was hit by anti-aircraft fire, dropped his payload over the radio towers on the island's tip before turning back out into the sea, and getting the hell out of there. It's hard to know what he was thinking as he was peering out the window; he was lost in his own thoughts...

The turnout for President Bush's arrival was a little disappointing—I think only 1,900 of the 2,000 residents were there, screaming and waving and putting leis over anyone they could find. (I ended up with 5 draped around my neck.) The arrival of George Bush was the biggest thing to ever happen to this island. No American President has ever been there. The Emperor did come a few years ago, but they all whispered this was bigger. President Bush waded right into the crowd, shaking every hand, taking photos and even kissing babies. If they had an election tomorrow, he would be a shoo-in. The girls literally were screaming and hugging themselves as if they might pass out. Older people—some of whom might have been there in 1944—wiped away tears. It was truly an amazing sight, much more emotional and even louder than the Beatles' first appearance on the *Ed Sullivan Show*.

When 41 finally tore himself away, we boarded a small boat (about the size of a typical Maine lobster boat) and went out to the spot where his plane went into the water. Everyone but President Bush was fascinated by the fact that his plane was still down there. He was much more focused on the spot where he had drifted for 3 hours in a lifeboat, hoping and praying to be rescued. Someone from the American embassy had very thoughtfully arranged for two wreaths of flowers to be on board, and when we got to the right spot, 41 threw them on the water and there was a moment of silence for his two lost crew members.

Again, it's not possible to know what all he was thinking. We'll know more when CNN airs its documentary (more on that later). He has told me some things but typically not much. I don't know what the others were thinking, but for me it was all rather surreal, looking at this 78-year-old man who had been President of the United States, and trying to imagine what it must have been like when he was 20 years old and floating around in the water thinking he would surely die. After a while, at his request, President Bush got into a life raft, and paddled away from our lobster boat. He looked rather silly floating around out there, but I think he just wanted to be by himself for a while, away from the CNN cameras, away from the American embassy folks, away from his Japanese hosts, away from James Bradley and his Japanese girlfriend, and away from me. He did not totally escape the Secret Service who were so distraught by this move that they put two agents in the water who sort of swam laps around the boat but tried to pretend they weren't there. I'm sure he noticed.

After a while, he paddled back in and we headed back to shore. First stop was a lunch hosted by the mayor and attended by almost everyone on the island. Or so it seemed. More raw tuna, but this time we were allowed to wash it down with this amazing passion fruit drink that after the third glass I realized was slightly alcoholic. The tuna never tasted that good before or after.

We then toured the rest of the island, visiting the radio station he bombed that day (it still stands but is in shambles and has been since the war. James Bradley is convinced it was 41's bombs that did most of the damage which we all chose to believe although we have no proof of any kind). The most stunning stop was still to come, high atop a cliff where we met a Japanese veteran who had a most remarkable story. He had been born in Hawaii, the son of a Japanese father and American mother (or vice versa, I'm not sure). Two months before Pearl Harbor they returned to Japan to look after a dying grandfather. He was 18 at the time and immediately conscripted into the Japanese Navy. He was en route to Iwo Jima when "we" bombed and sank his boat. He and the other survivors were all taken to Chichi Jima where he spent the rest of the war. He became good friends with a captured American pilot from Texas who was executed in front of him, and he changed his first name to "Warren"[13] to honor his fallen friend. One day when he was digging a cave, some friends shouted, "we

13. His full name was Nobuaki "Warren" Iwatake.

got another one" and they all rushed to the side of the cliff where they could watch an American pilot bobbing in the water. The American planes overhead kept strafing the Japanese boats, trying to protect their friend below but finally had to give up and return to their ship and their squadron since their gas was low. "Warren" and his Japanese comrades watched as a Japanese boat set out to pick up the pilot but was stopped cold when out of the depths of that beautiful water, an American submarine suddenly emerged, plucked the pilot out of the water, and then just as quickly disappeared back into the water. "Warren" said one of his friends said surely America would win the war, if they cared so much for the life of one pilot.

It would be nearly 50 years before "Warren" would realize he had watched the rescue of a future American president.

Also in our entourage was another American veteran, Bill Connell of Minnesota, who had been shot down over Chichi Jima and captured in July 1944. He was the last American pilot who was captured but not executed and cannibalized on Chichi Jima.[14] He was tortured for 8 days, then for unknown reasons, put on a boat for Tokyo where he survived until the end of the war. He was funny and interesting and modest about his war experience. He was very excited to meet President Bush and very unaware of how excited 41 was to meet him! Both had lost the rest of their crew and 41 told me later they talked a great deal about that, away from the cameras and the rest of us.

---

14. The Japanese commander on Chichijima ate the hearts and livers of captured pilots and was convicted of war crimes after the war. President Bush liked to tease Mrs. Bush that he almost became an hors d'oeuvre.

President Bush hosted another tuna-laden dinner that night for all our new friends. He sat between "Warren" and Bill and the rest of us gave them lots of space. No passion fruit drink to wash down the sushi but a wonderful Japanese beer that under normal circumstances I probably would not like but which I guzzled in the heat and humidity.

After dinner, we learned that the local hula dance class had miraculously decided not to hold their lesson that night in the community center, but on the little beach in front of the tiny hotel where we stayed. President Bush was dead tired but agreed to go for 10 minutes. He stayed for more than an hour, enchanted by the beautiful girls from age 4 to 20 doing the hula and other island dances. When he unexpectedly joined them on the beach (but no hip swayer was he), the little girls nearly knocked him over, they rushed him so fast and crowded around him so tightly. Again, much screaming and adulation. The agents looked alarmed; the boss looked happy. (He did later confess to me that he thought they might bowl him over and sit on top of him and he inquired how I would tell his wife and children that the "old man" had been killed by a gang of 4-year-old hula dancers in Chichi Jima, accomplishing what the Japanese military had failed to do in 1944.)

The next morning we got up and retraced our steps back to Tokyo. President Bush met the prime minister, attended a dinner, gave a speech…the usual stuff…

We were gone slightly more than 4 days. It seemed forever.

President Bush said the journey was all he wanted it to be. He said it did give him closure. I think meeting "Warren" and Bill helped a lot. He said it was easier than he thought it would be. He said he was so overwhelmed by his welcome and the hospitality of the Japanese people that he was having too much fun living in the present to really dwell on the past. I loved that.

I was blessed to go on this journey. We are all blessed to know 41 who has made all our life's entire journey infinitely more interesting and worthwhile. I don't even want to think about what would have happened if that American submarine had been somewhere else 58 years ago. I won't go there if you won't.

Jean

On the way home from the trip, President Bush confided to me that he was surprised by how excited the islanders were to see him. "Don't they know I bombed their parents and grandparents?" he wondered. "How many did I kill?"

He told me about a visit he made to the Philippines while he was vice president, to an island that he had also bombed during the war. Throughout the very celebratory dinner welcoming the vice president of the United States, during which there were many toasts in his honor, he said he had a hard time paying attention as he kept looking at all those smiling faces, wondering, "Did I kill your grandfather? Your mother?"

In the spring of 2010, President Bush had spent a week at home, feeling under the weather, but one day he asked me to come over to the house and bring any work I had for him. Mrs. Bush was out, and we could have a good visit, he told me.

When I arrived, he asked if he could watch the end of an episode of the HBO miniseries *The Pacific*, produced by Tom Hanks and

Steven Spielberg. "There's only twenty minutes left," he promised me. The series had not aired yet, but President Bush had been so anxious to see it that we reached out to Tom Hanks, who very kindly sent him an advance copy.

The television was on very loud, and the battle scene was brutal. Americans were trying to land on a Pacific island that I think was Peleliu—I am not sure—and they were getting mowed down by the Japanese. It was horrific, and I could barely watch. Finally and thankfully, American planes arrived and started dropping bombs on the Japanese, silencing their guns and allowing the Marines to safely come ashore and take the island. The episode ended with dead bodies everywhere (history records that sixteen hundred Americans died on Peleliu) and one Marine saying to another, "Where the hell were the flyboys? Where the hell have they been? Thanks a lot, guys."

I was so grateful the show was over—it had been loud and bloody and hard for me to watch. I turned to start my visit with President Bush, and there were tears coming down his face. I was taken aback and wasn't sure what to say. "I was one of those flyboys," he finally told me. "Where the hell were we? Why did it take us so long to start taking out the Japanese? Why were we so late?" His agony was palpable.

I tried to assure him this was not his fault, that he was a young pilot following orders. It took a while to console him, and my heart broke just a little.

One observation I made over the years about President Bush being shot down and almost captured: The man was fearless. He was not reckless, but he also wasn't afraid of anything, either.

Once, while flying with him on a tiny plane through a thunderstorm, the Secret Service agents and I were terrified. We knew we were going down. I was sitting across from President Bush, who never quit reading a newspaper while we were being tossed about. I finally asked him how on earth he could read through such turbulence. He looked at me over his reading glasses and said: "Jean, I was shot down during World War II. This does not scare me." Then he went back to reading.

Another time, a big storm was approaching Walker's Point, and President Bush was concerned that the grandchildren's boat, the *Maine Coaster*, was still moored in the bay. He told the Secret Service he would be leaving shortly to "take the boat around" to the dock where he kept his boats. The supervisor on duty, John McClellan, came flying into my office, wanting me to tell President Bush it was too late. The seas were too high, and there was no way he could make the mile-long trip to the mouth of the river. I told John this was a life-or-death issue, which meant he had to tell the president. But I did offer to go with him.

President Bush heard John out, and then said: "John, it's the anniversary of my being shot down over Chichijima. If I could survive that, I can survive this." And off they went.

If I had to pick President Bush's most fun idea of the nearly twenty-five years I was his chief of staff, I think it would be "Let's call George Clooney."

What many Americans do not realize is that just twenty-six days after Hurricane Katrina, Hurricane Rita came ashore and chewed up what was left of Louisiana's coastline. With Katrina dominating the headlines, disaster relief from the private sector was slow in coming to Rita's victims. Some months after Rita, a man named Richard Zuschlag called President Bush's office, seeking help for his hometown of Cameron, Louisiana. He said what Cameron needed more than anything was for the hospital to be rebuilt, beginning with the emergency room. Without access to medical care, explained Richard, people would be slow to come back. Plus, Cameron's emergency room facility was used heavily by the workers from the oil drilling platforms located in the Gulf of Mexico, just off the town's coast.[15]

President Bush had a soft spot in his heart for Cameron, dating back

---

15. Unfortunately, in August 2020, Hurricane Laura hit Cameron hard. Despite the horrific damage, I was relieved to learn that at least the hospital survived, although it was without power and water for several weeks.

to his own offshore drilling days when the town was his jumping-off point to visit his oil wells in the Gulf.

So we went to work. Our goal was to raise $2 million, which would allow for the emergency room to be rebuilt. Shortly before Christmas 2006, the money was raised, and President Bush planned to travel to Cameron to present the check and help break ground for the new ER.

What does any of this have to do with George Clooney?

While reviewing his schedule for his visit to Cameron, President Bush complained that it was a bit boring. I remember him telling me: "Jean, these people have had a terrible year. We need to make this day more exciting."

Perhaps with a tiny bit of attitude, I replied that I felt a former president coming to town with a check for $2 million the week before Christmas was pretty darn exciting.

He then pitched his idea: Why don't we invite George Clooney to go with us? "You know, Jean, the star of that TV show *ER*. Get it? *ER*."

Yeah, I got it.

What he didn't get was that Clooney had left the show seven years earlier and was now a huge movie star. Most Americans likely had forgotten he was ever on *ER*. When I reminded him of that, he argued, saying he and Mrs. Bush watched him every single night on *ER*.

Aha. Yes, they did. In reruns on TNT.

I then argued that we didn't know George Clooney; I had no idea how to call George Clooney; and it was likely he was not a fan. His politics were somewhere off to the left of President Bush's.

However, President Bush's entire life could be defined as "Never Say Never." He had already figured out that his good friend Jerry Weintraub was the producer of all "those *Ocean* movies." So he called Jerry. Who called George Clooney. Who came.

The "two Georges" were a huge hit. It's possible they shook every hand in town as they turned over the $2 million and smiled and waved to an adoring crowd—which, oddly, was about triple the size of the population of Cameron. Yes, word had leaked out about who was coming.

The press was clamoring to interview the two Georges. I was painfully aware that Diane Sawyer was still annoyed that President Bush's first post-9/11 interview had gone to Tom Brokaw and NBC, so we called her and she and her ABC crew made their way to Cameron and got the exclusive interview. I was finally forgiven.

On the flight coming home—I of course made this trip with the Georges—I asked Clooney why he came. His answer was something like this:

"I was so touched that he was raising money and making this huge effort for this tiny town that the TV cameras had yet to find. No one had ever heard of Cameron, Louisiana. But here is George Bush, raising money for their emergency room. It touched me. I had to come."

Once again, George Bush had a pretty good idea.

CHAPTER NINE

WHAT'S IN A NAME?

It wasn't long after leaving the White House that the Bushes became inundated with invitations to receive awards or have something named for them.

As for the awards—many of them meant a great deal, especially for President Bush when President Obama presented him with the Medal of Freedom in 2011.

Mrs. Bush swore she was honored when in 1995, *Outlaw Biker* magazine named her "Biker Babe of the Century," featuring a cover cartoon of her speeding along on a motorcycle, wearing leather boots and her trademark pearls.

The Bushes also knew that often the award and the event were tools used for fund-raising, and as long as it was a cause or an organization they liked, they were happy to say yes.

But what really surprised them was how many people wanted to name things for them. While President and Mrs. Bush would tell you it was always a great honor, it was often overwhelming, and maybe occasionally a little embarrassing.

There were George and Barbara Bush sandwiches, pizzas, gardens, roses, streets, and highways. Mrs. Bush has six elementary schools named for her, and President Bush has two. There were George Bush Awards for this and that, and a few named for Mrs. Bush as well.

"Who would want this award?" President Bush once mused to me when we were discussing possible recipients for the George Bush Award for Excellence in Public Service, given for many years by his library foundation and now by the George & Barbara Bush Foundation. As it turns out, a lot of people, with honorees ranging from Ted Kennedy to Mikhail Gorbachev to Billy Graham.

They were both funny about things named after them. When President Bush's presidential library was close to completion, he did a final walk-through before it became too late to make changes. He was very pleased, but as soon as we got in the car for the ninety-minute drive back to Houston he told me he had three issues:

- The color red used in the exhibit about his time served in China was not the right color red.
- A woman had donated a large collection of glass, porcelain, and ceramic elephants to the library, which was part of the exhibit about President Bush being chairman of the Republican National Committee. He thought the collection took up too much space. "I don't even like elephants," he admitted.
- The library was too much about him. "My name and photo are everywhere," he worried.

I pointed out that it *was* the George Bush Library.

One of Mrs. Bush's favorite naming honors was the little girl who wrote and told her she had named her heifer Barbara Bush. Mrs. Bush loved it, and the two became pen pals. Mrs. Bush was relieved, however, when the little girl wrote with the bad news that her heifer did not win any award at the Houston Livestock Show and Rodeo. As Mrs. Bush loved to joke in her speeches: "I was sorry for my friend but I was relieved. Can you just see the headline? 'Barbara Bush Wins the Fat Stock Show.'"

In addition to Barbara Bush the Heifer, Mrs. Bush would admit that for her the biggest naming honor was when the Maine Medical Center in Portland built a new pediatric wing and called it the Barbara Bush Children's Hospital. She visited at least once every summer, often on her birthday, to give some love to the patients and to read a book to those well enough to gather.

For President Bush, the first honor that he admitted thrilled him was when, in 1997, Houston renamed its biggest airport George Bush Intercontinental Airport. The day the new name became official, after a big dinner in a hangar at the airport, Continental Airlines filled a plane with Bush family and friends and circled Houston and Galveston, Texas, while we ate dessert and drank champagne. President Bush always smiled when sitting on a plane and the pilot would announce the flight time to "Bush Airport." Christopher Buckley, at a Celebration of Reading event in Houston, observed that he had flown out of Ronald Reagan Airport in Washington, DC, and into George Bush Airport in Houston. "I'm starting to think there really is a vast right-wing conspiracy," he mused.

We, the staff, were amused (mostly) by the occasional phone calls to the Office of George Bush complaining about lost luggage or delayed flights. Our receptionists, Melinda Lamoreaux and Mary Sage, told me that their explanations of why we had no control over baggage claim at George Bush Airport often fell on deaf ears.

The very next year President Bush was even more honored when then congressman Rob Portman of Ohio (now a senator) introduced legislation to rename the CIA headquarters in McLean, Virginia, the "George Bush Center for Intelligence," a bill that President Clinton signed into law. Despite the fact that President Bush was head of the CIA for barely a year, he was one of the more popular directors of Central Intelligence (DCI). He took the post in 1976 at a tumultuous time, as Congress was looking into illegal activities at the CIA. President Ford brought in George Bush to clean up the agency and restore its reputation, which he largely accomplished before newly elected President Carter replaced him in 1977.

Whenever President Bush visited CIA headquarters, he would always be met with thunderous applause from the intelligence officers who gathered to see him. As one of them emailed me right after such a visit, "Elvis has left the building."

The naming of CIA headquarters did not come without some teasing from the family. As Mrs. Bush used to say in her speeches: "It was a tremendous honor…but frankly bewildering. Why would an agency dedicated to *intelligence* name their headquarters after someone who celebrated his seventy-fifth birthday by jumping out of a perfectly good airplane at 12,500 feet?"

There was one rather odd hiccup in the decades-long romance between the forty-first president and the CIA. Like all former presidents, President Bush was offered a daily intelligence briefing—a much-scaled-down version of what the sitting president receives every day. For years, President Bush received his in person from a CIA officer, Monday through Friday. In 1997, one of his briefers chose to pose nude for *Playboy*, causing quite a stir within the agency. So much so that some of the top people flew from Washington to Houston to tell President Bush and apologize.

He was rather nonplussed by the entire affair—amused, even. For the sake of full disclosure (pun intended), I did send a staff person out to retrieve a copy of that particular *Playboy*. For years it was hidden in the bottom of one of my desk drawers, beneath a bunch of other files—a fact I conveniently forgot until one spring when one of our interns, Jason Denby, was helping me pack my office for the summer migration to Maine. I still remember the look on his face when he found the magazine beneath some very legitimate and even important files. It was rather hard to explain.

As much as President Bush appreciated the new name of the CIA building, I think he would agree that the biggest honor was when Secretary of the Navy Gordon England decided to name the Navy's newest aircraft carrier the USS *George H. W. Bush* (CVN 77). (A number of people have taken credit for the idea, but former Virginia senator John Warner—who was also a former secretary of the Navy—swears it was his. President Bush believed both of them.)

President Bush followed the building of the ship closely and was in attendance when the keel was laid in 2003; when the seven-hundred-ton island[1] was put into place on the flight deck in 2006; and later that year for the christening when the ship's sponsor, Doro Bush Koch, broke a champagne bottle on the still-unfinished vessel, officially giving the *Bush* her name. When the island was installed, President Bush put his World War II aviator wings into the foundation, following an old maritime tradition of burying something valuable on a ship as it is being built. Both Doro and President Bush's aide, Tom Frechette, remember there was not a dry eye on the deck.

President Bush could hardly wait for the ship to be commissioned and was crushed when I told him at some point in 2008 the ship would not be finished until sometime in 2009. The problem? His son would leave office on January 20, 2009, and it was important to him that President George W. Bush officiate over the commissioning of his ship.

It was at times like this when I admit having friends in high places was helpful. After going through the usual channels and getting nowhere, I sent an SOS to President Bush's friend Bob Gates,[2] who just happened to be the secretary of defense then. When I told Bob the problem, his reaction was: "Well, not every bolt needs to be in place. As long as the ship looks finished, we are going to commission that ship."

The next day I got a call from my point of contact at Northrop-Grumman/Newport News Shipbuilding, the company constructing the ship. As it turns out, the ship would be ready for commissioning on January 10, 2009—ten days before the forty-third president left office.

Technically, the Office of George Bush was not in charge of the commissioning, to be held in Norfolk, Virginia. Among the groups who

---

1. The island of the aircraft carrier is the command center that towers above the flight deck.

2. See the Glossary of Names for more about Bob.

thought they were in charge were: the Pentagon; the local Navy League; and the White House advance office.

But as the head of the Navy League admitted, they had never commissioned a ship whose namesake was still alive. President Bush had definite ideas on the program, the invitation list, and what other events would take place before and after. At the end of the day, he was the man in charge, who put his chief of staff in charge. Thank you, Mr. President.

The day before the commissioning, I was on board the ship with my team meeting with the White House advance team, the Navy's team, and the ship's team, going over the final details of who would do what when and who would sit where when I got an urgent phone call from Jim McGrath.

He was outside on the pier with a group of press, going over the details of the next day, when he happened to look down the pier and notice a group of people walking toward the ship. He was fairly certain it was President Bush, out for a stroll. As the group got closer, he confirmed that *yes*, it was President Bush. He and Mrs. Bush were staying on the Navy base, and President Bush had decided to walk over to "check out the action."

It might be my favorite memory of that weekend, watching the ship's company snap to attention, and both the outgoing and the incoming captains, Kevin O'Flaherty and Chip Miller, race through the ship to meet her namesake on the pier.

The next day, an estimated twenty thousand people watched as an emotional president of the United States commissioned the ship named for his dad. "So what do you give a guy who has been blessed and has just about everything he has ever needed? Well, an aircraft carrier," he teased his dad during the remarks.

The Navy—especially the captains of his ship—soon learned that President Bush would be a very hands-on namesake. He went out to sea twice, for one night each, while the ship was conducting training exercises in the Atlantic. Doro accompanied him the first time; Mrs. Bush went the second. He enjoyed in-person briefings from the captains before and after the ship deployed, and email reports during deployments. The relationship was such a close one that a year or so before he died, President Bush asked all the captains of the *Bush* and all the admirals who had been in charge of the Bush Carrier Strike Group to serve as honorary pallbearers at his state funeral.

And of course the captains were not totally immune to President Bush's penchant for coming up with ideas. He had a doozy regarding his aircraft carrier: Wouldn't it be fun if it were to cruise up the Atlantic coastline on one of its training missions and visit Kennebunkport? I first pitched the idea to Captain Chip Miller, who was all for it but said it was his boss's decision. So I emailed Admiral Nora Tyson, who said since the ship was getting ready to deploy soon, it just wouldn't work out. "You're not going to email the secretary of defense, are you?" she asked. I promised her I would not.

However, I did not forget that this was something President Bush hoped might happen one day, so I waited patiently until the ship returned from her seven-month deployment, spent a few months in dry dock, and then started training exercises before being deployed again. That's when I started my campaign anew. I didn't want to ask the Navy to do anything inappropriate, but it wasn't as if I was asking the ship to come to Iowa.

The ship's new captain, Brian "Lex" Luther,[3] loved the idea but said it could not be his decision. I wrote numerous memos to different people in the Pentagon who kept kicking it upstairs. (Bob Gates was long gone.) At one point, Captain Luther was so frustrated he told me that it was just possible when the ship was coming out of the river in Norfolk to leave on a training exercise, it might get lost in the fog one time and end up in Maine by mistake.

Finally, after months of lobbying and I think some scheming by

---

3. I learned almost everyone in the Navy has a nickname. The aforementioned Captain Chip Miller, for example, is really DeWolfe H. Miller III. Yes, we called him Chip.

Captain Luther, someone with authority saw the light and approved a training exercise that would take the ship north. I am guessing he or she realized there was a former Navy pilot who had been shot down in World War II who became president of the United States and who had an aircraft carrier named for him and who lived on the Atlantic Ocean and who secretly hoped the ship might come up his way while on a training run...Well, why the hell not? A training run was a training run.

Or maybe the ship did get lost in the fog? I never knew for sure.

The ship sailed into view of Walker's Point early on a Sunday morning in June 2012, and I was lucky enough to be on a golf cart with President Bush when we both spotted her. It was a breathtaking sight. I asked President Bush how it felt to know that majestic ship had his name on it. He had no words. We both just cried the rest of the ride up to the house.

The Bush family who were in residence—which included the forty-third president—all helicoptered to the ship, where the two presidents reenlisted seventy-seven sailors and promoted eleven officers. Then a contingent of officers and sailors came ashore to have lunch on the driveway of Walker's Point. In the meantime, the entire town of Kennebunkport came to a standstill and lined Ocean Avenue, taking photos and following the ship's every move. By the time it sailed out of sight that evening, we were an exhausted but happy bunch, but none more so than President Bush.

During the ship's three deployments, President Bush followed the ship as closely as he was allowed and fretted especially when it went into the Mediterranean Sea or the Persian Gulf. And he was right to fret, as F-18s flying off the ship were involved in military strikes on numerous occasions during all three deployments.

I remember telling him I was a little surprised the ship's captains were allowed to email him details—even photos—of events such as their going through the Suez Canal. It seemed to me that might be classified. Giving me the patient but slightly bemused look I knew only too well, he pointed out that it was hard to keep an aircraft carrier transiting a canal a secret. The whole world knew where the ship and the entire Bush Strike Force armada was at that moment in time.

Although an aircraft carrier is a warship, President Bush loved the ship's motto, "Freedom at Work." He felt in his heart that her main mission was to keep the peace, which he felt strongly she accomplished the minute she sailed into sight.

As proud as he was of that aircraft carrier, the namesake closest to President Bush's heart was the George Bush School of Government and Public Service, a master's degree program that opened at Texas A&M University in 1997.[4] President Bush hated what he called the "L word"— "legacy"—but he knew the school and her graduates would be one of his greatest legacies. All doubts of that were erased when he made the decision that he wanted the Bush School to receive all the "in lieu of flowers" donations when he died.

When Texas A&M lobbied hard for his presidential library, President Bush lobbied right back: As a companion to the library, he wanted a school of public service. He didn't want an institute or a foundation or a center. As he once said to me: "I don't want to reinvent the wheel. There are enough institutions and foundations doing good work."

He wanted a school. As he said in many speeches about the school, "Public service is a noble calling, and we need men and women of character to believe that they can make a difference in their communities, in their states, and in their countries."

That quote is now on his bust that sits inside the front door of the school. Former Bush School dean Bob Gates remembers that when he told President Bush the students rubbed the bust's nose for good luck before tests: "He looked at me and, with a perfectly straight face, said, 'Thank God it's only a bust.'"

(I've been told that before takeoff, some of the pilots who fly off the

---

4. You can find more information in the Glossary of Names.

USS *George H. W. Bush* rub a foot of President Bush's statue on the air-craft carrier. I've never been told that spies rub the nose of his bust that sits in the main lobby of the CIA headquarters, but they keep a lot of secrets there.)

His dream was that his school would inspire, train, and provide tomorrow's leaders. He was not disappointed. As of this writing, more than 70 percent of Bush School graduates are working in government positions on the city, county, state, and federal levels—including in the foreign service and at the CIA—or in the nonprofit sector.

President Bush loved interacting with the students. Once, just a few days before we were leaving for Maine for the summer, someone from the school called to ask if some of the students and professors could have a photo session with President Bush for a new school brochure. President Bush was incredibly busy, but I knew he would want to do this. I told the caller they had fifteen minutes on his schedule. He spent two hours with them, just visiting, answering questions, asking questions. Every time I went into his office to pull the plug, he gave me the look that said, "Not now, not yet."

The night he died, the students spontaneously showed up at the statue that sits on the campus of the Bush School, holding a candlelight vigil for the man this group of students unfortunately never met. But they cried anyway and returned the second night in even bigger numbers.

"President Bush is so much more than our namesake; he's in the DNA of this place," says Mark Welsh, the current dean of the Bush School. "Our students choose the Bush School because they want to serve their fellow citizens, as he served. They strive to live up to his example of respected and respectful governance. President Bush is not just our namesake; he's our North Star."

I never doubted the dean's words, but a letter to the Bush School's advisory board chairman, Neil Bush, from a Bush School student touched my heart deeply and made me realize the influence President Bush still has with today's students. The letter was written during the

2020 presidential election, shortly after the first and tumultuous debate between Donald Trump and Joe Biden. It said in part:

"I went to school early that morning and sat with your father. I really needed to feel his calm, prudent, thoughtful presence...I just sat and appreciated his leadership, honor, humility, integrity, graciousness, and faith in the whole of America."

CHAPTER TEN

THIS ISN'T THE WHITE HOUSE ANYMORE

There were several hints over the years that the Office of George Bush was maybe not the well-oiled machine President Bush had left behind at the White House.

But before we get into details...you probably assume that it took a huge operation to support all of President Bush's travel, causes, projects, correspondence, and, of course, ideas.

There were ten of us—sometimes. Our numbers now and then dipped as low as eight—including three people who worked part-time.[1]

We did have a large group of volunteers—fifteen to twenty at any given time—who would come to open and sort the mail and send out Eagle Scout and military retirement congratulatory letters. They were almost all women, and most of them had started volunteering for George Bush back in the 1960s.

After a while, I established an internship program with Texas A&M, to get some younger, computer-savvy help in the office.

Now that I think about it, how on earth did we do it?

---

1. You can find all their names in the glossary at the front of the book.

For the most part, I think we served the Bushes well, with the occasional hiccup or two.

You already know way too many of my faux pas—simple things like accidently inviting the president of the United States to the Houston Livestock Show and Rodeo.

One confession I have not made (and something I swore I would take to the grave) is about the time that the now-deceased Washington heavyweight ambassador Richard Holbrooke kept calling me to ask a favor of President Bush. The answer was no, but he didn't seem to hear me. He obviously thought he could wear me down.

President Bush had ordered me to hold the line and not to give in to what he wanted. (No, I am not going to tell you what the favor was, as it involved someone still alive and well.) About the fifth time he called, I thought I had asked our receptionist to please put him on hold for a few minutes. While gathering my thoughts on what to say to him, I vented to staffer Laura Pears, who just happened to be sitting in my office. Swearing like a sailor, I told her I had just had it with this jackass.

Well, Ambassador Holbrooke was not on hold; he had been put through and had been on the line during my entire tirade. I was so taken aback when I realized this I hung up. Not cool.

I immediately called General Scowcroft to get his advice on how to fix this mess. He felt I should not call him and apologize. His argument: You are not sure how much he heard. He said I should just let it play itself out.

Almost immediately, General Scowcroft's partner and collaborator, Ginny Mulberger, called to ask if she could release the entire incident to the *Washington Post*'s gossip column, "Reliable Source." She felt it would make me very popular among the DC crowd. I told her *no*.

I am not proud of this incident—my behavior was everything George H. W. Bush was not—but I did win the day: Ambassador Holbrooke never called me back. Case closed.

President Bush and Mrs. Bush welcome the Clintons to their new home on January 20, 1993. President Bush found something to smile about while the incoming president greeted the Bushes' dog Millie. *(George H. W. Bush Library and Museum/ Carol Powers)*

President Bush would call this "heaven." He made this jump on his seventy-fifth birthday in 1999 to help raise money for MD Anderson Cancer Center. *(George H. W. Bush Library and Museum/Michael Kellett)*

In 2000, forty-seven years after her death, President and Mrs. Bush moved their daughter Robin from Greenwich, Connecticut, to their gravesite on the grounds of the George H. W. Bush Library Center at Texas A&M University. With them are Reverend Larry Gipson and his wife, Mary Frances, and staffer Michael Dannenhauer. *(George & Barbara Bush Foundation/Chandler Arden)*

President Bush channeling Johnny Carson's Carnac the Magnificent character at Mrs. Bush's seventy-fifth birthday party in June 2000. He surprised the White House press corps when he did the same as president at a Gridiron Dinner. *(George H. W. Bush Library and Museum/Susan Biddle)*

In honor of his wife's birthday and with the help of photoshopping, President Bush revealed to the family for the first time the members of the highly secretive Ranking Committee. Sitting on the left is staffer Linda Poepsel; on the right is me. Yes, with President Bush's face superimposed on ours. *(Alexanderportraits.com)*

Barbara Bush took this photo of President Bush and me on the phone in their bedroom at Walker's Point in September 2000. My guess is we are talking to Karl Rove. Not sure why President Bush looks concerned and I'm smiling. *(Barbara Bush)*

A proud father reaches for his son's hand after President George W. Bush spoke at the National Day of Mourning service a few days after 9/11. *(George W. Bush Library and Museum/Eric Draper)*

Lunch with just a few of the five thousand friends who came to his eightieth birthday party. The "formers" are, starting from President Bush's right: Mikhail Gorbachev of the Soviet Union; Shimon Peres of Israel; Gorbachev's interpreter, Pavel Palazchenko; Mila Mulroney; John Major of the United Kingdom; Barbara Bush; Carlos Salinas of Mexico; Brian Mulroney of Canada; and Ana Paula Gerard Salinas. *(Alexanderportraits.com)*

Just for the fun of it, the Bushes had their own mock Summer Olympics in 2004. Here they compete in the hotly contested Segway race, won by Mrs. Bush. CBS sportscaster Jim Nantz showed the video during an NFL broadcast that fall. *(Office of George Bush)*

A birthday present from the Oak Ridge Boys, depicting all the milestones in President Bush's life. Mrs. Bush hated this jacket and gave it away. The Oaks found out and gave President Bush another one. He mainly wore it to tease her. *(Barbara Bush)*

Presidents Bush and Clinton visit with children in Indonesia during their trip in February 2005 after the tsunami that ravaged large parts of Asia. *(Joe Reilly)*

President and Mrs. Bush trying out for the Aggie Wranglers dance team at Texas A&M. They didn't make the cut. *(George & Barbara Bush Foundation/Chandler Arden)*

In December 2006, George Clooney helps President Bush bring joy to Cameron, Louisiana, most of which was destroyed by Hurricane Rita shortly after Katrina. *(Cyndi Sellers)*

President Bush interviews me about the life and times at Walker's Point, for a time capsule he buried near the flagpole. None of us were sure why he wore this aard-vark hat for all the interviews. *(Office of George Bush)*

President Bush teaches a Bush School class in November 2007. With him is the then head of the Bush School, Chuck Hermann. *(George & Barbara Bush Foundation/ Chandler Arden)*

President Bush arrives by parachute for the tenth-anniversary celebration of the opening of the George H. W. Bush Library. The jump was a secret and had people scratching their heads about where the heck he was. His tandem jumper is Army Golden Knight Mike Elliott. *(Lorraine Eden)*

Presidents Bush and Clinton, Secretary James Baker, and Galveston Mayor Lyda Ann Thomas hold a press conference shortly after Hurricane Ike chewed up the Texas Gulf Coast in September 2008. Secretary Baker chaired the Bush-Clinton Ike Fund. You can still see debris floating in the water. *(Mark Burns)*

President Bush and his longtime friend and staffer Don Rhodes. Don idolized President Bush, but even Don appears to be questioning his boss's wardrobe choices. *(Office of George Bush)*

President Bush became famous for his colorful socks. These Superman socks were among his favorites. *(Doro Bush Koch)*

President and Mrs. Bush on their seventieth wedding anniversary, January 6, 2015. *(Evan Sisley)*

President Bush shaved his head to support the son of one of his Secret Service agents, who lost his hair while undergoing chemo-therapy treatments for leukemia. Patrick was two and a half when this photo was taken. He's now a happy, healthy ten-year-old. *(Doro Bush Koch)*

This might have been the last formal family photo, taken on the occasion of Mrs. Bush's ninetieth birthday in 2015. All five of the Bushes' children and most of their spouses are here; we are missing a few of the grandchildren. Front row from left: Pace Andrews, Alexander Andrews, President Bush 41, Pierce Bush, Walker Bush, Sam LeBlond. Back row from left: David Lauren, Lauren Bush Lauren, Margaret Bush, Ashley Bush, Marshall Bush, Barbara Bush, Laura Bush (holding Mila Hager), Jenna Bush Hager, Henry Hager, President Bush 43, Marvin Bush (with his mother standing in front of him), Columba Bush, Jeb Bush, Maria Bush, Neil Bush, Doro Bush Koch, Gigi Koch, Ellie LeBlond Sosa, Nick Sosa. *(Evan Sisley)*

President and Mrs. Bush took this photo with the staff at the 2015 office Christmas party. Front row from left: Melinda Lamoreaux, President Bush, Barbara Bush, Hutton Hinson Higgins. Back row from left: Evan Sisley, Linda Poepsel, Catherine Branch, Laura Pears, Jean Becker, Nancy Lisenby, Jim McGrath, Mary Sage. *(Office of George Bush)*

The former presidents do some catching up while waiting to go on stage for a Hurricane Harvey fund-raiser in October 2017 at Texas A&M University. Long-time advance person and Bush family friend Therese Burch asked my permission to sneak in and get a photo. Then I decided to photobomb her photo. *(Pete Souza)*

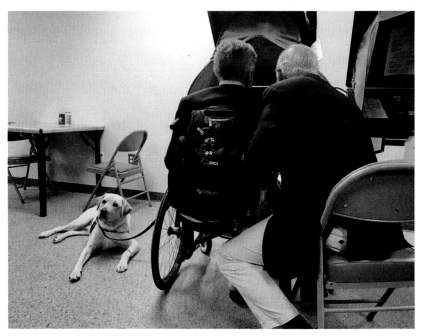

This was the last time President Bush was seen in public, early voting with his friend James Baker before the November 2018 midterm election. Sully did not vote. *(Evan Sisley)*

Sully guards President Bush's casket, December 2018. *(Evan Sisley)*

Presidents Trump, Obama, Clinton, and Carter and their spouses watch as President Bush's casket passes by at the state funeral at the National Cathedral. *(Paul Morse)*

A group of Texas cowboys pays the respects as President Bush's funeral train makes the journey from Houston to College Station. From left ar Casey Rice, Will Nichols, and Mat Nichols, all from Richards, Texas. promised Matt I would tell you tw things: There were more cowboys but the train whistle spooked the horses, and his son Will took his hat off right after his mom took th photo. *(Dayna Nichols)*

Together again. Journey complete. *(Marshall Ramsey)*

Now that I have thrown myself under the bus, there are so many other stories to tell.

There was the incident in 1997 when President Bush was in London, and he asked the staff to set up a lunch with a friend of his, a man named Sir Peter Middleton. The volunteer advance man, Josh Bolten, found a Sir Peter Middleton and arranged the lunch. He does remember Sir Peter seemed surprised, but pleased, at the invitation. And no wonder. While Josh was briefing President Bush about his schedule, the two of them figured out the wrong Sir Peter had been invited; the man was a complete stranger. President Bush felt strongly it would be rude to cancel lunch at such late notice and kept the date. He did tell Sir Peter the truth, but they had a good laugh and a great lunch.[2]

There was another time when a seemingly perfectly legitimate man with good credentials asked to meet President Bush to discuss giving significant amounts of money to the charity of President Bush's choice. About fifteen minutes into the meeting, it became obvious the man was a complete phony and we hustled him out the door as quickly as possible. I learned when in doubt to ask the Secret Service to do background checks on President Bush's visitors, or in the case of international guests, the CIA.

But it was the mistaken phone calls that became somewhat legendary in our office.

I asked Mary Sage to track down a phone number for President Bush's friend Tim Timken, whom the Senate had just confirmed as the U.S. ambassador to Germany under President George W. Bush. She provided a cell phone number, which President Bush promptly dialed and said, "Mr. Ambassador, congratulations!"

"Well, Mr. President, unless you know something I don't know, I don't think so. I'm playing golf in Aspen, Colorado, and I don't think I

---

2. The incident did not derail Josh Bolten's career; he served as President Bush 43's White House chief of staff from 2006 until 2009. He is now president and CEO of the Business Roundtable.

am headed to Germany." The receptionist had given President Bush the number for Tim Finchem, commissioner of golf's PGA Tour.

Then there was the time when President Bush was told that the former mayor of New York, Ed Koch, had called him. He knew and liked the mayor but had not talked to him in a while, so was curious as he returned the call.

Imagine President Bush's surprise when Mayor Koch, a Democrat, told President Bush he had decided to run against Hillary Clinton in the New York senatorial race. President Bush asked his friend, "You are going to run against her in the Democratic primary?"

"Well, no, sir, I will run as a Republican," said the caller.

"Ed, what have I missed here? When did you change parties?"

Well, he hadn't. President Bush was talking to Edwin Cox, the husband of Tricia Nixon Cox, not to Ed Koch. (A staff person did call Mr. Cox back and explained what had happened.)

Yes, there's more. Right after the devastating earthquake in Pakistan, President Bush wanted to talk to someone about how best to fill his new role as the United Nations' special envoy for earthquake relief. He was frustrated by how long it was taking to do anything, so he asked Mary to please get the ambassador from Pakistan to the United States on the phone. A few minutes later she buzzed to tell me that Ambassador Ryan Crocker was on line one.

The Pakistani ambassador's name was Ryan Crocker?

"No," she said. "You told me to get the American ambassador to Pakistan on the phone."

President Bush was not displeased—he knew and respected Ryan Crocker and was happy to hear he was our man in Pakistan. The problem: It was the middle of the night in Pakistan. We had gotten him out of bed.[3]

---

3. Both President Bush and Ambassador Crocker were happy to work together again, and when Ryan retired from the foreign service a few years later, he became dean of the Bush School.

★   ★   ★

One of the most regrettable staff mistakes was made by Jim McGrath, who on Labor Day weekend 2013 released a statement to the world saying how sad President Bush was to learn of the death of Nelson Mandela. Mandela had been ill for some time, so we had a statement ready to go. Jim woke up early one morning and saw a news bulletin on his cell phone, "Nelson Mandela Di—," and then the headline fell off the edge of the screen.

Assuming Mandela had died, he jumped out of bed and hit the "send" button on President Bush's statement. If he had gone to the next screen, he would have seen that the entire headline was "Nelson Mandela Discharged from Hospital."

Oops. The press went nuts, assuming we knew something that they didn't. Eventually the country of South Africa had to put out a statement assuring the world Mandela was still alive. Jim felt horrible and spent the rest of Labor Day weekend agonizing over the mistake. Jim rarely screwed up—this maybe was his only time—and I felt worse for him than about what happened. I assured him that "stuff" happens, and also promised him I was not going to tell President Bush. There was no need for him to know.

It was a great plan, until Secretary Baker called and asked President Bush why he told the world Mandela was dead when he wasn't. So President Bush called me to see what the heck Jimmy Baker was talking about. As usual, he was a forgiving soul.

The Mandela mishap is the perfect segue to what certainly was a pet peeve of President Bush's, Jim's, and mine—and, my guess, of all former presidents and their staff: the tradition of putting out statements when someone of note dies.

On a certain level, President Bush understood their usefulness, but he found it to be something of a hollow gesture. Why couldn't he just write the deceased's family? I think of him almost every time a famous person dies now, immediately followed by endless tweets about the recently departed. He would not approve.

As for Jim and me, we had one major complaint: Famous people all died on the weekend. Just a few examples: Betty Ford died on a Friday night; John McCain, President Reagan, and Pope John Paul II on a Saturday; Nancy Reagan and Princess Diana on a Sunday morning. President Ford was kind enough to die on a Tuesday—but the day after Christmas.[4]

No one ever died on Wednesday. This affected Jim more than me, since it was his responsibility to put these statements out. He would tell you most of these people died when he was coaching his son's Little League game, or when he was at a movie or out on the golf course. I was actually in a bar in Kennebunkport when I learned of Princess Diana's death, which, for us, was a Saturday night.

This was one reason why Jim begged President Bush for the two of them to work together to put statements "in the can," so we would be ready at a moment's notice, especially for late-night or weekend deaths. (I think we stopped this after the Mandela incident.) The other reason Jim and I felt "ready to go" statements would be smart was President Bush's age. As he used to quote Milton Berle: "All my friends are dying in alphabetical order." Putting out statements after someone died was becoming a way of life for us.

Both Bushes were particular and very hands-on about statements. They did not want to declare that someone was a great person if they really didn't think so. Or that they loved them if they didn't. President Bush stubbornly refused to put out a statement when longtime White House reporter Helen Thomas died. "I didn't like her," he declared.

Mrs. Bush was careful about what she said when Nancy Reagan died in 2016. By that time, their rivalry was well known. When I got word of her death on a Sunday morning, I called the Bushes first to let them know. Mrs. Bush immediately informed me she would not use the word "love" in her statement.

---

4. Another example: I am rereading this chapter the Saturday after Justice Ruth Bader Ginsburg died on a Friday night.

My next call was to Jim, who thankfully answered the phone. "Good luck," I said, informing him as I hung up that Mrs. Bush was expecting his call.[5]

President Bush's former secretary of state Larry Eagleburger[6] died early on a Saturday morning—of course—in June 2011. Margaret Tutwiler kindly called to let us know before it hit the news. President Bush knew immediately what he wanted to say about his friend, so I quickly got the statement out, without bothering Jim.

Up until then, it had been a quiet morning in the Kennebunkport office, where I was catching up on a few things. Suddenly the phone lit up like a Christmas tree, with all four lines buzzing. As it turns out, the Eagleburger family had not announced his death yet, and the press was calling to confirm.

I guess I announced his death. Or you could say President Bush did.

The Eagleburger family could not have been more gracious about it all. After all, unlike Mandela, their loved one *had* died.

Another statement on which I soloed was when Supreme Court Justice Antonin Scalia died very unexpectedly in 2016—on a Saturday. Despite the fact I knew Jim was in Corpus Christi, Texas, at his brother-in-law's wedding, I selfishly tried to call him anyway. I called in the middle of the ceremony, so he didn't answer.

This was going to be a tough one. Jim was so good at doing these; I really was not. I called the Bushes, who were quite sad, but the only words President Bush could give me were that he "loved him" and Scalia "was a great man."

---

5. The statement Jim and Mrs. Bush wrote together: "Nancy Reagan was totally devoted to President Reagan, and we take comfort that they will be reunited once more. George and I send our prayers and condolences to her family."

6. Eagleburger became acting secretary of state in 1992, when Secretary Baker left the State Department to become White House chief of staff. After he lost the election, President Bush made sure Eagleburger was simply secretary of state—without the "acting"—through a recess appointment. He was the first career foreign service officer to have the job.

I needed more than that. But as I was doing some quick research to add substance to President Bush's personal feelings, the forty-third president's statement hit the news. It pretty well said exactly what I had drafted at that point.

So I called my sister Millie—a lawyer, a constitutional scholar, and a huge fan of Justice Scalia's. When I told her I needed her help writing the statement for President Bush, she started crying. She had not heard the news and was upset. I told her to pull it together because I needed her. Through her tears she managed to give me some excellent talking points on Scalia's impact on the Supreme Court.

I wrote the statement, then called and read it to the Bushes. They loved it—Mrs. Bush raved over it—so I told her the truth: Most of the language had come from Millie.

Then I put it out to the media, and just minutes later, I heard CNN commentator Dave Gergen reading President Bush's statement. After he did so, he took off his glasses, peered meaningfully into the camera, and basically said the following: "I've read a lot of statements in my life. This one was not written by some staff person. This is straight from George Bush's heart."

Immediately my phone rang. It was Mrs. Bush, who was watching CNN, too. She was dying laughing and pointed out that the statement had really not been written by a staffer, but a staffer's sister.

For the record, before we leave this topic, President Bush died at about ten o'clock on a Friday night. Mrs. Bush, God love her, died on a Tuesday.

By now you must think our office was rather haphazard, and it's true that we could be at times. In our defense, we were extraordinarily busy, and, unfortunately, juggling too many balls. Multitasking does lead to mistakes.

I'm not even sure we realized how busy we were until 2016 when a few misguided congressmen and senators got it into their heads that the federal government should no longer provide funding for the offices of former presidents. Because President Bush was more or less the dean of the former "Presidents Club," and also because of his age—this bill would affect us less than the others except for President Carter—it fell largely to me and my team to take the lead on fighting back.

The staff went on a mission to collect as much data as they could to paint a picture of what all went on in the former presidents' offices, using ours as an example. Here are just a few key points from my report:

- President and Mrs. Bush have helped raise $670 million for key projects and charitable causes, including literacy, volunteerism, and cancer.
- In addition, they have attended scores of fund-raisers for nonprofit groups all over the country, but especially in their hometown of Houston, Texas. (I provided a list of all of them in the report.)
- One of the more prolific activities of the Office of George Bush is to send items to be used for charitable auctions. Signed photos and books, personal items of the Bushes, and signed paintings and baseballs are just a few of the items donated over the years. At least $1 million has been raised through the donation of these items.
- At one time President Bush received an average of one hundred to two hundred pieces of mail a day.
- Since 1993, the office has sent an estimated 149,700 congratulatory letters to Eagle Scouts.
- We send two hundred to three hundred military retirement letters a month.
- Since 1993, an estimated 43,500 congratulatory letters have been sent to mark special occasions: births, weddings, birthdays, anniversaries.
- We have not kept track of letters written to be read at special events or to mark certain occasions. They would number in the thousands. Right now, for example, we are providing letters for numerous twenty-fifth-anniversary Desert Storm reunions happening around the country.

- President Bush has served as honorary chair of 491 events and organizations over the years. (A complete list was attached to my report.)
- President Bush has recorded literally hundreds of public service announcements—560 in the eleven-year period between 1997 and 2007—and "greetings" to be shown at various events over the years.

The proposed legislation was a bee in my bonnet for months. You might detect some of that attitude in the cover letter I sent to Congress, along with the more detailed report:

"As a lifelong fiscal conservative, President Bush (41) applauds the efforts of Congress to amend the 'Former Presidents Act of 1958' to assure that the tax dollars spent to support the former presidents and their offices are used appropriately and efficiently.

"However, eliminating all funding to support the work of presidents is not fiscally meaningful, politically impactful, or even patriotic. The former presidents willingly perform—as they are expected to do—a wide variety of services for their country and their fellow citizens, all in their unofficial roles as former presidents...

"Without their staffs, the presidents would likely try to step up to the plate to help raise money, promote causes, provide leadership during crises, represent their country at official events and provide constituency services. But realistically, without staff support, little would happen. A team is needed to handle correspondence, receive and process incoming requests, schedule appointments and travel, coordinate logistics, and oversee special projects."

Thanks to the staff's hard work and the great efforts of two key players in Washington, DC—Ron Kaufman and Tom Collamore, both former staffers and longtime friends of the Bushes—the bill eventually died a natural death.

Before I get into the whiny part of this chapter, I want to be clear on one indisputable fact: We all loved our jobs. We knew working for George Bush was a great honor.

But it also was a wild roller-coaster ride. While researching this book, I found a speech I gave in Houston in 2004, specifically about my job. Sixteen years later, this paragraph made me laugh out loud:

"I feel incredibly blessed to work for them, yet there are challenges. I have been told by Mikhail Gorbachev to shut up, but I've been kissed by Tom Selleck; I've been yelled at by the President of the United States but blessed by the Pope. I have picked up the phone at 7 a.m. only to hear Barbara Bush say to me, 'Have you totally lost your mind,' but next week I move my office for five months to Kennebunkport, Maine... Yes, I think the highs greatly outweigh the occasional lows."

There were many long days that turned into long weeks, filled with challenges both big and small. They also were filled with just plain annoying crap. I tried to find a better, more sophisticated word, but I fear the right word here is "crap."

One small example: President Bush was famous for writing thank-you notes for thank-you notes, which might sound endearing—unless you are Linda Poepsel and in charge of his correspondence. We finally made a deal with him: Either Linda or I would email people and tell them how much President Bush appreciated their note.

So yes, occasionally, I sometimes would get into a mood. And to prevent the onslaught of ulcers, I often shared that mood with the staff, usually in the form of rambling emails or memos. Rereading them, I wonder: Why didn't they all run for the hills? Or at least to the closest bar? Now that I think about it, they probably did go to a bar. They just didn't invite me.

You also might have noticed by now that sometimes I got a little—

well, sassy with President Bush. Just a little bit of attitude would somehow seep into what I had planned to be well-measured arguments. The good news for me was that President Bush not only loved the sassiness but encouraged it. Mrs. Bush—not so much.

I am going to share just a few of my more infamous memos with you. (One of our volunteers, Margaret Voelkel, kept her favorite ones; I would never ever have saved these things.) If nothing else, they will illustrate some of the ups and downs in an office of a former president and maybe provide a bit of behind-the-scenes color.

This first memo was sent to all the staff and volunteers in the office. It is not dated, but the subject line is: **FIRST CRANKY MEMO OF 1995**. Here are some excerpts:

"Don't say I didn't warn you: This memo is going to be cranky. But there are a couple of things I need to bring to your collective attention.

1. When President Bush is in the office, we really do need to be mindful of the noise level in the lobby and his side of the hall. For some reason, noise seems to tunnel right down that hall into his office. I was sitting in his office yesterday going over some work, and it sounded like a three-ring circus outside. I do not consider this a problem when he is out of the office. In fact, I would like to suggest you talk louder so I can be sure and hear everything.

2. If you are traveling with President or Mrs. Bush or if you are out on a business assignment, **WEAR A PAGER**. Please don't make me ask you again.

3. Please file this under friendly advice: we have had a number of events lately, dating back to the [library] groundbreaking, where all of us had the occasion to be with the Bushes in a social situation. Keep in mind, that as staff and volunteers, we have the opportunity to see the Bushes

almost every day. Therefore, when we're out in public, 'face time' should be at a minimum. They don't want to see us; they want to see their friends and even family whom they don't get to see as often...you should not be a groupie and should keep face time to a minimum—at most, a quick hello...Most of the people in this office have been guilty of this at some time or another; so please everyone, spend a few minutes feeling really guilty about this, then get over it and swear you won't do it again. And no, I will not under any circumstances name names, so don't ask.

"OK, I'll get over my crankiness. After all, it's almost Friday."

Many of these notes were written from Maine. In the summer, from May through October, the staff split in half, with me and the Bushes' two personal aides going to Maine and everyone else staying in Houston.

And yes, those who went to Maine were the lucky ones with one small exception: As I once said in an interview, the troublemaker went with us. Yes, that would be President Bush.

July and August were especially complicated, when most of the Bush family descended upon Walker's Point. Some would come and stay awhile. Some would come and go. They all brought friends. Walker's Point slept anywhere between thirty-three and forty people, depending on if you counted couches and the bunk beds in the dormer room of the main house.

Mrs. Bush's aide was in charge of keeping track of who was coming when and where they would sleep. I used to tease the aides that in the summer, they had an additional title: concierge of Walker's Point.

It was mostly fun to have the family around.

It was always chaos.

Several of my emails back to the team in Houston best describe the bedlam:

Walker's Point Houseguests

August 20, 1996

At last count we had sailed past 100. Seriously. Among the luminaries have been Clarence Thomas, Lech Walesa, Freddy Couples, Billy Graham, and Richard North Patterson.[7] We've had one cat, one rabbit, and several dogs. It was NOT a smart move on the part of anyone who brought these animals to do so... The numbers will continue to skyrocket next week with the arrival of the Oak Ridge Boys and their wives.

---

7. A Supreme Court justice, a Polish head of state, a golfer, a man of God, and an author.

Subject: Complete Nervous Breakdown

July 30, 1997, 2:43 p.m.

We have grandkids eating things off trees.

The local barber Emile Roy (sort of a Roy Orbison look-alike) wants to go out with me.

Paula Rendon the housekeeper is lost somewhere between here and Houston because her flight was cancelled.

The stupid ass restaurant where the Bushes are having dinner tonight has now called 4 times to make sure "they have it right."

Gian-Carlo wrecked one of President Bush's boats.

They shut the water off.

President Bush's fishing buddy wants to go out with Quincy[8] and she doesn't want to.

Some tourists took my picture when I went to lunch.

I'm sick of the Chinese and hope they lose Hong Kong, Taiwan, Tibet, and Mongolia. (Do they have Mongolia?)[9]

---

8. Quincy Hicks, who was Mrs. Bush's aide at the time. Now Quincy Crawford, she lives in New Orleans with her husband, J.T., and two sons.

9. My guess is a Chinese delegation wanted to come see President Bush, which was quite often. Not to offend a country of one billion people, but they were always higher-maintenance than most.

Quincy and I want cheese enchiladas and there are none for 800 miles.

We're still getting dead dog mail.[10]

We got a letter written in German and we don't know any.

And because it's a gorgeous day, we are running away. In fact, we probably are gone.

Don't call. Don't write.

Send help. Or money.

We'll come back tomorrow. Maybe.

This next one was written the summer of George W.'s first campaign for the White House, and the reality of having a family member return to 1600 Pennsylvania Avenue was beginning to sink in. I was in Maine, and I sent this email to Linda Poepsel, Laura Pears, and Mary Sage.

---

10. Mrs. Bush's beloved dog, Millie, had died.

Subject: Today's random thoughts

July 26, 2000, 5:50 p.m.

What will we do if George W. wins? Will the whole world write/call/e-mail George H. W. Bush with their suggestions, complaints, and ideas for the President? It's going to be a nightmare, girls. White House tours? Oh my god I can see it coming. We might have to hire a new person just for that. I'm so sick of people asking us for convention credentials and tickets and meetings and access, etc., that I've had this terrible vision of what's maybe to come.

Yesterday, UPS and FedEx delivered 10 huge boxes of stuff. We couldn't even walk into the kitchen. I thought Kimberly[11] was going to cry.

1. A huge box of neckties with parachutes on them.
2. Two boxes of golf clothes from the people the Bushes stayed with in Chicago.
3. A huge box of potato chips from the Snack Food Association. To my dismay, Doro took them.
4. My new computer. My current one is dying an ugly, slow death.
5. Some gizmo for Mrs. Bush's computer.
6. A Houston box. Yes, we cursed you all.[12]
7. 3 boxes of fishing equipment.
8. GB's laundry, which he had shipped from the road.
9. A box of Turkish towels he had bought in Istanbul.

---

11. Kimberly Hamlin, our summer intern.

12. During the summer, the Houston office sent us a box of mail at least once a week.

Wait, this is more than 10 boxes—it was a mess and a sight to behold. I was not amused by the laundry[13] or the stupid ass neckties…

The [Republican] convention wants to play "the devil with the blue dress" when Mrs. Bush walks out. Now I just have to talk her into it.

I hate the phone, fax machine, and mail in that order. E-mail is still pretty sacred although way too many reporters have gotten my e-mail address somehow and my home phone number…

Why don't we all get six weeks of vacation like Arabella????[14]

This is a major question. The Bushes almost threw up when they heard this and are in denial. Tom [Frechette], Kimberly and I have not left this office before 7 p.m. the entire time the Bushes have been [traveling] except for this Friday when I told Tom I had to leave or die…the next sound you hear might be the door slamming as I leave. My theme song, "I'm leaving on a jet plane." Wasn't that a song?

Yet, despite the madness, the Office of George Bush was a joyous place to work, because President Bush made it so. He not only was full of

---

13. I am not sure why I was not amused by the laundry. It's not as if I had to do the laundry.

14. Arabella Warburton, chief of staff to former British prime minister John Major and my English soul mate.

energy and ideas, he also knew how to have fun. And he made our lives more fun.

Just reading his memos brought more smiles than listening to a stand-up comic.

So I am going to share two of my favorites.

This first one he wrote to the volunteers on December 12, 1997, and left it in a basket full of coffee cups in the volunteer room of our office. It even had a cover page:

Coffee Cups

By

George Bush

"A Cri de Coeur"

Yes, this is all about coffee cups.

Here is a large basket, courtesy of the U.S. Government. It is filled with a wide array of coffee cups. It appears that no two cups are the same. A wide variety of cups that have been given by numerous charitable, sports, sororital, and fraternal organizations.

Note the use of the word "sororital." Given that so many of our fantastic volunteers are of the female gender, I think it best to strive for correctness here. (I must chortle however at how Hillary was heaved out of the University Club in N.Y.—spraying perfume was the charge. She did it and a lot of my friends were offended.)

Back to Cup, coffee:

Too many cups have worked their way from the bacteria kitchen[15]
to the executive kitchen. It may be a "dishwasher thing." I am not
trying to blame anyone. I am simply saying that the shelves in the
executive kitchen were groaning under the load . . .

I used to dream of sports and religion and well frankly, physical
things—yes, things having to do with sex. This dream pattern I am
told is normal for a guy 73.

But that was long ago, before the shelves near the oven on the left
side as you walk in were laden down with coffee cups. Now instead
of feeling the pull of a striped bass on my fly rod I see dirty cups
coming out of the ocean in Kennebunkport.

As I go to fire my shot gun, I see cups instead of quail. When I
wake up I vaguely remember the covey—I vividly remember the
cups.

In one of those dreams, oddly, I saw a bikini-clad Sharon Stone—
saw her fleetingly emerging from a steam bath. But up front up top
were two coffee cups—one saying, "Preferred Savings"—the other
simply saying "MMMC."

Below on her bikini was the outline of another cup. This one simply
said "Pennsylvania." She turned seductively around and there were
two more cups. On the left it said, "DCI Communications Center"
while on the right side it said, "Tupelo Children's Mansion."

What is going on here?

---

15. The Office of George Bush had two kitchens—a general-use kitchen for everyone
and a bigger kitchen considered President Bush's but that we all used. It had the only
microwave and the only dishwasher.

I am an old man. Not a tired old man. Oh no! But time is running through glass. I want to dream nice, sweet dreams.

Please help me. Whoever is in charge back there in the volunteer room, please help. If a committee decision is needed—fine! Form a committee . . .

I love you all. I hope you understand, not taking this as a criticism but rather taking [it] as a cri de couer, a "cri" from a guy whose Prozac[16] can no longer do the job, a patient who needs help right now.

P.S. Oh yes, normally I use Times New Roman #14*—yes, a fine font. But for emphasis here I have gone to* Amherst #18*—a bold departure; but when one's very id, his mantra too, needs help, when his karma is under siege then dramatic change is in order. Help me!!!*

I will add this note to President Bush's wonderful ode to coffee cups: We were overrun with the darn things. Coffee cups, T-shirts, baseball caps, and tote bags became the bane of our existence, as every single group and sometimes individuals thought the Bushes would just die to drink coffee out of a cup with their logo while wearing a T-shirt or a baseball cap with the same and carrying their tote bag on their arm. My advice: Don't. Send flowers. Better yet: Donate to one of their causes.

The topic of this second memo centered on a broken toilet seat in the office at Walker's Point, written right before the Bushes' grandson George P. Bush got married in Kennebunkport and right before the Bushes left for Greece to head the U.S. delegation to the Summer Olympics and spend some time cruising the Aegean Sea.

---

16. For the record, President Bush was not taking Prozac.

Subject: Chief of Staff

I address this to our "Chief" asking that she enlist the summer lads[17] or someone to solve this problem:

All of you, each in your own way, have done a good job on paper towels, Kleenex, soap, and toilet paper. Indeed, we have had very few glitches.

But now there is a new danger. The toilet seat upstairs here appears to be misaligned. There is grave danger that if it tilts further someone can fall off and get hurt. What if Laura [Pears] re-broke her arm just before the cruise. What if Tommy [Frechette] or I had the embarrassment of having to call for help whilst writhing on the floor. How could we explain to Brian[18] if M got seriously hurt in this unseemly, undignified, unladylike manner?

Jean—this may seem a tiny matter on this big BBQ day, just as wedding plans come to fruition, just as final decisions on the cruise must be made, security problems wrestled with; but please attend to this matter. Delegate! Lead us!

---

17. President Bush's nickname for the yard workers at Walker's Point.

18. Michele Whalen was Mrs. Bush's personal aide; Brian was her then boyfriend. Now Michele Stanton, she lives in College Station, Texas, with her husband, Clay, and two daughters.

Do not ask Ariel—the man cooked all night long. Do not ask Teresa or Alicia or even Paula—they have other duties.[19]

Perhaps this crisis can safely wait until after we all leave, but suppose we have all gone cruising and special, dear Amanda, while soloing in there, falls off—unattended.[20]

Please Jean. Please do this.

P.S. Do not call a plumber. After Robin's Nest pond work, increasing demands for champagne, more ordering-out-for pizzas, more "can I borrow the car or the truck?," more "just have me met in Boston by People Movers," I am feeling broke so we must fix this ourselves.

The more I think about it: "Tommy just bring me a monkey wrench!"

*Sincerely, George Bush,
41st President of the United States of America*

---

19. The household staff: Ariel Deguzman, Paula Rendon, and her daughter Alicia Huizar. Paula's daughter Teresa was visiting.

20. Amanda Biedrzycki was our summer intern and would be holding down the fort while we were in Greece.

★   ★   ★

Before we leave this chapter about life in the Office of George Bush, we must go back to phone calls. Phone calls could have been an entire book!

One of my favorites was one evening when I was having a quiet night at home until President Bush called. He was on the road with his great friend Brian Mulroney, who had a terrible cold. The two of them were in a Walgreens trying to decide what to buy, and President Bush for some odd reason called me for advice. He remembered I'd just had a cold and he told his friend I would know what to take.

I was hesitant to give medical advice to two former leaders of the Free World, but I told President Bush I was a big fan of NyQuil. It would help him sleep and clear up his congestion. As I told President Bush this, I heard him yelling, "Brian, Jean says to buy NyQuil!" and then he thanked me and hung up. It would have made a great commercial.

Then there was the day that Lynda Webster, the wife of former CIA and FBI director Judge William Webster, called to give me a heads-up that a former head of the CIA (I have forgotten which one) was dying and she thought he might appreciate a call from President Bush. She gave me the direct line to his hospital room.

As soon as I gave President Bush the message he picked up the phone and called, and a woman answered. As it turned out, the former CIA chief had been moved to another part of the hospital.

That didn't stop President Bush from having a chat with the current room occupant. He asked her what she was in for, how she was feeling, if she was in pain—all the usual. She gave him all the answers, by this time having figured out to whom she was talking. She was screaming into the phone, she was so excited, and then put one of her nurses on the phone, so the nurse could confirm to the patient's family that she had indeed talked to the former president.

When he hung up, President Bush said something to me like, "Nice visit." It didn't seem to bother him that she was a stranger.

He didn't mind talking to strangers and in fact rather enjoyed it. My sister Millie called just a few summers before President Bush died to tell me that while on a trip to Chicago, her cabdriver started talking to her about what a huge fan he was of President Bush No. 41. He was an immigrant from another country and felt President Bush had saved his people. He had *no* idea Millie's sister worked for his idol. The conversation was unprovoked and random.

Millie got his name and cell phone number, telling him she might call him during her Chicago visit for more taxi rides. She told me the story, I told President Bush the story, and he of course said, "Well, get him on the phone." I placed the call, explained who I was and why we were calling. He asked to pull over to the side of the road—thankfully, he had no passengers—and compose himself before I gave the phone to President Bush. "Really nice guy," President Bush reported back to me.

Not long before he died, I got a message from a family member of a man named Donovan who was on the USS *Finback* when the submarine plucked President Bush out of the Pacific Ocean. The man was dying and told his daughter he would love to hear President Bush's voice one more time. When I told President Bush the man's name, he did not remember him. I said I would call the daughter and explain he just wasn't up for a phone call. President Bush told me that was nonsense.

"He doesn't need to know I don't remember him," he chided me.

"Let's call Donovan," President Bush said.

We placed the call, and President Bush bellowed his "friend's" name when Donovan got on the phone. I was always amused at how President Bush was never shy about asking sick and dying people about their ailment. "What's getting you?" he asked. When he hung up, he told me and Jon Meacham, who happened to be visiting at the time, "Great visit. But I think he's almost gone." (He died that night.)

Another "stranger" phone call resulted in my finding this note on my desk one Monday morning:

April 16, 1995

Jean:

It's Easter, and I am doing case work; for I answered the phone here in the office.

A [name omitted], unemployed welder, called in. He wanted Barbara for he has a reading problem.

When queried, I told him "It is I."

He then told me his problem. A good welder, he cannot find work because of his dyslexia and bad reading overall.

He is in construction and makes, sometimes, $15 per hour. Because of his reading failure he can't get work now.

He hates welfare. He doesn't want a handout.

I gave him the usual disclaimer "out of office, unemployed myself, call the Congressman."

Can someone call him [Name omitted and phone number omitted].

Maybe BPB knows of an adult reading program. Just any call back might encourage the guy. Even if we said, "We've checked, and have no suggestions."

Can we help ?—GB

We did call him back and hooked him up with a literacy program at the Houston Read Commission.

One of the more complicated phone calls I ever placed for President Bush was when he decided one Saturday morning, in either 1996 or 1997, he would like to call Dan Rostenkowski in prison.

Rostenkowski—a legendary Democratic politician who rose from being a ward boss in Chicago to chairing the powerful Ways and Means Committee in the House of Representatives—was in federal prison, having pled guilty to two felony counts for mail fraud. He had faced seventeen different charges, all based on his misuse of taxpayers' money, including things like keeping a slush fund and showering gifts on supporters.

Despite their political differences, he and President Bush had become great friends while serving together on the House Ways and Means Committee in the 1960s, then working on getting legislation passed through Congress when President Bush was in the White House. President Bush felt the charges and eventual conviction of his friend were unfair. "That's how Danny was raised in Chicago," I remember him telling me at the time. When he died, even the *Chicago Tribune* said in his obituary all the charges against him were "time-honored methods of conducting political business in Chicago."

I am not sure why President Bush thought of his friend on this particular Saturday morning. I told him I did not think prisoners could accept phone calls. He asked me to make sure. So filled with doubt, I cold-called the main switchboard number at the prison, which I found on the internet. "Yeah, this is going nowhere," I thought to myself.

An operator did answer and listened to what I had to say. He asked for my number and hung up. Just what I thought: a dead end. A few minutes later our office phone rang. It was the warden. I think he asked me to repeat who exactly was calling to talk to whom. Again, he heard me out. Then he asked if I could put the request in writing on stationery that would prove this was President Bush calling.

I typed and faxed the memo. In less than thirty minutes, the phone rang and it was Dan Rostenkowski. "Did President Bush try to call me?" he asked rather tentatively.

They had a wonderful visit, and I know Rostenkowski never forgot that while in prison, a former president of the United States called to "check in."

President Bush was the best at calling people who maybe were not having a great day. He did not hesitate to call the sick or dying, their grieving relatives, obviously people in prison, or anyone making unwanted headlines. We tracked down Arnold Schwarzenegger, for example, the day it was announced Maria Shriver was leaving him. I argued with him over that call—after all, Maria had left Arnold because it became public he'd had a love child with their former housekeeper. President Bush won the day by arguing that probably no one was calling Arnold, and he just wanted to let him know he still considered him a friend. "That's when you call people, Jean," I remember him telling me. "When you know they are down and need a friend."

He then asked me if I could think of anyone else he should call; anyone else who could use a lift. I reminded him that earlier that week U.S. Special Forces had captured and killed the world's most wanted terrorist, Osama bin Laden, so maybe he should call his four widows. I think he called me a smart-ass, which I deserved.

One of his more out-of-the-box phone call ideas was the morning after the first Democratic primary debate in 2008. There were eight candidates on the stage, but the questions went predominantly to Senator Barack Obama, Senator Hillary Clinton, and Senator John Edwards. "Get Joe Biden and Chris Dodd on the phone for me," he said as he walked past my office. "I am outraged how they were treated last night."

"I've been where they are," President Bush said, referring to his 1980 run for the White House. He felt both men were qualified to be president and deserved a chance to make their case. I would have loved to have been a fly on the wall of the offices of the two Democratic senators when they were told President Bush was on the phone to discuss the debate the night before. I never met Senator Dodd but have interacted with President Biden several times over the years. He never failed to bring up that call and what it meant to him.

Except for the Prince Bandar story, it's possible that my favorite-ever phone call incident was the summer of 2000, right before we left Kennebunkport to fly to Philadelphia for the Republican National Convention, where George W. would officially accept his party's nomination for the presidency.

I was leaving on Sunday morning; the Bushes would arrive about midday on Monday. President Bush and I were both in the office all day Saturday, frantically trying to get some work done before the big event.

Finally, around 5 p.m., I told President Bush I had to go home, do laundry, and pack before catching my 7 a.m. flight. I think my exact words were, "If I don't go home and do laundry, I will have no clean underwear for the convention." In my defense, I needed for him to understand the urgency of the situation.

I ran to the store to buy detergent and raced home, only to find more work messages on my home phone. One was from Leslie Goodman, the director of communications for the convention—she and I talked several times a day since the Bushes were going to do a ton of interviews in Philadelphia. She said she needed to talk to me ASAP.

I started my laundry—first things first—and then called Leslie.

She told me that when she called the office, President Bush answered the phone—she recognized his voice immediately—but she politely asked if she could talk to me.

To which he said, without missing a beat: "I'm sorry, but Jean just left. Apparently she has no clean underwear."

Leslie worried he might be giving this message to others. I called the office but, thankfully, he had left for the day. Whew. As for Leslie, she was so unnerved that President Bush had said the word "underwear" to her, she forgot why she had called in the first place.

I loved working for someone who believed that telling the truth should be one of life's rules. But once in a while, President Bush took that tenet maybe just a little too far...

CHAPTER ELEVEN

THE WORST OF TIMES

There were times, but not often, when the roller-coaster ride of the Office of George Bush seemed like one very long uphill climb.

Obviously, dealing with the president's and Mrs. Bush's declining health and aging issues, and their deaths, was challenging. Yet, because of their deep faith and their full acceptance of the realities of life—the last few years actually were not the worst of times. They made it easier for all of us.

The best way to explain "the worst of times" might be to answer two questions I often get:

- What was the hardest issue you faced as President Bush's chief of staff?
- What was the toughest decision you had to make?

The answer to the first is hard to talk about, even now.

The fall of 2017, for several weeks during the height of the #MeToo movement, several women came forward to accuse President Bush of inappropriate behavior. It was crushing to see his name linked with the likes of Harvey Weinstein and Jeffrey Epstein.

None of his accusers knew him. Almost all the "incidents" happened in photo receiving lines, and almost all of them happened after he was in a wheelchair. We also knew his specific kind of Parkinson's disease often resulted in "involuntary behavior," which was a contributing factor.

Nevertheless, I took the accusations seriously and interrogated all of President Bush's personal aides, going back to his White House days, to see if there was anything we needed to be worried about. Although I knew that I had seen nothing inappropriate in my twenty-three years as his chief of staff, I was not always with him. The aides were.

The answers came back a resounding no. None of them had seen anything resembling abuse.

As Jim McGrath told the media, "George Bush simply does not have it in his heart to knowingly cause anyone harm or distress, and he again apologizes to anyone he may have offended during a photo op."

After a few weeks, the media agreed that President Bush was not a part of this story and we all moved on.

Now to the second question: The hardest decision I had to make had to do with Jon Meacham.

We first met Jon in the fall of 1998 when he was the young National Affairs editor of *Newsweek* magazine. Our relationship with *Newsweek* had not been great—most of Bush World had not forgiven the magazine for the infamous "wimp" cover in 1987 when then vice president Bush announced he was running for president, and the *Newsweek* cover story questioned if he had what it took to be president. They called it the "Wimp Factor."

So how on earth did someone from *Newsweek* even get through the door?

Jon had asked his good friend and highly respected presidential historian Michael Beschloss to review President Bush and Brent Scowcroft's soon-to-be-released book, *A World Transformed*. Michael thought an interview would help him in writing the review. President Bush heard the idea and thought, "Ugh, *Newsweek*!" General Scowcroft heard the idea and thought, "Book sales!" His argument won the day.

Then Michael complicated my life by asking if he could bring Jon with him to do the interview. It was only to be a half hour—President Bush wanted them in at 7:30 a.m. and out at 8 a.m. so he could salvage the rest of his day—so I thought no harm done. President Bush grumpily agreed.

They arrived promptly at 7:30 a.m.

They left at 5 p.m.

The interview obviously had gone well. Then Jon and Michael were invited to join the houseguests—David Rubenstein[1] and John and Norma Major—for pancakes.

Then I lost control.

They got a tour of the house from Mrs. Bush, including the master bedroom bathroom; went shopping with the former president in downtown Kennebunkport; and last but certainly not least, earned a ride on *Fidelity*. I silently questioned the wisdom of the boat ride as we went farther and farther out on a very windy day, which meant high seas. But President Bush was determined to show them Boon Island, where a long-ago shipwreck apparently led to cannibalism among the survivors. Michael and Jon seemed to enjoy the rough ride and felt safe with the former Navy man. I remember wondering—just briefly—if President Bush was going to leave them out there. (I don't remember if the houseguests had already left or were too smart to go with us, but they were not on the boat.)

When I asked Jon recently for his help in remembering how this friendship began, he admitted the following, more than twenty years later after that first meeting:

"I was riveted by the president's quiet, persistent charisma, his reassuring presence, his command of his surroundings, and of those who surrounded him. I had been an undergraduate through much of his presidency and so had a kind of a caricatured view of his years in office—

---

1. David, a philanthropist and good friend, was cofounder and codirector of the Carlyle Group.

he was more Dana Carvey[2] to me at that point than George Herbert Walker Bush."

The friendship grew over the next few years as Jon interviewed President Bush now and then—about his son running for president and about 9/11, for example. President Bush liked him and began to trust him

During this same time period, although he eventually became editor in chief at *Newsweek*, Jon also began his career as a historian by writing about the friendship between Franklin Roosevelt and Winston Churchill in *Franklin and Winston*. President Bush loved the book and wrote Jon a long fan letter telling him so. Somewhere in here, I think Jon was beginning to realize he wanted to write about President Bush, whom by now he considered maybe the most underrated president of the twentieth century.

The big turning point came in 2006, when Jon came to President Bush's library to attend the event where the Reverend Billy Graham received the George Bush Award for Excellence in Public Service.

In a conversation in the living room of the Bushes' library apartment, Jon remembers President Bush asking him if he wanted to read his diaries. (For the record, I thought Jon asked, but he insists President Bush brought it up first.)

I do know that once again, I almost fell off my chair.

The diaries? They were under lock and key in President Bush's Houston office. *No one read the diaries.*

The next thing I knew, Jon came to Houston to read the diaries. I do think he was a little concerned when we put him in the conference room where President Bush's extensive gun collection lined one entire wall. We'll never know if this was by design, but while Jon was in the room reading away, staffer Don Rhodes came in and started cleaning some of the guns. I had to admit it was interesting timing on his part.

At one point, Jon came breathlessly into my office and said these

---

2. Dana Carvey played the role of President Bush in political satires on NBC's *Saturday Night Live.*

diaries were the most important presidential document since John Quincy Adams's diaries had been released. His idea was to edit the diaries with commentary, modeled on the book Michael Beschloss had written based on LBJ's White House tapes.

President Bush had a different idea. He suggested to Jon he use the diaries to write a biography, promising him full access to the diary with zero editorial control from us. A diary book, if necessary, could come later, but only after he had died. Or, as Jon remembers President Bush putting it, after he was "paws up."[3]

There was only one problem: President Bush did not want to do any interviews for the book. He thought Jon could write the book without any input from him, but just by reading the diaries, doing research at the library, and talking to staff, friends, and family. "You won't need to talk to me," President Bush assumed.

This time I did the peeling from the ceiling—Jon—while explaining to President Bush that of course Jon would need to talk to him about the story of his life.

It was a leap of faith. I didn't sleep for days after we formalized the agreement with a letter from President Bush to Jon. It was a decision made, after some vetting, on pure gut.

When word got out, the reaction was—well, not great. Marlin Fitzwater, President Bush's White House press secretary, told me I had lost it. The family also questioned my sanity, including the forty-third president of the United States. At issue especially was letting Jon read the diaries. I remember having such a "spirited" discussion about it with President Bush in the staff office kitchen at Walker's Point that it triggered a hot flash (me, not him). As I emphatically and somewhat bravely stood my ground, it was as if someone up above had turned a fire hose on me. The president was kind enough not to mention the sudden water-

---

3. Jon plans to publish the diary book as part of President Bush's one hundredth birthday celebration, June 12, 2024.

works, but even as I write this I still wonder what he thought at the time. (I never had the nerve to ask.)

I reminded everyone this was President Bush's decision, not mine. But the prevailing attitude was that I was the one with the foot on the pedal and, more important, the one with the combination to the safe where the diaries were kept.

The controversy abated a bit in 2009 when Jon won the Pulitzer Prize for *American Lion: Andrew Jackson in the White House.* I used that Pulitzer as a coat of armor—I loved being able to say "Pulitzer Prize–winning author Jon Meacham..."

In addition to concerned family members and former Bush staffers, I also heard from several disappointed historians who had been hoping to write the definitive biography of President Bush. Why Jon? How did he get in the door? Was I aware he once worked for *Newsweek*? As I remember, the hits just kept on coming.

By the time the book was published in November 2015—it took Jon only ten years to write *Destiny and Power: The American Odyssey of George Herbert Walker Bush*—Jon was like family. Both President Bush and Mrs. Bush adored him. He had interviewed President Bush so many times that all the walls had come down. As for Mrs. Bush, even she agreed to turn her diaries over to him to read—a decision I completely opposed. It would be an understatement to describe her diaries as blunt.

She did have one caveat: Jon needed her permission to include any of her diary entries in the book. (For the record, even Jon was shocked when she approved every single diary entry he proposed to use.)

As much as I liked—and trusted—Jon, there were times I gently reminded the Bushes: *He is not family.* He is an author who is going to write a book about you. You might want to be a little cautious. He does not need to know every detail of your life; you do not need to share with him every single thought that comes into your mind.

Despite my concerns, I chose not to sit in on the interviews. By this time in his life, President Bush relied on me too much to remember things—even when I wasn't there. For example, more than once through the years, I had to gently remind President Bush I was not in the Oval Office when his team decided to send troops to the Middle East to kick Saddam Hussein out of Kuwait. His memory was much better than he thought—and, most important, it was accurate. He maybe forgot some details, but what he remembered was almost always right.

So Jon and President Bush were alone for all the interviews. I did barge in once when I could hear through my office wall President Bush sobbing—they were talking about Robin. I think I gave Jon a look and stormed out of the room.

As the publication date approached, I couldn't help but be nervous. Would all the trust we put in Jon pay off? Or would the naysayers be right? Was it possible I had, after all, totally lost it?

When I finally read it, I loved it. Jon gave me an early draft (just for fact-checking purposes), and I thought Jon had brilliantly captured the essence of George Herbert Walker Bush. Did I agree with everything in the book? Of course not. But for the most part Jon had gotten it right. I felt he truly understood George Bush's heart and soul.

I was feeling pretty smug. The Jon Meacham decision had been a brilliant one. Maybe I would claim it had been my idea all along.

But then the first weekend the book was out it all fell apart—at least in my mind. The media of course were most focused on any hint of controversy in the book, especially any disagreement between the two Presidents Bush. They zeroed in on a quote from President Bush where he talked about his former secretary of defense and George W.'s vice president, Dick Cheney. President Bush had told Jon he thought Vice President Cheney—although a good man and a good friend—had made a hard turn to the right after 9/11 and was sometimes too strident. He partially blamed his wife, Lynne, whom he called an "iron ass."

Except the media reported he had called Cheney an iron ass. It went viral. I remember lying on my couch in the fetal position watching NBC's *Meet the Press*, during which host Chuck Todd questioned why on earth President Bush the Elder would say such a thing for public consumption. "I sure wouldn't want to be at the Bush family Thanksgiving table," one of Todd's panelists said, speculating all of this must be causing tension in the family.

I was crushed and convinced once again that life as I knew it was over. I considered driving over to the Bushes' house and apologizing—and doing something I had never considered before or would after: offering to resign. The book was a disaster, and it was my fault.

Then I decided this act of bravery on my part could wait until Monday. I spent a miserable Sunday wondering how this would all end. Then I randomly turned on the television that Sunday evening and there—live on CNN—was Jon Meacham with President George W. Bush, doing an interview at the George W. Bush Presidential Center in Dallas. The forty-third president was raving about the book, and he and Jon had a very spirited discussion about *Destiny and Power* for the next hour. I was in a state of shock and hugely relieved.

The next day I did talk to President Bush about all the controversy surrounding the book and showed him the passages that had inspired the intense Sunday talk show chatter. President Bush read it, sort of shrugged his shoulders, and said, "Well, I did say that. He got it right." He then asked me why I was so worried.

Jon recently reminded me that he did come to Houston before publication to read some of the quotations to President Bush—not to change them, but to remind the president of what was likely to get a lot of early attention. President Bush's reaction was terse: "I said it." And that was that.

President Bush did fret about hurting Cheney's feelings. He called and apologized, and Vice President Cheney was most gracious. In fact, the Cheneys told Jon that they had "Iron Ass" hats and shirts made up for the family.

A few months later, when it was time to attend the annual Alfalfa Club dinner in Washington, the organizers graciously offered for President Bush to choose who sat next to him besides his wife. He looked at the list of possibilities and immediately picked Cheney. At the dinner, when one of the speakers in good humor referred to the "iron ass" quote, the former vice president grabbed the former president's hand and lifted their arms in triumph. It was a class act.

The whole episode was such an important lesson for me—mainly that one has to be comfortable with the truth, and to own the truth. If you said it or did it, admit it. If you feel it was a mistake—say that, too. It wasn't that I had the habit of lying—I was raised better than that—but there are creative ways to sometimes dodge admitting to things you did or didn't do or say.

And I think that is why President Bush so trusted Jon with probably the most important "legacy" project of his post-presidency. Instinctively, he liked Jon a lot and thought he was a good man. He also liked being around him. Jon was funny, smart, and didn't take himself too seriously—all qualities President Bush valued in people. Spending a lot of time with Jon Meacham for a few years was an idea that did not scare him after all.

But more important, President Bush was also a man comfortable with who he was, what he had done, and what he had accomplished. As he told Jon, "I got some things right, some things wrong. You sort it out."

A few years later, in 2016, I was reminded again of this important lesson. Points of Light brought a group of supporters and stakeholders to Walker's Point for an annual get-together. Among the guests was Kathleen Kennedy Townsend, daughter of Bobby and Ethel Kennedy. During a photo receiving line in the Bushes' living room, President Bush inexplicably decided to whisper into her ear that he was going to vote for Hillary Clinton and not for Donald Trump in November.

Kathleen then, even more inexplicably, posted the conversation on Facebook. It went viral.

I was furious. First, I wasn't even sure it was true. And second, even if it was, it was *not* her news to tell. She had made public a private conversation with a ninety-two-year-old man.

I will forever be grateful to Angelina Jolie, who announced the following day she was divorcing Brad Pitt. I was sorry their romance had ended but was thrilled the media no longer cared for whom President Bush would vote. But by that time the damage had been done.

When I asked President Bush about the conversation, he sort of shrugged and said, "I think I did tell her that." Case closed.

That same year, Mark Updegrove did a series of interviews with President Bush for the book he was writing called *The Last Republicans*. When he asked President Bush how he felt about then candidate Donald Trump, President Bush admitted he didn't like him much and called him a blowhard.

By the time Mark was going over the final galley of his book, Donald Trump had been elected, and out of respect for President Bush and how he feels about the office of the presidency, Mark felt it only fair to give President Bush a chance to change his wording.

So I read the "blowhard" passage to President Bush and told him if he wanted, he could have a slight rewrite.

At this stage in his life, President Bush was a man of few words because of his Parkinson's. But when he spoke, every word mattered.

After a few minutes, he said, "I am fairly certain I said that."

Then a few minutes later he said, "I meant it."

Then he said, "And it's the truth. So what's your question?"

The book was published as is. Once again, the quote went viral, to the point that "blowhard" was the most searched word on the Merriam-Webster dictionary website the month of publication.

This time I didn't worry.

CHAPTER TWELVE

LIFE LESSONS

The end of the last chapter raises the question: What else did I learn from George and Barbara Bush? My answer is typically quick and short:

- Think big.
- Think of the other guy.
- Make a difference.
- Don't be afraid to get into the ring.
- Live life with joy.

But when I give real thought to the query, the answer is a little more complicated and more profound:

Be open to new ideas. Don't be afraid to change your mind. Don't be afraid to say you were wrong. Don't judge. Don't hold grudges.

It was great fun to work for someone who was a big thinker.

When I thought Cameron High School Band, he thought George Clooney.

In 2004, I seriously considered saying yes to a job offer from the *Atlanta Journal-Constitution* to be an op-ed columnist. It seemed like a dream job, so I flew to Atlanta to check it out. When I told President Bush I would be gone a few days and why, he was more or less supportive but sent me an email while I was gone: "Another idea—maybe you should consider buying a paper."

What? Buy a newspaper?

Not long before President Bush died, his aide Evan Sisley told him that he had decided to apply for medical school. President Bush thought for a few minutes and then said, "I think that will be an excellent résumé builder."

What? Becoming a doctor was a résumé builder?

For President Bush, he always thought there was something bigger on the horizon if you just looked for it. He lived his entire life open to new ideas and often doing the unexpected.

After all, he shocked his family after graduating Yale when he chose to move to West Texas rather than accept a safe job on Wall Street. He shocked President Ford when in 1974 he offered George Bush a chance to serve as ambassador to the most popular postings—London or Paris—and the answer came back: Send me to China. Right after becoming president, he shocked the country when he decided to attend Emperor Hirohito's funeral, the man who'd led Japan during World War II. (The critics were quickly silenced when President Bush reminded them he knew all about Hirohito—it was his military who had downed his airplane and killed his two crew members.)

He surprised, if not shocked me, at least once a week, in both big ways and small.

I was very surprised, for example, when in the summer of 2003, he decided to buy a potato gun. He just felt it sounded like a lot of fun. The whole idea was to take this plastic cannon-looking device, stuff it with cut-up raw potatoes, use any kind of aerosol spray for the fuel, then shoot potatoes out of the cannon. He and his brother Bucky, ably assisted by Tom Frechette, tried it out first, standing outside the office on Walker's Point and pointing the cannon at the tourists across the bay. There was no danger of anyone getting hit, but as I wrote the Houston-based staff on July 23:

"If suddenly I quit writing, you'll know he apparently actually managed to hit a tourist and I had to go into full 'spin control' mode, trying to explain to the injured, bystanders, and the rest of the free world why the former President and the father of the current one believes shooting potatoes out of a potato gun is a worthwhile activity."

I actually credit President Bush's fascination with gadgets as being the reason why he bought the potato gun. Both President Bush's and Mrs. Bush's willingness, when they were much older than I am now, to learn new skills and new toys was amazing. The wonders of computers, cell phones, iPads, digital cameras, the internet—they were eager learners of all, sometimes outpacing me—okay, almost always outpacing me—in learning new technology.

A note he wrote Hugh Sidey in 1999 shows just how addicted President Bush had become to technology:

Dear Hugh,

It's 11:05 a.m. here in Houston.

I feel horrible and alone—unloved and even scared.

Why? might you ask. Well Michael[1] just rushed in and said our E-Mail must be closed down for 4 days. He announced, firmly almost defiantly, "Our server will be turned off in exactly five minutes."

---

1. Michael Dannenhauer was the acting chief of staff while I was putting together *All the Best.*

No time to notify family and friends, no time even to say goodbye
to my wife of 54 years, Barbara. Cut off as if Norad[2] had told us a
theater nuclear weapon was coming right here to suite 900, and here
alone, in exactly five minutes . . .

Michael was too busy rushing from office to office to explain why,
but it has to do with a nationwide virus. Some evil little computer
nerd out there is spreading a virus; and to hear Michael tell it, if
we don't turn off our server and close out our own E-Mails in five
minutes disaster could strike.

This virus might come right into my machine and wipe out all my
files, all "documents sent." Michael tells me if it strikes, then virus-
laden messages will go out to everyone in my global file and in my
Personal Address file. Every single person in those files will get a
contagious message; and then their modems, their e-mails will crash.
It's that serious. It's like Armageddon and there's nothing even Bill
Gates can do about it . . .

Twelve months ago I was a Fax man or a phone man. Now I
e-mail everyone in the office and tons of people outside the office.
I am hooked. I know how to hit the "reply" button and to use the
paper clip that lets me forward documents. I can spell check and
thesaurus words. I can use color and different fonts to emphasize
things . . . I even listen for the little chime that quietly sounds when
an incoming e-mail hits my modem. When I hear it I look for that
tiny little envelope icon on the bottom right hand corner of my IBM.
It comes right on, saying by its very presence someone is writing you,
someone cares . . .

---

2. North American Aerospace Defense Command, based in Omaha, Nebraska.

*It's 11:15 AM. We are now shut down, off-line, disconnected
from each other, alone in a world that is still tough in spite of the
implosion of the Soviet Union.*

*When I was [a] kid we didn't have TV. We didn't know about
faxes or computers. And, of course, Al Gore hadn't even made his
contribution to connectivity back then.*

*But then came E-mail right into my life. I resisted at first . . . I had
not then discovered the absolute essentiality of e-mail, but our server
has been down now for 6 minutes and I feel lonely and lost.*

Call me . . .

George

Despite his love of email, President Bush never got into social media. Jim McGrath did finally convince him to open a Twitter account, as a vehicle to make known now and then what he was thinking. However, we rarely convinced him to use it. He just didn't think other people would find his thoughts all that interesting.

But the toys themselves fascinated the Bushes. I think it bothered them less than it did me when BlackBerrys became a thing of the past and we needed to learn how to use cell phones that could do everything but wash our clothes.

And of course President Bush loved installing new gadgets on *Fidelity*, especially those that gave him permission (at least he thought) to traverse even denser fog and rougher seas.

There was one very unfortunate incident when President Bush was out in a heavy fog. He was relying on GPS but still somehow managed to run *Fidelity* (and another boat that was following him in the fog) aground on the beach in Kennebunk, Maine. Despite the fog at sea, the shore was bathed in sunshine, so the beach was packed. Fortunately, he didn't run over anybody as the boat came ashore. Mrs. Bush's aide that summer, Hutton Hinson,[3] happened to be on the beach when all this transpired. She said the most amazing thing was that President Bush simply climbed out of the boat, waved and smiled at everybody, and got into a waiting Secret Service car that had been rushed to the spot. She said the whole scene reminded her of a war movie she had seen of Douglas MacArthur coming ashore in the Philippines during World War II.

And even though I was not present for this incident, you could say once again I learned something from the forty-first president: how to stay cool in a situation that likely would have made others die of embarrassment.

Finally it's time to talk about Don Rhodes, how he fit into the Bushes' lives, and the valuable lessons I learned from their friendship.

I first encountered Don at the White House and immediately wondered who on earth this person could be. He sort of looked like a homeless person wandering around. It did not appear he bathed often or even changed his clothes. I later found all this to be true.

Don came into the Bushes' lives in 1964 when President Bush was running for the U.S. Senate, a race he eventually lost. Don was a convenience store clerk, and he would come into campaign headquarters between shifts to mainly stuff envelopes.

He was deaf in one ear and hard of hearing in the other. He lacked social graces and maybe drank a little too much.

Despite the fact he was a proud graduate of Texas A&M, he didn't have much of a career. He was a bit of a lost soul.

---

3. Now Hutton Higgins, she lives in Houston with her husband, Taylor, and their daughter.

Until George and Barbara Bush came into his life.

When the campaign was over, President Bush retained Don's services as an assistant. Over the years, Don was the one who ran errands, paid the bills, arranged for things to be fixed. (It was Don who ran out for me and bought the *Playboy* magazine with the CIA agent on the cover.)

He also kept the books and the finances for the Bushes, including signing all our paychecks, until he died in 2011. He pretty much lived in the same city where they lived, except he did not follow the Bushes to New York City during the United Nations days or to China. And he came to Maine only to help open Walker's Point in May and to close it down in October. Otherwise, he needed to return to Texas—or, as he called it, God's Country.

And yes, he had an office in the East Wing of the White House.

After work every night, he would go over to the Bushes' house and have a beer with the man whom he called Mr. President. I understand this was also true in the White House if the president was available.

Don was kind, smart, funny, stubborn, honest to a fault, and would walk on hot coals for George Bush.

When I became the Bushes' chief of staff, it took a while to gain his trust. When I did, I knew I had crossed a very important threshold.

There are many wonderful Don stories, but my favorite is when the Bushes were living in China, and Doro called Don to ask him for some money (he was controlling the Bushes' finances in their absence) to buy a bridesmaid dress. He asked her if she wasn't in another wedding earlier that year. When she said yes, he asked why she couldn't wear that dress; it was probably still plenty good. And hung up. (Doro sent an appeal to China to her mother; she got the money to buy the dress.)

Over the years Mrs. Bush tried many times to get Don to clean his act up a little bit but failed. What I love is that the Bushes saw the man he was, despite the dirty blue jacket he wore every single day and the unfortunate aroma that often emanated from his body. It didn't matter. He was a good man and a good and loyal friend.

When Don was dying of cancer, a childhood friend of his surfaced in our lives for the first time. It was then we learned that Don's mother was a prostitute and that it was not unusual for her clients to sometimes abuse her little boy. He then would run down the street to his friend's house, seeking refuge. His friend guessed that Don was not born deaf but had lost his hearing through such abuse.

President Bush was devastated when Don died in 2011, tracking me down in Washington, DC, and telling me through sobs that Don was gone. For a while I was so sad that Don had died, but as the Bushes' health continued to decline, I was grateful Don left first. He was not meant to be on this earth without George and Barbara Bush.

One day, right before he died, Don asked me while I was visiting him in the hospital if I believed in heaven. Don was agnostic, and he admitted to being worried about what was next for him. The question made me nervous—I didn't want to give spiritual advice without a license, so to speak—so I briefly excused myself from his room and called my brother the priest. Eddie still remembers exactly what he told me to tell Don: God loves us beyond anything we can imagine whether we believe in him or not. And nobody knew better than God what a good person Don had been. So we could have faith that God would take good care of Don.

At his memorial service a few days later, Mrs. Bush said in her eulogy, looking up to heaven:

"Don, now you know there is a God. I was right and you were wrong." She added it might be the only argument she ever won with him.

His ashes are scattered on the Bushes' gravesite.

I grew up on a farm in Missouri surrounded by mainly plain folk. But before working for the Bushes, I am not sure I would have hired a Don Rhodes. Shame on me.

One of my more interesting dustups with Don actually leads me to another life lesson from George Bush: Live life with humor and joy. No one did it better, and sometimes in surprising ways.

First, a little background.

While I was editing *All the Best*, Don occasionally would put a letter or a folder on my desk, telling me this might be something for the book. After a few of these incidents, I asked Don where he was getting all this material, as I had spent hours and hours tracking down letters. He seemed to be pulling stuff out of thin air. He nonchalantly told me that President Bush had given him some papers he wasn't quite ready to turn over to his presidential library as they were very personal. So Don had put them in the safest place he knew: his oven.

Probably responding to the look on my face, Don quickly assured me he never used his oven and the papers were safe.

I insisted he bring all the papers to the office but agreed he could keep them in a safe in his office. He didn't offer to let me look at them, and I didn't ask. I might have been chief of staff, but I knew better than to get into Don's business. (After Don died, I did dispatch a staffer to Don's house to check the oven. It was empty.)

Which brings us back to the main story and one of the folders Don put on my desk for the book.

"You might want to see these," he said. "I am not sure they work."

With great anticipation and even some fear and trembling, I opened the folder.

It was filled with a series of essays about farting.

Like many times in my life as President Bush's chief of staff—I didn't see that one coming.

As it turns out, while he was vice president of the United States, President Bush had attended an event where the mayor of the town he was visiting—a woman, no less—apparently had some digestive issues during the ceremony. For some odd reason, the vice president decided to put it all on paper, which he continued to do for several years after similar incidents. I shall share no names—you don't need to know the offenders. But I will share one such essay, for the first time ever.

You might ask why. Well, I'm not even sure. Except that one of the things that has always bothered me, and what I am hoping this book will fix, is how so many Americans truly did not understand the George

Bush that I knew—especially the fact that he lived every single minute of life and knew how to make the most of every situation, no matter how bizarre.

So here goes…

November 30, 1986

1986 has almost come and gone and I have made no contributions at all to my life's work—my thesis on farting.

That isn't to say that 1986 hasn't been a fine year, indeed a vintage year. It is simply to note that I have been less than diligent in the recording.

There was the dinner in Israel. I think it was the president's wife, before the dinner. She was very pleasant and very pretty but she was in slight discomfort. I know that I saw a smile of relief cross her lips… I've been there and know it was a fart "slud" out, as Dizzy Dean would say, that gave her some relief.

The Secret Service guys are under great pressure on farts. They are human like anyone else—disciplined, yes, polite—but last month all windows up and locked, the big 1986 Cadillac fully armored heading towards Chicago, having just left O'Hare, there was a moment of crisis. I moved my hand rapidly to the automatic window locks, two of them on my side, one for my window, the other for the other passenger window. Both were firmly locked… that's the rule—better to drive with the windows up and locked. Anyway, there is a little clicking noise when you activate the "open" button, even if it is locked. I clicked, calmly at first, then more urgently. I

*didn't want to say, "open the windows." The fart had taken over. I
know it wasn't the governor—in fact, I'm sure it came from the front
seat, but we couldn't discuss it man to man as it were—pride you
know. I finally said, "stuffy back here, crack the locks will you?"—
a definite command—nicely done. The locks were released. I pushed
both buttons and the fresh air rushed in—instant relief. Everyone
knew, no one spoke.*

When Don gave the fart essays to me, I immediately went into President Bush's office to confront him with his "life thesis." He was beyond delighted they had been found. He thought they had been lost forever. It was like finding an old friend.

He decided to use them to tease Mrs. Bush a bit. While we were working on his book of letters, I typically would give him a folder of letters every night as he walked out the door. His job was to go through them and pull any he did not think should be in the book. That night he of course tucked the newly discovered essays in the letters folder.

The next morning, as the Bushes were going through their homework in bed, President Bush hid the essays in a stack of letters meant for the book and gave them to his wife. He admitted he told her that I felt strongly this entire stack should be in the letters book and asked for her opinion.

She called me at home—I think it was six o'clock—and asked what the hell I was thinking. At that hour, I had no idea what I was thinking or why she was asking. I had no idea the "thesis" was now in her hands. For President Bush, this was a twofer—a good joke on both his wife and his chief of staff. It was going to be a very good day.

To close the loop on the papers in Don Rhodes's oven: Except for the files I brought home to write this book, they are all now at President Bush's library. I promise my book files will end up there, too.

★   ★   ★

Since Don Rhodes was one of the most honest people I knew, the perfect segue from his story to another lesson learned from President Bush is one that should be so obvious:

Tell the truth. Always.

It seems so simple, but I think a lot these days about President Bush's absolute belief that only the truth should be spoken. Honesty should be a given, but I am not so sure of that anymore, especially considering the epidemic of lies, made-up stories, and fake news that can be found on the internet.

All of that was and would be so foreign to him.

And yes, of course, I have a story, which actually began in World War II.

When the submarine USS *Finback* rescued President Bush after he was shot down near Chichijima, he shared a bunk with Lieutenant Junior Grade Albert Brostrom. They called it "hot bunking"—when one man was on duty the other went to bed. (President Bush had night lookout duty while on the *Finback*, so he slept during the day.) When it was time for President Bush to leave the *Finback*, he decided to give his service revolver—a .38-caliber Smith and Wesson—and its leather harness to Brostrom as a thank-you for sharing his bunk.

The revolver resurfaced in 2007, after Brostrom had died and his son Ron found the revolver hidden below the floorboards of the attic. After President Bush became vice president, his son thinks his dad realized the value of the revolver, so he hid it. Ron does remember his dad saying in 1980, when the Reagan-Bush ticket won the election, "The kid did okay." The family was aware of the revolver but wasn't sure what happened to it.

Realizing the historical importance of the revolver, Ron tracked down longtime Bush staffer and volunteer advance person Topper Ray, who, like Ron, lived in Philadelphia. Ron wanted to return the gun. After many phone calls back and forth, it was decided the gun would be given to President Bush during an upcoming visit to the National

Constitution Center, also in Philadelphia and of which President Bush was then chairman of the board. The president and CEO of the Constitution Center, Joe Torsella, was thrilled. It would help shine a light on the center and its work, so he arranged for the press and even a group of schoolchildren to witness the occasion.

But on the flight to Philly, President Bush became concerned that the revolver was not his. "How do they know it's mine? Maybe another pilot gave Brostrom their revolver. Maybe it got mixed up with other revolvers."

He fretted for the entire flight and thought we should call the whole thing off. I felt it was too late. It *was* too late. And my modest opinion was that even if it was the wrong revolver, who would know?

President Bush said he would know.

As we nervously arrived at the Constitution Center, President Bush agreed we should proceed as planned, and if it turned out it was *not* his revolver, we would deal with that issue later. As I stood off to the side, I watched President Bush examine the gun and holster carefully, then he sought me out in the crowd of schoolchildren and other onlookers and gave me a broad smile and a slight nod. It was his gun.

I was so relieved, as was Topper Ray, who swears: "The look I got from Jean at the event that day made me think that if the gun was not real, that she may have turned it on me." (Never!)

Later that day, on the way back to the airport, I asked President Bush how he knew for sure.

"The minute I touched it, Jean, I knew," he said, choking up a bit. "I'm not sure how, but I knew."

Yes, the truth really does matter.

Another great lesson learned from watching President Bush was the simple fact that holding grudges was a waste of time.

Mrs. Bush would be the first to admit this was a tough one for her—especially if the offense in question was something said about her family.

I am not a grudge holder, despite having an Irish mother who most certainly was. But after watching President Bush, I know I can do better.

It's possible he went to his grave not liking only three people: Saddam Hussein, Ross Perot, and Dan Rather.

The best and most famous story was, of course, his friendship with Bill Clinton. A lot of people just didn't get it, but that didn't bother President Bush. He genuinely came to love the man who had served up one of the most humiliating moments in his life.

No other stories approach the Bush-Clinton bromance, but there are two I would like to tell.

We'll start with Geraldine Ferraro.

Ferraro, a congresswoman from Queens, made history in 1984 when the Democratic nominee for president, former vice president Walter Mondale, chose her to be his running mate, making her the first woman to be nominated for national office on a major party ticket. For women, it was exciting and glass ceiling shattering.

For then vice president George Bush, it was a bit of a nightmare. As he wrote in *All the Best*: "I will confess that I was a little apprehensive to be the first man to run against the first woman. It was uncharted territory."

During their only debate, Vice President Bush worried that if he came on too strong against his opponent and questioned her qualifications for the office, he would be accused of being condescending and patronizing.

And that was exactly what Ferraro herself said during the debate while answering a foreign policy question; and it was exactly what the Mondale-Ferraro campaign and some members of the press said and wrote after the debate.

It didn't help when the following day, while President Bush was visiting with some longshoremen in New Jersey, one of them held up a sign that said, "George, you kicked a little ass last night." President Bush gave him a thumbs-up, repeating what the sign said. A TV boom mike picked it up and it made news—not in a good way for the vice president, as the comment was interpreted as being antifeminist.

Mrs. Bush further complicated the situation when a few weeks later, while talking to the press on the campaign plane about the Ferraros' finances, she said that she and her husband never tried to hide their wealth, unlike that "$4 million...I can't say it but it rhymes with 'rich.'"

She later tried to claim the word she didn't say was "witch." And she also later admitted that wasn't exactly true.

So how was it that when Ferraro was on her deathbed in 2011, President Bush wrote her this note:

I often think of our strange but wonderful relationship, and I hope you know that I consider you a real friend. In fact I hope it's okay I say I love you.

I wasn't sure of the answer—how two political rivals became the kind of friends who said "I love you" to each other. So I called Ferraro's daughter, Donna Zaccaro, who said she did know the story and had made it part of a documentary she did about her mother's life.

It started the night of the election in 1984, when her mom called Vice President Bush to congratulate him and President Reagan on their win. The vice president thanked her and said he would like to have her over for lunch. Donna said that surprised her mom, who assumed he would never follow up.

But of course he did. They had a wonderful lunch, each bringing the person who had helped them prepare for their debate against each other: Ferraro brought her friend and Democratic consultant Bob Barnett; the vice president brought Lynn Martin, a congresswoman from Illinois who went on to become his secretary of labor when he was president.

From that lunch, the friendship blossomed, with the two of them occasionally exchanging notes, particularly when something was going on in their lives.

"They just liked each other," said Zaccaro. "They had a sense of humor. They had the same values. They maybe went at things a little differently, but that didn't matter. They wanted the same thing."

Although I was vaguely aware of the friendship, I didn't truly understand it until 2008, as the vice presidential debate between Joe Biden and Sarah Palin approached. Jamie Gangel, still with NBC's *Today*, wanted to interview President Bush and Geraldine Ferraro, the only other man and woman to debate each other in a general election. They both loved the idea. President Bush wasn't thrilled to do an interview—he never was—but he loved and trusted Jamie, and he was excited to have an excuse to invite his friend Geraldine to come to Kennebunkport for a visit.

Ferraro readily said yes, despite the fact she was already ill with the disease that eventually would kill her, multiple myeloma. She brought with her Donna and Donna's thirteen-year-old son, Matthew.

"Mom wasn't sure how President Bush would feel about a thirteen-year-old coming along, but the answer was 'Of course.' I think President Bush was deeply touched that it was important to Mom for her oldest grandchild to meet him."

Donna remembers that President Bush tried to race through the interview, as he was most interested in taking the Ferraro family out on *Fidelity*. And he was disappointed that they didn't spend the night. Donna said her mom wasn't feeling well enough for an overnight visit and needed to go home and sleep in her own bed.

At some point during the day, Donna had a chance to tell President Bush that his friendship with her mother was very important to her. "He kissed me on the head. It was so sweet."

Her other big memory of that day was Mrs. Bush still fretting over the "rhymes with 'rich'" incident from 1984. "Mom kept telling her to stop worrying about it and reminded Mrs. Bush that she had called Ferraro immediately after it happened, and she had forgiven her then. I brought the Bushes some homemade brownies, and Mrs. Bush sent a thank-you note. She apologized again to me in that note."

Donna added one footnote to the visit. Her daughter Natalie—who had helped bake the brownies—was not happy she did not get to come: "Natalie sent a note up with me for President Bush in which she expressed her disappointment at not being allowed to make the trip with her older brother to meet President Bush and said that she thought it was age discrimination. President Bush got a huge kick out of the letter and sent a handwritten response back to Natalie immediately agreeing that it was age discrimination, that he too was disappointed to have not met her—and that he hoped to meet her someday. Which he did when I interviewed him and Mrs. Bush in 2012 for the documentary about my mom. I, of course, brought Natalie along."

Three years later, knowing she was dying, President Bush mailed but also emailed his last letter to Ferraro. "I heard Mom's BlackBerry pinging and I checked and found the note from President Bush. I read it out loud to Mom. It was the last words she heard that weren't from family."

The other "rival to friendship" story was President Bush and Senator Bob Dole. When they competed for the Republican nomination in 1988, they had several ugly exchanges of words, some of which occurred during an interview I had with Senator Dole. They just did not like each other.

But when the election was over, it didn't take them long to find common ground and eventually to become good friends. As the minority leader of the Senate, it was Senator Dole's job to help President Bush get some of his legislation enacted—a tough task given the House also had a Democratic majority. But together they managed to pass several pieces of major legislation, including the Clean Air Act and the Americans with Disabilities Act.

President Bush was deeply touched by Senator Dole's tribute on the Senate floor, given the day after he left office. It ended with these words:

"In March of 1991, President Bush stood in the House chamber to tell the nation that the war in the Gulf was over. And at the conclusion of his remarks he said that 'we're coming home now—proud, confident, heads high.' And because he changed America and the world for the better; because our children are safer—George Bush had every reason to leave the White House in the same way: proud, confident, and his head held high. On behalf of…the American people, and the men and women around the world who now live in freedom, I say, Thank you, Mr. President."

They kept in touch over the years, and on the seventy-fifth anniversary of Pearl Harbor in 2016, Senator Dole came to President Bush's library to receive the George Bush Award for Excellence in Public Service. At dinner the night before, sitting side by side in their wheelchairs, they talked and drank like old war buddies. Which in many ways they were.

One of the most memorable moments of President Bush's funeral events was when Senator Dole was wheeled into the Capitol Rotunda to pay his respects as President Bush lay in state. Suddenly, an aide helped him struggle to his feet so he could salute the casket. It was a stunning moment.

After the funeral, during one of his "checking-up-on-you phone calls," I asked Senator Dole about the salute. I asked him why he just didn't salute from his wheelchair. "Oh, Jean," he said. "I had to stand for the president. It didn't feel right to be sitting down when I saluted that amazing man."

If I had to pick just one of the life lessons the Bushes taught me that I feel the world needs to hear right now it would be this: Listen to others and be open to new ideas. Don't live life with a closed mind.

There may be no better example than their complete change of heart on the issue of same-sex marriage.

As recently as 2004, President Bush wrote in an email to his friend and former political adviser Mary Matalin that the idea of gay marriage confused him.

I personally find it hard to cope with. You know something, I am getting old at just about the right time. I know I am not "with it"... but those of us who are against all this are made to feel guilty, intolerant, bigoted—whatever. I confidently expect to live at least until 2008 because I must go to sea aboard CVN 77,[4] but after that I will be ready to move on because so much of what I have been taught, and so much [of] what I believe, will be in the dust bins of history.

I am not sure exactly where the journey to understanding, acceptance, and support began, but, oddly, it predates this email to Mary Matalin. In 1998, while I was working on *All the Best*, he asked Michael Dannenhauer, his former personal aide, to be his interim chief of staff. Michael confided to me one very rainy night sitting in my car that he was gay, and he was very nervous President Bush would not approve of a gay man heading his office. I assured him I did not think that would be the case. Michael asked me not to tell him, but also not to lie about it, either, if President Bush ever brought up the possibility.

Not long afterward, President Bush and I were together at his library when he began quizzing me about why Michael had been so quiet as of late. My face obviously revealed I knew something he did not—I am a terrible poker player—and President Bush started guessing dreadful things like Michael was dying of cancer.

So I told him Michael was gay; he was just now coming out of the closet but didn't know how to come out to him.

I asked him not to say anything until I had a chance to come clean and tell Michael I had spilled the beans.

My mistake was not calling Michael immediately because President Bush beat me to it.

---

4. Maybe it's time to explain why "CVN 77" is part of the official name of the USS *George H. W. Bush*: C—Carrier; V—Aircraft (fixed wing); N—Nuclear Powered. It's the seventy-seventh Navy aircraft carrier.

While I stayed behind at the library to continue researching *All the Best*, President Bush returned to Houston. And of course the very next morning, he called Michael into his office, asked him to close the door, and told him not to kill me, but I had told him that Michael was gay.

President Bush told Michael that he loved him, nothing would ever change that, that he was family, and he should not worry about this.

If there were any doubts left of his acceptance of Michael's sexuality, it would have been erased a short time later when Michael Huffington came to see President Bush. Michael is the son of President Bush's good friend Roy Huffington, had worked for him in various jobs over the years, and had served as a congressman from California. His marriage to writer and journalist Arianna Huffington was about to crash and burn as Michael prepared to announce that he was bisexual. When he called for an appointment to see President Bush, he explained he wanted President Bush to hear this news from him and not from the media.

The two men had a closed-door visit and then decided to go to lunch. While Michael Huffington was "freshening up," an excited President Bush came into my office to declare he had—yes—an idea. He was going to invite Michael Dannenhauer to join them for lunch. "Jean, they are perfect for each other."

I told him it was a terrible idea. First, both Michaels were just now beginning to deal openly with their sexuality. And I did not think either of them would really want the forty-first president of the United States and their former or current boss to be their matchmaker. President Bush promptly dismissed my concerns and went down the hall to ask Michael Dannenhauer to lunch.

Michael somehow managed to get out of it, and as soon as the other two left, he stormed down the hall to ask if I knew what had just happened. I tried to get Michael to see the bright side of this odd occurrence—President Bush not only didn't mind that he was gay, he wanted to help find him a partner.

I should have reminded Michael that President Bush was a famous fixer-upper, including trying to match up George W. Bush with Tricia Nixon, the daughter of President Richard Nixon. It did not go well. And he tried to fix up two of Mrs. Bush's personal aides with popular athletes—Quincy Hicks with Houston Astros first baseman Jeff Bagwell; and Hutton Hinson with then Denver Broncos quarterback Tim Tebow. They didn't work, either.

After Mrs. Bush died, Michael wrote a long note to President Bush about what the two of them had meant in the life of "this small-town Ohio boy":

"During the most difficult struggle of my life, YOU were the one that lifted me the highest because it was you that I respected and admired most in life and never wanted to disappoint or embarrass. It's been 20 years since you called me into your office that day, and we had the talk about my being gay. It wasn't a long conversation, but it had the most profound impact and lifted an incredible weight off my shoulders. As you always do, you showed me unconditional love and more understanding than I could have hoped for—and that short conversation changed my life. From that moment forward I was able to hold my head high and not worry about what others may think."

It wasn't until 2013 when I knew President Bush had truly come full circle on the issue of same-sex marriage. It would still be two years before the U.S. Supreme Court made it legal in all fifty states, but the state of Maine had done so the previous year. A lesbian couple in Kennebunkport—Bonnie Clement and Helen Thorgalsen, who ran the town's general store—decided to get married the following summer. They invited the Bushes to attend the small ceremony, which was to be held in their apartment over the store.

That was not an option as President Bush's Parkinson's disease had put him in a wheelchair, and the only access into their apartment was a steep set of stairs.

President Bush fretted over this and confided in me he was disappointed he could not attend. "I've never been to a same-sex wedding," he told me, as if this piece of information might surprise me. I *was* surprised this was on his bucket list, but he said he wished he could go in support of their decision.

I slept on this for a few days, then casually asked Bonnie and Helen if they would like to get married in the front yard of the summer cottage I had rented for several years. It was an old carriage house, now a guest-house, of one of Kennebunkport's grand turn-of-the-century houses that line Ocean Avenue. The view from my front yard was the Atlantic Ocean.

They were touched and surprised, and even more so when I told them the real reason for my offer.

So on a cold, blustery fall day, Bonnie and Helen got married in my front yard, with George and Barbara Bush among the small group of attendees. I was not happy when it leaked to the media that the Bushes had attended the wedding. The news went viral. I think it bothered me more than President Bush—my point was if President Bush wanted to make a major statement about same-sex marriage, we would have issued a statement. He *had* made a statement, but in his own way. He was a believer that actions speak louder than words.

He, on the other hand, did seem amused by how popular he was on the gay websites. This was a first for him.

A few years later, in October 2015, Jon Meacham asked the Bushes if he could bring historian Tim Naftali, whom they had not met, to lunch. I was not there, but apparently Tim and Mrs. Bush had a rather lively dis-cussion about gender transitioning, which had been big on America's mind that year when Bruce Jenner became Caitlyn Jenner. Tim wasn't sure what Mrs. Bush had thought of him or their talk until Mrs. Bush wrote Jon a note a few days later about how much she enjoyed meeting Tim and how he had educated and changed her mind on transgender people.

When Mrs. Bush died in April 2018, Tim ended his essay about Bar-bara Bush for the *Atlantic* with this insight:

"There will be much written about Barbara Bush in the next few days. She deserves enormous praise as a strong mother, wife, grand-mother, and first lady, and as an advocate for literacy and civility. What

I will hold especially dear is the personal experience of her willingness not only to learn about people she didn't understand, but to recognize she might have been wrong about them. And she did this at
90—and at a time when her son was running to lead a party whose
voters mostly believe America is too accepting of transgender people.
Now, in this even more tribal moment, America can even less afford to
lose her."

In late 2015, President Bush's personal aide, Coleman Lapointe, left us to
work for Governor Jeb Bush's presidential campaign. Coleman told me
that one of the home health-care workers, Evan Sisley, was the perfect
person to fill his shoes.

Evan was not only a paramedic, he was also a combat veteran, having completed a tour of duty in Afghanistan as a Navy medic attached to
a Marine Corps infantry division. He was indeed perfect to absorb the
duties of a personal aide—overseeing President Bush's daily schedule,
running errands, being his troubleshooter—while also overseeing his
medical regimen and the home health-care workers.

Evan came to my office one day before he officially said yes and asked
me if I knew he was gay. And did the Bushes know he was gay. I think
my exact words were, "Oh, honey, that glass ceiling was broken a long
time ago." And yes, we knew. In fact, when Coleman and I recom-
mended Evan to President Bush, he asked us, "Is he a gay lad?"

The Bushes proudly sat in the front row when Evan and Ian were
married in December 2017. And Evan was in the room the day Barbara Bush died, and the night George Bush died. He, too, had become
family.

Jon Meacham, when writing *Destiny and Power*, asked President Bush
if he had changed his mind about same-sex marriage. He admitted that
he still believed in "traditional marriage," but with a huge "but": "People should be able to do what they want to do, without discrimination.
People have a right to be happy."

★   ★   ★

I am not sure a week went by in the twenty-four years I was President Bush's chief of staff that I did not learn something from him, mainly by watching the way he lived his life. In 2003, his friend Henry O. Dormann, chairman and editor in chief of *Leaders* magazine, asked him to write a piece answering this question: "What is the greatest challenge you have had to overcome in your life?" His answer was classic George H. W. Bush—simple, yet profound:

I cannot single out the one greatest challenge in my life. I have had a lot of challenges and my advice to young people might be as follows:

1. *Don't get down when your life takes a bad turn. Out of adversity comes challenge and often success.*

2. *Don't blame others for your setbacks.*

3. *When things go well, always give credit to others.*

4. *Don't talk all the time. Listen to your friends and mentors and learn from them.*

5. *Don't brag about yourself. Let others point out your virtues, your strong points.*

6. *Give someone else a hand. When a friend is hurting, show that friend you care.*

7. *Nobody likes an overbearing big shot.*

8. *As you succeed, be kind to people. Thank those who help you along the way.*

9. *Don't be afraid to shed a tear when your heart is broken because a friend is hurting.*

10. *Say your prayers!!*

Lessons learned.

CHAPTER THIRTEEN

FAMILY FIRST

When writer George Plimpton asked President Bush, "How do you get through something like that?" referring to the 1992 loss to Bill Clinton, President Bush's answer was one word:

"Family."

Because this book was written from my perspective—my stories, my observations, my memories—there remains at this point a gaping hole in this version of George Herbert Walker Bush's life story: his deep love for and extraordinary relationship with his family.

They always came first.

President Bush was the patriarch of a very large clan that included not only his five children and their spouses, the grandchildren and the great-grandchildren, but also his brothers and one sister, nieces and nephews and their children, first cousins and their children—there were hundreds of them.

Linda Poepsel in our office kept the family tree, which was a monumental task. (It didn't help that there were so many men named George Walker that it was impossible to keep track of who belonged to whom.) She dutifully recorded deaths and births, the latter outpacing the former. She knew it was important to her boss to keep track of every single family member.

Just how big this family was came into focus right before George W.'s first inauguration. A first cousin of President Bush's called to complain to me that she and her children were not being treated as generously as they had been at her cousin's inauguration on January 20, 1989. Yes, they were invited, but their seats were not nearly as good, nor were they invited to as many parties.

I reminded the not-to-be-named cousin that she was *not* the first cousin of the president-elect this time around; she was the second or third cousin—depending on how you defined these things. I also reminded her of just how many first cousins the president-elect had—all the children of President Bush's siblings—Prescott, Jonathan, and Bucky Bush, and his sister Nancy Ellis; plus all the Pierces from his mother's side.

"I am sorry, but you have moved way down the family tree," I reminded her, hopefully with compassion.

President Bush made time for all of them, particularly in Maine where he had an open-gate policy for every relative who wanted to use the pool or tennis court at Walker's Point: nieces and nephews, cousins, their children and their children's children, and some people who fit in, though I never figured out exactly how. But they were all welcome.

Of course at the center of President Bush's life was Barbara Pierce Bush, their children, and their grandchildren. He would move heaven and earth for them. The night he lost the election in 1992, he told his crowd of supporters he planned to "get very active in the grandchild business." His face would light up when one of them called or when he was told someone had just driven through the gates of Walker's Point. Off he would race to be the welcoming committee and start planning big adventures.

He loved organizing games and contests, making up all sorts of rules on who could play and who couldn't. For years he swore it was not him, but a top secret committee who made these decisions, ranking family members on everything from joke telling to tennis and horseshoes. Finally, in honor of Mrs. Bush's seventy-fifth birthday, he decided to reveal the members of his so-called Ranking Committee. Each family member received a copy of a photo with the five committee members: a golfer, a businessman, a biker, a secretary, and a sheik. Thanks to the magic of Photoshop, they were all him, of course.

Besides loving them, he teased them—especially the grandkids. One of his favorite ongoing jokes was to claim that he was the person who invented the phrase "You da man." He insisted those words were first shouted out by him in the 1960s at a Houston Astros baseball game as he watched Astros slugger Rusty Staub circle the bases. The phrase then caught on—or, as we would say now, "went viral." Somehow his claim to coining this phrase even made its way to Wikipedia. I don't know how many times I walked into a room with him and the grandchildren to hear a heated argument on the truth of this issue.

When the family descended on Walker's Point in the summer, the staff held their breath. As I have mentioned before, it was pure chaos. But it was also pure joy. I loved watching them just be a family, as normal as possible given there were always tourists watching from across the bay. The family became quite adept at ignoring them and just focusing on each other.

One year, right after the Fourth of July weekend—which always brought a lot of family to town—I was sitting in my office watching CNN, waiting for the president of the United States, George W. Bush, to come out and make a statement to the nation about some missile testing North Korea had conducted over the weekend. The reporter on TV was whispering into her microphone, "We expect the president to come into the briefing room any minute," when our summer intern buzzed and told me the president was on the phone. I think I asked which president. His answer was, "Well, *our* president."

I was surprised. Was it possible he wanted my opinion on North Korea? Well, maybe.

As it turns out, he was curious about who had been at Walker's Point over the weekend, who slept where, what did everyone do, who would be there when he came up in August. He also hoped his dad didn't have any fishing trips to Canada scheduled during his visit. I told him what he wanted to know, and just a few minutes after we hung up, he did indeed walk into the press briefing room to talk about North Korea.

He might have been president, but he was also a son and a brother, a father and an uncle.

Rather than try to describe the relationship with his family, I'd like to share just a few of the letters and emails President Bush wrote to them—or about them—during his post-presidency years. They are much more entertaining than anything I could write.

January 6, 1994

For: Barbara Pierce

From: GHWB

Will you marry me? Oops, I forgot, you did that 49 years ago today! I was very happy on that day in 1945, but I am even happier today. You have given me joy that few men know. You have made our boys into men by bawling them out and then, right away, by loving them. You have helped Doro be the sweetest greatest daughter in the whole wide world. I have climbed perhaps the highest mountain in the world, but even that cannot hold a candle to being Barbara's husband. Mum used to tell me: "Now, George, don't walk ahead." Little did she know I was only trying to keep up—keep up with Barbara Pierce from Onondaga Street in Rye New York. I love you!

(To his grandson Jeb, who lived with his grandparents for several summers.)

August 28, 1996

Dear Jeb,

It's not the same around here. I have nobody around here to tease any more. I have no one who likes to fish as much as I do. And there is no one left out here that loves the boats . . .

I love you. Work hard. Stay out of trouble. Play hard. Read a lot. Give your Mom and Dad a big hug every day, for they love you so much and they are the greatest.

And if you ever get discouraged or a little down, think of the stripers off the rocks, or that huge trout in Newfoundland; and remember that your old grandfather is in your corner.

Devotedly,
Gampy

(In 1996 President Bush bought a small Zodiac boat for the grandkids to use during the summer. He created a contest to name the boat, with Don Rhodes serving as the impartial judge. Here is his letter as written.)

February 18, 1997

To: All the family

Re: Boat Naming Contest

WE HAVE A WINNER!

Yes, The Judge just reported in. After hours of deliberation during which he considered the speed of the boat, where and how the name might be applied to the boat and other serious things, Judge Rhodes narrowed the list down to two names 1) Gull (submitted by Neil Bush family) and 2) Maine Coaster. At exactly 3:48 Judge Rhodes announced that the winner is:

Maine Coaster[1]

And the winning name submitter is:

Margaret Bush, mother of Walker and Marshall, wife of Marvin.

---

1. This would be the same boat President Bush rescued from a big storm on a September 2.

OK, Let's hear it for Margaret—to whom the prize of 25 U.S. Dollars is being mailed as I type. C'mon no sulking let's hear it for her! That's better!

Attached is the full list of names as submitted to Judge Rhodes.[2] You will note that the good Judge was totally unaware of the submitters' names. We did it the old-fashioned way—**FAIRLY!**

All five families sent in entries. Everyone entered in. It was a heavenly contest. The boat, properly named now, will be ready for all of you by Mid May.

Oh yes, a couple of families tried to bribe the judge by sucking up to him, saying nice things about him, etc. He never saw those comments, though.

Thanks for what I can only term superb cooperation. Devotedly,

Gampy

_____

2. I am not attaching the list; it's two pages long.

(Nothing brought more joy to President Bush than family fishing out-
ings. He wrote this for Christopher Buckley at *Forbes FYI* magazine.)

September 10, 1998

Dear Christo,

You asked me about fishing. Well, OK, here goes. I love it . . .

*Let me tell you about fishing for the little tinker mackerel right here
in the bay by our house in Kennebunkport . . .*

*The best mackerel fishing for me is when I take a couple of grandkids
out in my new very fast boat. It is a 31, center console, Fountain
fishing boat named* Fidelity II *. . .*

*My new Fountain flies and handles big Maine seas with ease. My
grandkids love it when we speed to our fishing waters. They get
restless if the mackerel don't bite. "C'mon, Gampy, let's go fast."
They need to learn to calm down and to relax when we troll or cast.
They need to learn the joy of just being out on the sea, watching the
gulls, seeing the waves crash against the rocks, watching for a fish to
break the water. They need to grow up, but I don't want them to do
that.*

*When my grandson Walker pulls in 4 squirming mackerel and starts
yelling "I got four—look at what I caught, Gampy," that is heaven
for me . . .*

*I'm 74 now but I don't feel old. I meditate a lot when I am out
fishing. I wonder how many more years I will have to fish with my
sons, my grandkids.*

I count my blessings of health and family. I want to keep on fishing.

I want to teach Gigi, our youngest grandchild, now 2½ years old, how to fish. When the fish aren't biting I want to listen to her tell me what makes her happy and what makes her cry. Maybe I can start next year.

I won't tell her I was President. I'll just try to tell her about the wonders of life and have her understand that our family is what matters. Out on the boat she is a captive. She can squirm but she can't hide.

I will tell her I love her.

And when she says, "Are you crying?" I'll say "Yes but these are tears of joy. Older guys do that, Gigi."

See, you can do that kind of thing when you go fishing.

Though you are too young for the tears, Chris, be sure to take [your children] Conor and Caitlin out fishing.

George Bush

(When the Bushes' daughter Robin died from leukemia in 1953, she was buried in Greenwich, Connecticut, in President Bush's parents' burial plot. But once the president and Mrs. Bush's burial plot was established at the George Bush Presidential Library Center at Texas A&M, they moved Robin to Texas. President Bush wrote this note to their priest, Dr. Larry Gipson.)

May 16, 2000

Dear Larry,

. . . I have been slow in writing to tell you just how much your coming up to A&M meant to both Barbara and me.

It seems funny after almost 50 years after her death how dear Robin is to our hearts. My tears flowed when you said those lovely prayers. But they were not the same tears of devastation, loss, and pain that I felt when Robin died. Instead they were tears of gratitude that we had her at all and maybe even tears of joy that she was still with us.

I remember when Robin was about to die another parent of another leukemia victim who had also fought the good fight told us, "Well, I guess Jesus was right when he said 'Let the little children suffer so they can come unto me.'" She got it wrong, Larry, but maybe she also got it right, too. Her kid and ours did suffer and indeed in their innocence they went to heaven. Of that I am certain.

Friday's peaceful, private, moving little ceremony was not about suffering nor death—those were both a long time ago. It was about happiness and memories. We are very comforted to know that when we are buried the body of our beloved little four-year-old will be tucked in right there beside us—right next to her parents who love her so much.

Thank you, Larry, for making this tiny service so special for Barbara and me.

Con Afecto,
George Bush

(President Bush wrote this note to Brian Mulroney after the 2000 Republican convention, when George W. accepted the Republican nomination.)

August 5, 2000

Dear Brian,

. . . There is no way I can tell you of the emotion we felt when we saw George W. up there in front of the Convention.

One good thing—when George finished his acceptance speech, it was like a new day had dawned on our family. I felt that finally my political days were over—the record sealed and finished, with the historians left to decide. The baton had indeed been passed; and when Bar and I left the hall, proudest parents in the world, we felt that a wonderful chapter was closed, finished!

For us, the mission is now to stay off stage and pray for our "boy." When the road ahead for him is rocky, and it will be, we will be here for him, our arms held out to him, just as they were 50 some years ago when he'd fall on the rocks right out this window and come in with a cut on his legs. We are his loving parents. He is our loving son. That, dear Brian, is what this is all about right now . . .

Your friend,
George

(President Bush wrote this email to the president's aide, Logan Walters, in preparation for spending Christmas at Camp David with the family. While in office, the forty-third president referred to Camp David as Camp Marvin.)

December 18, 2001

Logan, my Lad. Please relay this important message to all those who have a "need to know."

Re: The Bowling Championship:

Count me in, unless of course my 77-year-old hip acts up. My backhand style should minimize the chance of any flare-up, however. I am ready for the fray. Please enter me in the Championship Flight.

On another subject: One minor suggestion. Why, when considering a name change for what was known as Camp David, can't the name go up, not down? Ike went down two generations to find Camp David. Now #43 appears to be going down by a few years for Camp Marvin. But doesn't it make sense to honor age? Really!

Please, dear Logan, ask the President to consider "Camp Gampster." This would mean a lot to my wife Barbara and would undoubtedly be universally approved by AARP and by my grandkids, who are hoping against hope to be remembered in my will. Just a thought, Logan. Have a great Christmas and if you dare enter the Oval Office feel free to share this thinking with THE PRESIDENT. He'll love it.

GB

(An email to granddaughters Jenna, Barbara, and Lauren.)

Subject: Nervous grandfather

March 9, 2003

It is Sunday morning. I am at my duty station in the office. I am worrying about three of my older granddaughters. Spring Break causes the worry. I wonder—are all three off somewhere trying to get on the Wild College Women TV show? Are they having a good time? Are they sticking near their three campuses so they can do what, well, what I used to do during spring break back in the good old days, circa 1946–47–48. Namely, stick near the Library. I found it was almost free of noise and people during spring break. Maybe you three have discovered the same thing. I am here all week in Houston in case you need adult leadership. Despite these worries, maybe because of these worries, I love all three of you "guys" (who says the Gampster can't be "with it"?).

Devotedly,
Gampy

(An email to the grandchildren, or, as he called them, wieners.)

April 19, 2003

Subject: Easter

*I am at our apartment at A&M. The Easter Bunny just hopped
in here—right into my office, sneaked past Sadie[3] and gave me
a present for each of you. The Bunny scrunched up his nose
like rabbits do and said something that sounds like this, "Hey,
Gampster, please send this folding stuff to each grandchild, provided
they check in within two weeks' time."*

*I told the Bunny, "Hey, Rabbit, this is great. I will email them,
and if they respond they get a neat Easter present from you."*

*Those that check in by email will get the rabbit's present. Those that
don't, well, they can wait until next year, hoping the bunny hops
back into our lives next Easter. . .*

*In the meantime this brings along all my love. My pride in all of
you. My hopes that you will all have a Happy Easter. Ganny feels
the same way, sending her love as I type.*

*At this special time of year, as old age creeps up, I love to count my
blessings. All 14 of you are my most precious blessings.*

---

3. The Bushes' English springer spaniel, who came after Millie died.

(Another email to the "wieners.")

October 12, 2003

Subject: Leaving and crying.

In exactly 69 minutes we drive out the gate of the Point we love so much. The trek back to Houston begins. We speak at West Virginia Monday, then fly back to Houston Monday evening . . .

The only thing wrong with the last five months is that none of you were here enough. Oh I know some got to stay as long as usual, but there never can be enough of having all of you here. Next year, promise this old gampster that you will spend more time with us here by the sea.

I am a very happy Gampy. My legs don't bend too well. As you know I have had to give up fly fishing off the rocks, but there is plenty left to do—plenty of wonderful things.

I think of all of you an awful lot. I just wonder how each of you is doing—in life, in college, in school.

If you need me, I am here for you, because I love you very much.

This comes from your devoted,

Gampy

(President Bush wrote this note to his granddaughter Ellie LeBlond Sosa after she had a tough semester in college.)

December 3, 2007

Dear Special Wonderful Ellie,

Your mom told me you tried to call me, and she told me what it was about. My message back to you is that I love you, I am proud of you, and I will always be in your corner. We all hit bumps in the road of life but you will get past this bump and go on to great things.

Here are some worry beads. If you ever worry, rub these beads and the worries should fade away. Also, you can pawn them if you go broke in Tanzania. For, as Doro once asked, "Are they real?" Well they are, so if you need a Starbucks double latte mocha special, peddle them.

One last point—if you ever need a shoulder to cry on, an arm to lift you up in the years ahead, or just plain someone to say, "I love, Ellie," I'm "da man." Also, if you need a back to rub, I am "da man." And I pay folding green.

Good luck in your fascinating life ahead. Out of difficulties come new exciting challenges. You will do well, of that I am sure.

Devotedly,
Gampy

(President Bush wrote this note to his grandson Pierce in 2008, after he ran *Fidelity* up on the rocks while trying to come into the dock at Walker's Point. He left it on Pierce's pillow.)

Pierce—

I remember days when I felt I could do nothing right. But then the sun would come up and a bright new day would embrace me. Do not worry about the boat or the car incident.[4] You are a good man who got a bad bounce, but all is well, believe me! I hate to see you worrying and down.

You brighten my life, so forget yesterday and today's little incidents—You da man! and I love you. Ganny does, too.

Gampy

---

4. The day before, Pierce had gotten into trouble with his grandmother when he took her Smart Car without permission.

(An email to his five children after Mrs. Bush had open-heart surgery.)

March 4, 2009

Subject: REPORT ON YOUR MOTHER!

Importance: High

Dear George, Jeb, Neil, Marv, and Doro,

The operation went very well. I just saw your mother in the recovery room. She couldn't speak or anything this early, but all the valves and gauges show that she is doing perfectly. They did put in the pig valve instead of the metal one, so she may be oinking around for a while when she gets home.

I am so relieved and so happy. I will see her at about 3:00 this afternoon, and she will be able to talk and respond. All in all, according to Dr. [Gerald] Lawrie, the operation could not have gone better. He said, "She is one strong woman," but I didn't need the operation to let me know that.

Anyway, I love you all; and cross your Mom off the worry list.

(Written to his first great-grandchild, Georgia Helena Walker Bush—yes, GHWB—daughter of his grandson Jeb and his wife, Sandra.)

August 18, 2011

Dear Georgia,

I haven't seen you yet and I love you already—more than tongue can tell. You are one very lucky little girl. You have two wonderful parents who will always be with you and love you. You have grandparents who feel the same way. And you have two really old guys, great grandparents, Barbara Bush and me, who worship the ground you will be walking on and who will be here for you, at your side, for as long as we live.

So have a wonderful happy life, dear Georgia.

Gampy

(This letter is slightly out of chronological order, but it is the perfect ending for this chapter about family—a letter to his five children.)

September 23, 1998

Dear Kids,

This letter is about aging. Not about the President's Conference on Aging and how we should play lawn bowling, get discounts at the movies, turn into skin-conscious sunblockers, take Metamucil and grow old gracefully. No it's about me, about what happened between last year and this, between being 73 and 74. It's interesting—well, fairly interesting to you maybe, therapeutic to me for I know I am getting older now.

Last year I could drop the anchor on Fidelity *and worry only a little bit about falling off the bow. This year if Bill Busch[5] or Neil isn't up there on the bow of* Fidelity II *to drop the anchor I can still do it; but I figure it's about a 75% chance that a wave will hit* Fidelity, *my balance will go and I'll be in the drink.*

Last year I could fly fish on the end rocks at the Point, and not be too concerned about losing my balance. Oh, if I'd been casting at one target for a while way back in the summer of '97, my spike clad feet firmly placed on two rocks, and then I turned fast I'd feel a little— what's the word here—not "wobbly" but "unbalanced"—that's the feeling.

---

5. President Bush's Maine fishing buddy, the one who wore the forbidden T-shirt.

This year if I turn fast, I wobble. I recover as I go from rock to rock, but I look like one of the Wallenda brothers going across Niagara Falls. Arms in the air are more important this year...

Then there's memory. I'm still pretty good at faking it. "Well, I'll be darn, how in the heck are you?" or "long time no see!" or "What you been up to?" or if I want to gamble "How's your better half?" Careful of this last one at both 73 and 74 though. The better half crop is getting a little thinner. Death has claimed some "better halfs" and over the years some have been dumped...

The twins invited friends from Biddeford Pool over to Walker's Point this summer. Mystery guests in a way for they'd leave one day midst warm embraces and farewells only to mysteriously reappear the next.

Jenna introduced me to them on Day 1 and on Day 2—then gave up on me when failing to recall names I kept saying "Biddeford Girls—I am sure glad you came back. How long are you going to be with us?" They were very nice about it, and after a week of seeing them eating here they wedged into my heart—always room for more nice kids...

One last point on memory. I can remember things very clearly that happened a long time ago. The longer ago, it seems, the clearer my recall.

Examples:

I can vividly remember the bottom of my mother's feet. Yes, she played a much younger woman named Peaches Peltz in tennis back in 1935 or so. Peaches was smooth. Mum was tenacious. Mother literally wore the skin off the bottom of her feet. But I can't remember whom I played tennis with last week...

I remember a lot of detail about all five of you when you were little—all happy memories I retain; but alas I am vague on recent details in your lives. I am passionately interested but factoids escape me.

This summer, one or two of you, I am sure in an effort to be helpful, said "get a hearing aid" or "try listening." I heard you. I also heard a family member (I won't say of which generation) go: "The old fogy is getting deaf." But I had clearly heard what had gone before and I heard that "old fogy" thing, too. Come to think back on it I am not sure the word used was "fogy"—not sure, not sure at all.

But on the hearing thing, here's my side of it. Each year I have my hearing checked at the Mayo Clinic. They keep telling me "very slight hearing loss—no need for a hearing aid." So there!

What happens this year unlike last is I just tune out more: because I do not want to know when they are all thinking of going to the movies and I don't want to sign off on having someone take them all the way to Portland. So, on purpose, I either look confused or simply proceed on my way pretending to have heard nary a sound. It works . . .

I sleep about the same as last year, but I find I am going to bed earlier but I wake up when the first sea gull, beak wide open, sends out his earliest screechiest call. Sea gulls don't crow or scream, what is it they do? I forget.

This year I am more philosophical. I don't feel old at all, and I still love sports, but things are without a question different. I ache more after tennis—I mean I'm talking real hip and knee pain. Body parts hurt at night. Daytime is OK . . . Golf's a problem—less distance this year . . . Horseshoes, I can still hold my own . . .

Desire—no aging in the desire department. I still want to compete. I still drive Fidelity II *fast—very fast. My best so far—63 mph in a slight chop with one USSS agent on board.*

I desire to play better golf, but I am allergic to practice, so I just tee it up and play fast. I can still volley but I can't cover behind me. I have the desire though. I love being out on the course or court with the greats of today or yesterday. It's more than name dropping. It's being close to excellence that I enjoy. No aging in the desire category.

If I try to read after dinner I fall asleep on the third page no matter how gripping the mystery. Read a briefing paper in bed? No way— Sominex time!

A very personal note. Three times this summer—once in June, twice in August someone has sidled up to me and whispered, "Your zipper is down." Once I responded by quoting General Vernon Walters' memorable line: "An old bird does not fall out of the nest."

The other two times I just turned sideways, mumbled my thanks, and corrected the problem. But the difference is, 10 years ago I'd have been embarrassed. Now I couldn't care less. Tragic!

Actually I learned this zipper recovery technique from Italy's Prime Minister [Giulio] Andreotti. In the Oval Office one time George Shultz whispered to Andreotti that his zipper was down. Though speaking little English, Andreotti got the drift. Turning his back to all of us he stood up as if to examine the Gilbert Stuart picture of George Washington that was hanging behind President Reagan; and then with no visible concern zipped his pants up.

Last year there was only a tiny sense of time left—of sand running through the glass. This year, I must confess, I am more aware of that. No fear, no apprehension, just a feeling like "let's go—there's so much to do and there might not be a lot of time left." And except for an ache here a pain there I feel like the proverbial spring colt. There is so much left to do.

Your kids keep me young even if I don't bend as easily or run as fast or hear as well.

Maybe I am a little grumpier when there are a whole bunch of them together making funny sounds and having too many friends over who leave too many smelly sneakers around.

And, yes, I confess I am less tolerant about the 7-up can barely sipped—left to get stale and warm or about all the lights left on or about the VCR's whose empty cases are strewn around, the tapes themselves off in another house—stuck into yet another VCR machine.

Though I try not to show it, I also get irritated now when I go to watch a tape and instead of the Hitchcock movie or my Costner film in the proper cover I find a tape of Bambi or of that horrible Simpson family—always a tape that needs rewinding, too.

This summer when he came to the Point, Kevin Costner his ownself gave me tapes of 7 of his movies. I now have 2 tapes in proper covers, empty cardboard covers for two others, the rest of the covers and the other 5 tapes gone—vanished—MIA. Am I being unreasonable here?

I have given up trying to assign blame. I did that when you all were young but I never had my heart and soul in the blame game. Now I find I tune out when someone says, "Ask Jeb, he knows!" or "Gampy, I wasn't even in the boat when they hit the rock." Or after all five gallons of French vanilla turned to mush, the freezer door having been left open all night, "I didn't do it, and I'm not saying who did, but Robert took out two Eskimo Pies after dinner—honest!" I wasn't trying to find the culprit. I was trying to safeguard our future.

I realize "Keep the freezer door closed from now on and I mean it" lacks the rhetorical depth of "This will not stand" or "Read my lips," but back in the White House days Ramsey or George[6] worried about closing the freezer door while I worried about other problems. The lines were more clearly drawn back then.

No there is a difference now and maybe when we reconvene next year, you'll notice even more of a gentle slide. I hope not. I want to put this "aging" on hold for a while now.

I don't expect to be on the A team anymore; but I want to play golf with you. And I want to fish or throw shoes. And I want to rejoice in your victories be they political, or business, or family happiness victories.

And I want to be there for you if you get a bad bounce in life, and no doubt you will for the seas do indeed get rough.

---

6. James Ramsey and George Haney of the White House residence staff.

When I say "be there" I don't mean just showing up—I mean in the game, in the lineup, viscerally involved in your lives even though I might be miles away.

I don't want you to pull your punches. If I call Lauren "Barbara" go ahead and give me your best shot—I can take it. But try not to say "C'mon, Alph, get with it."

If I shed tears easier now try not to laugh at me, because I'll lose more saline and that makes me feel like a sissy, and it might make my mouth dry later on, and might be bad for digestion, too. And besides it's OK to cry if you are a man—a happy man (me) or a man faced with sadness or hurt (not me).

Hey, don't point the first finger at whomever is shedding the tear because all Bushes cry easily when we're happy, or counting our blessings, or sad when one of you gets bruised or really hurt inside.

As the summer finishes out and the seas get a little higher, the winds a little colder, I'll be making some notes—writing it down lest I forget—so I can add to this report on getting older. Who knows maybe they'll come out with a new drug that makes legs bend easier—joints hurt less, drives go farther, memory come roaring back, and all fears about falling off fishing rocks go away.

Remember the old song "I'll be there ready when you are." Well, I'll be there ready when you are, for there's so much excitement ahead, so many grandkids to watch grow. If you need me, I'm here.

Devotedly,
Dad

CHAPTER FOURTEEN

LEFTOVERS

O ne of my favorite things about my job was how random the Bushes made my life. But the key word here is "random."

Before we get to the end of this journey, there are just a few more stories I would love to share, but they don't fit into the theme of any of the other chapters. What to do?

Aha. Create a chapter just for the homeless—and yes, random—stories.

And what better place to start than with celebrities...

Getting to Know You

One of President Bush's most endearing qualities was that he was a self-professed and shameless name-dropper. In most people, that bad habit would be considered annoying and egotistical.

What I loved was that President Bush never figured out he was almost always the biggest name in the room. Jeb reminded me of the expression his dad always used about name-droppers: "Most name-droppers say, 'I know him' over and over again. The world-class name-droppers say, 'He knows me.' It always got a good laugh."

One of my favorite celebrity stories is about when parts of the movie

Tin Cup were being filmed in Houston. The entire city was abuzz as the movie starred Kevin Costner, Don Johnson, Rene Russo, and Cheech Marin. There were stories of sightings everywhere—some true, some not so true. (Some of my girlfriends and I managed to have drinks in the bar at the Four Seasons one night, waiting for the cast to come back to their hotel. We struck out.)

President Bush decided *not* to leave his sighting to chance. He arranged through his friend Jim Nantz—the CBS sportscaster who was doing a cameo in this movie about golf—to visit the movie set. Did I go along for the ride? You have to ask?

Costner took the lead in hosting us, and we sat in his trailer for a brief visit. We didn't stay long—they were, after all, making a movie. But before we left, President Bush asked Kevin if some of them would like to come over for dinner. He immediately accepted and said he would put together a small group.

A few days later, Kevin, Don Johnson, and Cheech came to dinner.

I almost passed out when President Bush told me the last seat at the table was mine. I had been his chief of staff for only a year, but I think he already knew it would be a mistake on his part not to wedge me in somehow.

There are four stories from the evening that stand out:

- During the cocktails, everyone was having a great time, talking on top of one another, except for Cheech. He seemed a little uncomfortable. As much as I wanted to mainly stare at Kevin, I couldn't help but watch as President Bush zeroed in on Cheech and got him to start talking. Given Cheech's history of edgy comedy during his Cheech and Chong days, I was curious about what direction the conversation would take. President Bush asked him where he grew up, and Cheech proudly told about his father, who had been a Los Angeles police officer. They talked until dinnertime.

- Before dinner, Mrs. Bush convinced Kevin to walk down the street with her and knock on the door of her great friend Mildred

Kerr. (Mrs. Bush's dog Millie was named for Mrs. Kerr.) While Mrs. Bush hid in a bush, Kevin told Mrs. Kerr he was on a scavenger hunt and needed an umbrella. Yes, she died. When Don Johnson arrived, just a little late, Mrs. Bush asked him to do the same thing. Unfortunately, Mrs. Kerr did not recognize him. How had Mrs. Kerr missed *Miami Vice*?

- This dinner took place during the trial of O. J. Simpson, whom almost everyone at the table (not me) had met. Kevin especially considered him a friend, and he was very honest about how hard it was to begin to realize that someone you knew and liked had maybe killed someone. For some odd reason, during this discussion, I finally found my voice. I made the point that there was a difference between someone who was a murderer—people like hitmen and serial killers who killed at will; and someone who committed *a murder*—murders of passion and rage. Not being able to stop myself, I added that all of us were likely capable of *a murder*, if pushed far enough. The reaction of the table was muted. And no, I really don't know what I was thinking.

- But Mrs. Bush saved me by announcing that O.J. was possibly the sexiest man she had ever met. She gushed over his smile and his charm. Finally President Bush interrupted her and said, "Darling, there are several people sitting at this table who maybe were hoping you considered them the sexiest person you ever met. That would include your husband of fifty years." Uncharacteristically tone-deaf, Mrs. Bush did not concede the point.

A few years later, when Kevin was in Maine filming the movie *Message in a Bottle*, he spent some time with the Bushes—fishing, golfing, eating dinner—and brought his children with him at least once. (I guess my invitation got lost in the mail.) He also was kind enough to come to the opening of President Bush's library in 1997, which caused a huge stir.

Years later, I received a phone call from a woman named Marian Heard, head of the United Way in Boston and a founding board member of Points of Light. She had spent the day with Don Johnson, who had agreed to help her raise some money.

At some point they discovered their mutual friendship with the Bushes, at which point Don told Marian there was a crazy woman who worked for President Bush who thought we were all murderers. "Jean, I think he meant you," she said with some hesitancy. I guess I had made an impression.

And for the record, I really do not think we are all capable of murder.

Another great celebrity story involved Taylor Swift, who came to Maine in 2010 to shoot a music video. President Bush's granddaughter Gigi lobbied Mrs. Bush's aide, Hutton Hinson, and our summer intern, Coleman Lapointe, to help lobby her Gampy to invite Taylor to Walker's Point. They were all-in.

At their urging, and after watching some of her music videos, President Bush wrote her this note:

July 8, 2010

Dear Taylor,

There are a lot of family fans of yours here at our lovely place by the sea. Please come over tomorrow afternoon for a swim and relaxation by our pool.

I believe in long shots, so I hope this works out.

Sincerely,
George Bush
old 41

He then dispatched the three of them to find her (it helped that Coleman knew all the local cops) and to deliver the note.

They managed to get past security and convince Taylor's assistant they weren't stalkers. (They sort of were.) They made their way to Taylor's mother, who took them to her daughter. Hutton remembers what happened next:

"Taylor was very excited by the invitation and asked if her whole team could come over to Walker's Point the next day. We said of course but realized there was one issue: We had not told Barbara Bush about any of this yet. Luckily, Mrs. Bush thought this sounded fun and said she would make sure there were lobster rolls or something special for Taylor and her team.

"Taylor signed photos and hugged everyone she met like old friends. When she came back later that summer to debut her 'Mine' music video on the grounds of St. Ann's Church, her first invite to come watch the debut was to her new friend, George Bush 41."

I was out of town when all this happened. I thought I had missed the Second Coming, excitement was so high at Walker's Point when I got back. It definitely had been a triumphant moment for Gigi, Hutton, and Coleman.

My last celebrity story belongs to Mrs. Bush. She once sat next to world champion boxer Evander Holyfield at a Houston Astros game. I was not there, but someone who was reported that the two of them had a lively conversation throughout the game and were becoming fast friends. Right around the seventh inning, she turned to him and said, "Now, Evander, tell me what you do for a living."

Keep Them Laughing

Mrs. Bush often told people that one of the many reasons why she married George Bush was that he made her laugh.

His sense of humor among family and friends—even among his

head-of-state peers—was legendary. It surprised me, and even irritated me a little, that so many Americans never realized just how darn funny he was. Then again, he did take his jobs as president, vice president—his jobs all the way back to World War II—quite seriously. So maybe I should be more forgiving.

He was the master of practical jokes, with his wife often his target. One of his more famous success stories had to be the day he managed to convince her she might be going to jail for trafficking porn.

During the summer of 1998, it came to light that someone in the house was looking up and printing porn off Mrs. Bush's computer. Several unnamed teenage grandsons were the immediate suspects and quickly acknowledged their crime. (Leaving some photos in the printer led to their downfall.)

A few days after the unfortunate incident, Mrs. Bush found in her stack of mail a letter from the Office of the Inspector General of the Federal Trade Commission. It read in part: "In doing a routine check, it appears you have recently been engaged in downloading pornographic material...We respectfully request that you report to our regional office in Portland, Maine, for a hearing on August 17, 1998, at 8:30 a.m...."

Lying next to her husband in bed as she was reading through her mail, she blurted out to him that she might be going to jail! I was not there when all this transpired, but I am told President Bush managed to keep it together for a few minutes before dissolving into laughter. Yes, he had written the letter, perhaps with the help of some staff members who had created the fake stationery. She pretended not to think it was funny but then again, she told the story for years, including in the sequel to her memoirs, *Reflections*.

Then there was the year President Bush invited a pig to Celebration of Reading. The annual event came just a month after Mrs. Bush's open-heart surgery where a pig heart valve was used to replace one of her defective ones. President Bush had the odd and yet brilliant idea that we needed to find a pig to come out onstage, playing the part as the relative of the valve donor. The pig was there, in theory, to protest.

Our production team and longtime Bush friends Danny Ward and Nancy Ames did manage to find a pig. They even got the pig to walk out onto the stage on cue, just as President Bush was explaining the surgery to the audience. What they didn't see coming was that in his excitement, the pig immediately defecated. Show business is tough.

President Bush not only was funny but he appreciated humor. He had a famous file of jokes that he loved sharing in emails with family and friends, and he loved funny people. I think it was why he and Dana Carvey became great friends.

Most of you likely know the story that when President Bush lost the election in 1992, he asked Dana to come to the White House to do a surprise stand-up routine for the rather depressed staff. No one was more shocked than Dana. He had been killing it for years on *Saturday Night Live*, imitating and making fun of the forty-first president.

It was the beginning of a beautiful friendship.

As it turns out, President Bush had always thought Dana's routine was funny, and even agreed to a cameo with him on *SNL*, done remotely from Houston.

They kept in touch through the years, and Dana graciously did a few fund-raising events for us. But the best was when Dana came to Houston in 2008 for a big charity event for a nonprofit group called Boys and Girls Country. He was the after-dinner entertainment, but Dana convinced his hosts to let him do a short stand-up bit before dinner, with no questions asked. He walked onstage and began his George H. W. Bush routine, when suddenly over the microphone came President Bush's unmistakable voice: "What are you doing? You are nothing like me."

Then President Bush walked out onto the stage and the two brought the house down. I was watching from the back of the hotel ballroom and noticed that even the waiters had to put their trays down, they were laughing so hard.

The whole cameo had been President Bush's idea. I think he always had a little stand-up comic inside of him.

What Do You Know and When Did You Know It?

I flew to Washington, DC, in January 2005 with the Bushes to attend the second inauguration of their son. I didn't see them at all after we arrived—they stayed at the White House and rode in presidential motorcades. I stayed with Michael Dannenhauer and rode on buses.

When I got home, I sent a full report to my siblings, including this tidbit:

"By far the best event of the weekend was the church service on Friday morning. To sit in the National Cathedral and hear Ronan Tynan sing 'How Great Thou Art' and then later in the program, 'Ave Maria,' was truly unbelievable. Add to that a rare public appearance by Billy Graham, and an opening procession that included the hierarchy of every known religion, it really sent chills down your spine and made you feel good about being American.

"So while I was feeling quite spiritual and enthralled, I look up and see 41's personal aide, Tom Frechette, walking down the side aisles obviously looking for someone. So I crawled out of my middle pew to see if he needed help. 41 had sent him to find me, because he wanted me to ride back to the White House with him to tell him…well, gossip. He felt cut off from the real world, I think, and although he had very high-level gossip of his own,[1] he wanted to know who I had seen and what I had heard. He was gossip-starved. It was very funny. I had been hanging out with many members of his extended family all week so was able to provide him with some interesting tidbits about this and that, who was behaving, who was being sort of a jerk. I don't think he was enjoying being in that 'presidential bubble.'

---

1. I hate to disappoint you but I don't remember any of this high-level gossip, which is probably a good thing.

"Mrs. Bush said during the service, when they took up a collection, both the President and the Vice President searched their pockets but had no money on them. So 41 put in a $100 bill and told the usher in a very loud whisper that he was covering all 3 of them. She said the whole front of the church saw and heard it and got the twitters. I was sitting too far back to catch this action."

Body Dysfunction

In 2005, while Hurricane Rita was ravaging parts of the Gulf Coast, I had an emergency hysterectomy in Maine. I had been feeling poorly for a while and finally cried "uncle" one day, then asked my houseguest, Mrs. Bush's former aide Kara Babers Sanders, to take me to the emergency room at Maine Medical Center in Portland.

The pain-causing culprit was a benign fibroid tumor that had grown into the size of a volleyball[2] and was wreaking havoc in my body, including shutting down all my body functions. I would not share this rather personal detail if it were not key to the story.

The morning after the long, complicated surgery I woke up to find the forty-first president of the United States in my room. (Mrs. Bush came later so we could have "girl talk.")

He was there when my wonderful surgeon, Dr. Hector Tarraza, came into my room, followed by a large group of residents, to report on my surgery. He was taken aback to find President Bush sitting there, and as professionally and gracefully as possible, told President Bush he was there to discuss my medical condition and it might be best if he left the room. Before I could answer, President Bush assured them he was like family and he did not need to leave.

---

2. The staff named the tumor "Wilson," after the volleyball that kept Tom Hanks company in the movie *Cast Away*.

Although I was in a morphine-induced state, I still remember with incredible clarity two things he asked during the briefing:

- When Dr. Tarraza described the tumor, President Bush asked if he could see it, wondering if I didn't want to see it, too. I really did not. Dr. Tarraza was rather startled and said it was in the lab where it was being dissected to confirm it was noncancerous (it was), and not available for viewing. President Bush was oddly disappointed.
- Dr. Tarraza explained to the residents that what finally made me realize I had a serious medical problem was the shutting down of all body functions. Again, President Bush was fascinated. "Number one or number two?" he asked. Dr. Tarraza looked at me to see if I wanted to answer. "Both," I told him, and I clearly remember pushing the morphine drip at this moment in time. "Fascinating," President Bush replied.

One last note about the surgery: Apparently while I was in recovery, I insisted to the nurses I had been kidnapped by Saudi and Kuwaiti insurgents and told them they needed to get help. They said I was most anxious and fearful and warned them we all were in danger. When I revealed my mad ramblings to President Bush, he said it would have been Iraqi insurgents who would have kidnapped me, not Kuwaitis or Saudis. He felt that was important to know. I found it amusing he was more or less fact-checking my hallucinations. I was told later that the recovery room staff was fairly sure the word "insurgent" had never been uttered in that room before.

Wedding Bells—Not!

The Bushes' great interest and concern about my private life was endearing but sometimes challenging. One of the bigger challenges was their attempt to marry me off to my best friend in life, singer-actor George Dvorsky.

Who also happens to be gay.

The Bushes became friends with the veteran Broadway performer before I did as they had seen him perform numerous times at Houston's Theatre Under the Stars, better known as TUTS. Since they always went backstage after every performance they attended, they had gotten to know George quite well. So much so that President Bush started asking George to sing for them in Kennebunkport for various fund-raisers and social events, which he was always happy to do if available.

Eventually George and I became great friends, as our paths kept crossing through the Bushes and other mutual friends. The friendship was cemented when he came to Houston in December 2009 to play Captain von Trapp in TUTS's production of *The Sound of Music*, and rather than stay at a hotel with the rest of the cast, he stayed with me.

The Bushes loved the show so much they went twice.

The morning after the last performance the Bushes called me bright and early while still in bed. They got straight to the point: They thought George and I were perfect for each other and we should become a couple.

In the interest of full disclosure, I am embarrassed to admit I was slightly hungover. My neighborhood annual Christmas party had been the night before, and since we all just walk from house to house for a bite to eat and drink, we typically let ourselves get a little tipsy.

So I was already struggling a bit with conversation when I had to tackle this unexpected issue. "No," I said to them. "We are just very good friends. You do know he is gay?"

One of them, maybe President Bush, asked, "How gay is he?"

Well, gay is gay.

Mrs. Bush argued, "Jean, I just watched him fall in love twice with Maria.[3] No one is that gay."

"Well," I replied, "he's a very good actor."

I called George, who ironically was at George Bush Airport waiting for his flight back to New York, to tell him of this development. He thought it was hysterical and dear.

---

3. Maria von Trapp, in *The Sound of Music*.

The Bushes revisited this idea a couple of times over the years. It was compounded when George rescued an adorable Pomeranian named Zeke, whom I occasionally babysat while George traveled. The Bushes felt if George trusted me with his dog, then surely he would want to marry me.

In April 2011, George was in Houston doing a show that ended about the time for me to make the annual trek to Maine. Typically one of my sisters helped me with the two-thousand-mile drive,[4] but that May George and Zeke were my copilots. Somewhere along the way, I had a very productive phone call with former White House chief of staff Andy Card, whom President Bush very much wanted to be acting dean of the Bush School. The current dean was Ryan Crocker, who was being called back into the foreign service by President Obama to be our ambassador in Afghanistan during a crucial time. On behalf of President Bush, I had planted the seed with Andy to take Ryan's place until his return, and on my drive to Maine, Andy called and said yes. I was ecstatic and couldn't wait to tell President Bush.

My first day in Maine, I had lunch with the Bushes and announced as soon as we sat down I had joyous news. Before I could say another word, Mrs. Bush blurted out, "George asked you to marry him! We just knew it would happen on your trip." President Bush added his congratulations.

Uh, no, that was not what had happened. I told them about Andy, and they were thrilled. But admitted disappointment, even surprise, that I was not engaged.

A few weeks later, when the Bushes' Houston minister, the Reverend Russ Levenson, his wife, Laura, and Karl Rove and his wife, Karen, were visiting Walker's Point, Mrs. Bush asked them if they knew I had a serious boyfriend and likely would soon be getting engaged.

---

4. I drove these two thousand miles twice a year for twenty-six years—from Texas to Maine in May, back down to Texas in October. Over the years President Bush offered to hire someone to drive my car or even to rent me a car in Maine, but truthfully—I loved the drive. It was three to four days away from the maddening crowd, and a good chance to catch up with whoever was my copilot. I am what you call a road warrior.

As Karl and Russ both looked at me for further explanation, I had flashbacks of President Bush's campaign to make my brother Eddie the next pope. I suddenly realized they were using the same strategy: If they talked about it enough, it would happen.

Hot Dogs and Apple Pie

I am not sure when exactly this tradition started, but for more than ten years I hosted *the* Fourth of July party in Kennebunkport. I would love to be able to claim that my party became famous because I was such a gracious host, or my cooking was sublime, or I was hugely popular.

It was because George and Barbara Bush started crashing my Fourth of July gathering, and the rest is history.

My party began small enough—whoever my houseguests happened to be and maybe a few local friends. The numbers grew every year until suddenly, by 2010, I had at least fifty people.

That was the year I was talking about my party with Mrs. Bush, and she confessed to me she was feeling rather tired and wondered if I would be willing to invite whatever Bush family was at Walker's Point. She said she could use a day off from large family gatherings, and, more important, she could give her exhausted household staff some time off.

I, of course, was delighted. I had never invited any Walker's Point residents, assuming they would have a family get-together, but I loved them all to pieces and they were tons of fun, so I was happy to invite one and all. I think that first year it was Neil and his family and Doro and her family.

Just as guests were beginning to arrive, my phone rang. It was President Bush. Mrs. Bush was not feeling well and had already gone to bed and he was starving. "Could I just drop by for a burger?" he asked rather plaintively. "Everybody else here is going to your house."

"Of course," I said.

He came and stayed for two hours, holding court on my patio. There were several people who had RSVP'd by saying they would only drop by but then had to leave for another party. They came and never left. Funny how that happens. And yes, I ran out of burgers.

After that, all of Walker's Point came every year. One year, the city police stopped by to tell me cars were parked illegally all around the house. They walked out to my patio and saw two Presidents George Bush, Barbara Bush, Laura Bush, and a host of Secret Service. The police officer tipped his hat at me and said, "Yeah, never mind," then left.

That was the same year that I was still making the burgers and getting organized when one of my houseguests came running into my kitchen to announce that two guests had just shown up about a half hour early. I told her to go back out there and entertain them. She said, "I think you better come."

As it turns out, the early birds were George W. and Laura Bush. His parents weren't far behind. So I think I sent George Dvorsky and his dog, Zeke, out to entertain them. The burgers had to come first.

Eventually the party became so large—one hundred people—that President Bush's brother Bucky offered to cohost with me and move it to his summer rental house, which had a large porch and backyard. It was great fun. Everyone brought a ton of food, and Ken Raynor, the local golf pro, grilled hamburgers and hot dogs for hours. At some point we would all stop eating and drinking and visiting and sing "God Bless America."

The good news, for me and for Bucky, was that you could not see the fireworks from his porch or my front yard. So by 8:30, everyone had cleared out. No one overstayed their welcome.

Nine Lives

One of the odder topics of conversation that President Bush and I occasionally had over the years was how many times he had almost died.

It began after one of his rather close calls with death when I teased him—after the crisis had well passed—that he had nine lives.

He asked me to help him count how many times he had cheated

death. He was fairly certain it was more than nine. I started with September 2, 1944; he pushed me back a few years. He had almost died of rheumatic fever while a student at Andover and had sat out a year of high school.

You might think we would then jump to his golden years, but not so fast.

Very few people know that the forty-first president almost died in a quicksand bog in Canada. Given how proud President Bush was of his "cheating death" record, I think he would want me to finally tell you.

Actually, I asked Johnny Morris—founder and owner of Bass Pro Shops and President Bush's favorite fishing partner—to tell the story. He was there; I was not.

Here is what happened, according to Johnny:

"It took place in the summer of 1995. We were the guests of great friends Craig and Elaine Dobbin from Newfoundland. Craig loved fly-fishing and was a committed conservationist; as CEO of Canadian Helicopter, he made access to remote rivers available to us with his aircraft.

"One particular morning, as we were flying off to fish the beautiful Hawk River, it got too foggy and we had to land. As soon as we did, the president went off into a wooded area to relieve himself. The Secret Service agents stayed a respectful distance behind, but after what seemed like a very long time they went to look for him. It turned out he had wandered into a bog and was up to his armpits in quicksand. Talk about a startling sight! Fortunately, the president, as he often did, remained calm and instead of thrashing around in a panic, which would have caused the bog to suck him completely under, he stayed still with his arms outspread, trusting he would be found. It was a tricky situation, and rescuing him from that quicksand was not easy considering he was already in it up to his neck.

"To this day, I don't believe many people, including his closest friends and even his family, realize what a very, very close call this was, how close we came to losing him in the quicksand."

It was one story President Bush did not like to tell; he felt it made the

Secret Service look bad. After all, if he had died, how would they have explained losing a president in a bog? "There probably would be a congressional inquiry," he told me.

But in the end, they were the ones who pulled him out. And they were the reason why I think the man knew no fear: He lived life trusting that the agents had his back. And they did.

Striking Out

Occasionally I am asked if President Bush ever became truly annoyed with me. We, of course, had our disagreements over the years, but I said one thing to him that he truly never got over.

It was all about baseball.

As you now know, President Bush had a huge love for the game and, until we went to Maine for the summer, was a constant presence at Houston Astros baseball games. As was Mrs. Bush, who dutifully kept a scorecard.

I occasionally tagged along with them, but I always managed to grab a seat when the Astros were hosting my team, the St. Louis Cardinals. President Bush went to his grave a tad annoyed he never convinced me to become an Astros fan—he really didn't get it. He took it rather personally and told me I also was hurting the feelings of then Astros owner Drayton McLane. (Drayton assured me that was not the case and swore he admired my loyalty.)

But my real sin was the day I told President Bush that Cardinals slugger Albert Pujols was on track to become the best hitter in baseball history.

When I shared this tidbit, we were watching Pujols trot around the bases after hitting yet another home run. I had just read that if Pujols stayed healthy, he could shatter all hitting records.

President Bush was appalled and told me so. I should add here that he had been quite close to Ted Williams, the legendary Rex Sox player who was the last major league baseball player to end the season with an average higher than .400—.406 in 1941.

Pujols would never, ever, be better than Williams, he informed me, with a hint of disdain in his voice.

For months, even years, random people would say to me, "Did you really tell President Bush that Albert Pujols might be better than Ted Williams?"

Well, yes I had.

"He's still really mad about it," the messenger would always report.

It didn't help that during the National League Championship Series in 2005, with the Astros on the brink of clinching and going to their first World Series, Pujols hit a towering home run in Minute Maid Park that won Game 5 for the Cardinals, sending the series back to St. Louis for Games 6 and 7. Despite the fact the Astros won Game 6 and went to the World Series (which they lost in four games to the Chicago White Sox), Astros fans never forgot Pujols's home run and always booed him when he came to the plate.

At home recovering from my hysterectomy, I was not at the game, but President Bush sent me this email from his BlackBerry on his way home: "I am trying to muster up some sincerity. What a homerun by Puhols [sic]. I know you are ecstatic and that does make me happy—well, less gloomy. So dear, Jean, sleep well, savor your victory. Meet you in St. Louis. Almost home to cry and try to forget Ahols. I mean Puhols."

He never really got over it. I think he felt it was perhaps my largest error in judgment.

A couple of notes to end this saga: Pujols did not stay healthy; he will not be remembered as the best hitter in baseball history. He's good, but he's no Ted Williams.

When President Bush died, former Cardinals manager Tony La Russa—another baseball friend of President Bush's—brought Pujols as his guest to the funeral at the National Cathedral. When Tony asked me if that would be okay, I said of course—and secretly smiled to myself. It was just a little ironic, given that Pujols had been the source of a funny friction between us for years.

But even in death, President Bush got the last word.

A few months after the funeral, as part of closing down the Office of George Bush, I spent one afternoon finally packing my office. Buried deep in one of my drawers I found something President Bush had given me nearly ten years earlier.

He had been invited to the HBO premiere of their documentary on Ted Williams. The name of the film: *Ted Williams: There Goes the Greatest Hitter That Ever Lived*. President Bush had left the invitation on my desk, attaching a note on a yellow stickie: "See, Jean!! Watch and Learn!!"

Yes, sir.[5]

---

5. I am looking at it right now, hanging on my office wall.

CHAPTER FIFTEEN

THE LONG JOURNEY HOME

I once told President Bush, with respect of course, that when he died we really should dissect him to figure out what made him tick. He had more energy than anyone I knew. He was a whirlwind of action, especially in Maine, where he could bounce from a 7 a.m. tee time (he was famous for playing eighteen holes in ninety minutes, admittedly not well), to dropping by the office to check his emails, then maybe a round of tennis with some grandkids, followed by a dip in the pool. There was always time for a fast boat ride, maybe to fish or spot whales or go to lunch—sometimes all three. Then back to the office to read and answer letters and tell me his latest idea, and maybe go jump into the ocean, after which he might call and invite twenty people over for cocktails.

It would be hard to pinpoint exactly when he began to slow down. But we all noticed that he was walking a little slower and sometimes with a bit of a limp. He took more naps. He had both hips replaced—the first in 2000, the second in 2007. And he had back surgery in 2008 from which I felt he never fully recovered.

I emailed my sisters in November 2007 that although President Bush's body was eighty-three, his spirit was sixty-five—and that sometimes was problematic:

"Today he is going hunting, the first trip of the season. He's so unstable on his feet, and he confessed to me he's slightly afraid of getting shot. He says if you wobble out there, you might fall in the path of another hunter. He was dead serious yet has no intention of not going. He just sort of said it matter of fact, 'I might get shot today, Jean.' Well, ok, then. These Texans are weird."

After all, he was getting older. This is what happens when you turn eighty, even if you did celebrate with a parachute jump.

What we didn't know for a few years was that there was something bigger going on than simply getting old. Around 2010 he was diagnosed with a form of Parkinson's disease, which eventually led to him walking with a pronounced limp, to using a cane, then to using a scooter for going distances much farther than across the room, and finally to being in a wheelchair.

Watching him deal with his new reality taught me another important life lesson: Grow old gracefully. Don't whine. Don't wallow in self-pity.

When first diagnosed, President Bush was disappointed he would not finish his life in full throttle. He went through a period where he was, simply put, down in the dumps. I know Mrs. Bush worried about him a great deal, and I have found notes I made to myself or others about his mental state.

But just as he had throughout his life, he eventually shook it off and accepted his new normal. He was ready to move forward and made the necessary adjustments. He continued to be out and about as much as possible and got used to needing help. He still loved throwing out the first pitch at baseball games when invited—which the Astros would do at least once a season—despite the fact he really couldn't throw at all. Once, he kept waving the catcher to get closer, and closer, and closer—until he handed him the ball. The crowd roared.

One afternoon, after having lunch in downtown Houston with President Bush, we walked a few city blocks. Well, I was walking and he was being pushed in his wheelchair. He was amazed at how easy it was to navigate the city sidewalks because every intersection had a wheelchair ramp. I loved reminding him that he was the president who signed the Americans with Disabilities Act, the equivalent of a Civil Rights bill for the disabled that made wheelchair access to all public places the law of the land.

"Ah, good point," he said.

There were several things left on his to-do list that he didn't get done. For example, he and his good friend Lex Frieden—one of the architects of the ADA, who had been in a wheelchair since a car accident his freshman year in college—were going to ride Houston's city buses to publicize how wheelchair friendly they were. Unfortunately, President Bush died before they went for their joyride.

Like most of us are as we grow older, the Bushes were in denial for a while about how frail they were becoming and the fact they needed more help, especially President Bush. I made a number of attempts to talk them into home health care but struck out. It was, in fact, a topic that irritated them greatly. So right before Christmas 2011, I emailed their five children and asked them to discuss the topic with their parents while they were all together in Florida during the week between Christmas and New Year's. They assured me they would get this settled.

Doro called me from Florida to tell me it had not gone well and I was in big trouble with her mom. Neil had decided to introduce the topic by saying, "Jean asked us to talk to you about home health care." I was hoping Mrs. Bush would forget all that by the time they came back to Houston. She did not.

Oddly, it was NBC anchor Brian Williams who saved the day.

One night while watching the *NBC Nightly News*, I became intrigued by a story about the high unemployment rate among veterans returning from Iraq and Afghanistan. By this time I had learned from the master: I had an idea.

The next day I told the Bushes about the very sad circumstances of these veterans and suggested we should find a few in Houston and hire them to help us. They both immediately agreed something needed to be done. President Bush said maybe they could do odd jobs around the office. I pretended to think for a minute, then said, "No, I really don't need more help at the office. How about if they did odd jobs around the house." They agreed that would be okay.

With the help of our good friend Tyson Voelkel, a Bush School graduate who was a major in the U.S. Army Reserve, we eventually hired three young men who just happened to have some kind of medical training. (It was how we eventually found Evan Sisley.) I asked Tyson to come brief the Bushes about the young men—another good move on my part. Mrs. Bush thought they only needed one aide; Tyson convinced her it was always good to have backups. And that was that. Starting in the fall of 2012, President Bush was surrounded until he died by an expanding group of dedicated veterans who took care of him and became part of our extended family.

And once in a while they did an odd job or two.

The older he got, the quieter President Bush became, partially because Parkinson's did affect his speech. He always knew what he wanted to say but couldn't always formulate the words.

But I told all visitors in those last few years, "Don't think he doesn't hear or understand everything you say." He did. But you had to give him a chance to respond. I would cringe when I saw people just talk and talk and talk—they weren't comfortable with the silence that would come between what they said and what President Bush eventually would say. (No one mastered this art form more than Jon Meacham, who knew how to wait and was almost always rewarded.)

My best example of someone who couldn't wait comes from President Bush's longtime friend Dan Gillcrist, who sent me this email about a lunch he had with President Bush and Secretary Baker at their favorite hangout, Christie's:

"I told him a joke and he did not laugh, so I said, 'Didn't you hear my joke...you didn't laugh.' He eventually responded, 'I heard the joke—I didn't laugh because I didn't think the joke was funny!'"

★   ★   ★

One of the more touching aspects of watching the Bushes grow old was also having a front-row seat to their seventy-three-year love story. I got a few hints back in the White House days—I remember one evening, for example, when the First Lady returned late from a trip. As her motorcade pulled up to the diplomatic entrance on the south side of the White House, from where the president and First Lady always came and went, the staff was fascinated to see a man wearing very old clothes and a cowboy hat waiting for us. Who on earth could that be? The president of the United States waiting to welcome home "his bride," as he called her.

One of my first summers in Maine, I remember being with Mrs. Bush in her bedroom, going over some work, when we heard President Bush's voice calling out to her as he walked into the house. Her instinct was to immediately look into a mirror and pinch her cheeks so they had a little more color. It was a sweet moment I never forgot.

Years later, as their assorted aging issues were interrupting their sleep, both Bushes complained to me more than once how much the other snored. I finally suggested to President Bush that maybe it was time they considered separate bedrooms. A good night's sleep was, after all, essential to their staying healthy.

President Bush was appalled. I remember exactly what he said: "Jean, I have to be able to reach out during the night and touch her and make sure she is there."

I never brought it up again.

They were so connected and devoted to each other that, for the last few years of their lives, if one of them was admitted, Houston Methodist Hospital automatically reserved the room next to them. It became inevitable the other would be checking in before long.

One such incident was just a few weeks before Mrs. Bush died. It was Good Friday, 2018. She had been in the hospital but had been dismissed a few days earlier. But now President Bush was in the hospital. Then I got word from Evan Sisley that Mrs. Bush was having trouble breathing and was headed back. I headed there, too, mainly to hold President Bush's hand, as I knew he would be upset.

Once she was settled into her room, he insisted he get out of bed, get into his wheelchair, and go visit. He looked like hell: He had on a hospital gown, his hair was sticking straight up, and he was wearing an oxygen mask. But it didn't matter—Mrs. Bush was more or less out of it. She was not in a coma, but she wasn't with us, either.

He just sat by her bedside and held her hand. I was getting ready to leave and as I peeked in to say goodbye, her eyes suddenly opened and she looked at him and said, "My God, George, you are devastatingly handsome."

With that she closed her eyes; he looked at me and shrugged as if to say, "Well, it is what it is."

They flirted with each other until the very end.

Discussing his funeral was oddly one of President Bush's favorite topics of conversation between us. About once a year he would ask me to dig out his funeral file, which began as one small folder, and grew to fill an entire credenza by the time he died. He liked fiddling with the details—honorary pallbearers, music to be sung, sequence of events. Several major themes never changed:

- He wanted it to be short and simple. For a while, this included no service of any kind in Washington, DC. A group of us finally convinced him—I think we really convinced Mrs. Bush—to change his mind, including to lie in state at the U.S. Capitol and then have a full state funeral at the National Cathedral. He agreed, as long as no one spoke too long.
- He wanted a simple coffin, similar to what his Navy comrades would have been buried in during World War II. Captain Kevin Wensing, on the secretary of the Navy's staff at the Pentagon, searched high and low for such a coffin, only to let President Bush

know they were not made anymore. I caught him more than once shopping for a coffin on websites, and he came home from Pope John Paul II's funeral with high praise for his simple wooden coffin: "It was plain brown wood, just like I hope to have for my own casket," he wrote Hugh Sidey.

- Likewise, he wanted a simple cross for a headstone—the kind used in the military cemetery in Normandy—with his Navy number inscribed on the back. He often sketched into his funeral memos how he wanted his gravesite to look.

- He worried the formal military part of the ceremonies would take too long. He came home from every presidential funeral he attended—Nixon's, Reagan's, and Ford's—and told me to please tell the military people to walk and march faster. (I did and they didn't.)

President Bush of course managed to find humor in all the planning and preparation that goes into a presidential funeral. About five years or so before he died, Jim McGrath let me know that Fox News had asked if they could do a walk-through of the gravesite, as they already knew that was their pool camera assignment for President Bush's funeral. I am not even sure why I told President Bush—maybe I knew he would be amused—but he immediately had an idea: "Jean, wouldn't it be funny if when the Fox team got to the gravesite, I was lying on top of the ground with my hands crossed, just like a corpse?" No, I didn't think it would be funny. Thankfully, I talked him out of it. (In the end, the burial was private; no press.)

Around this same time the military team in charge of his funeral was doing some practice drills, including standing post at the Bushes' Houston parish, St. Martin's Episcopal Church, where President Bush would lie in repose during the night. Again, I mentioned to President Bush this would be happening, and again, he thought it would be fun to just show up and walk into the church to see how the soldiers would react. I sort of wish I had not talked him out of that one.

And of course he had some big ideas. His favorite was that after the funeral service in Houston, the family should travel by train to College Station for the burial at his presidential library. "We can eat lunch on the train," he excitedly told me.

"Well, the family will appreciate that, giving them some time to rest, too," I pointed out. I fear my insinuation might have been, "No lunch for you."

"Don't forget, Jean, I'll be on the train, too. I might not eat lunch, but I'll be there." And of course he was right.

As their health problems grew in scope and seriousness, the imminence of the Bushes' funerals increasingly became a weight on my shoulders and those of the rest of the staff. I completely quit traveling—I was too nervous to go out of town, since I knew the minute they died, I had to hit the ground running. And sleep was fleeting, especially when they were in the hospital.

The day after we buried President Bush, I sat alone on my couch in my living room in Houston and cried for about two hours. It was the first time I had cried all week. I confess that mixed into my grief was also a healthy dose of relief. He was gone, and I already missed him terribly. But we also were done. And except for the military walking very slowly, it had all gone well. I felt we had served him well.

But the road to get there had sometimes been bumpy.

One day in Maine, when I had worked all day on the funeral, I came home to houseguests who were ready to do something fun for the evening. I was exhausted, and a little frustrated at some of the problems I knew I needed to solve. All I wanted to do was open a bottle of wine and collapse.

One of my friends was not amused, and with major attitude, she said something like the following: "I don't understand what the big deal is. You've been planning this funeral for years. How is it you are not done yet? What is the big deal?"

My answer:

"Just imagine you are in charge of an event that will take place over

six days in three—maybe four—different cities and involves a cast of
thousands including presidents and queens and kings and members of
a very large family that live all over the United States who need to be
moved from where they live to Houston to Washington back to Houston
to College Station and back to their homes, all of which will be carried
live on television, morning, noon, and night for six days.

"And you have *no* idea when the event is going to happen. *None.* But
when it does, you have about forty-eight hours to pull all this together
before the show begins—again on live television for the next six days.
You won't sleep. You won't eat. You won't even really think. You just
have to do."

She never asked again.

When all the planning was done for President Bush's funeral, the
team oversaw twenty separate events, which included developing the
guest list, writing and issuing the invitations, collecting the RSVPs, and
then organizing the events themselves. We had two funeral services, a
burial service, four airport departure/arrival ceremonies, twelve special
groups to pay their respects in the Capitol Rotunda, and one train arrival
ceremony.

The weight of it all sat there for about six years, as we survived one
close call after another with the Bushes. Were they coming or going?

The first real brush with death was Christmas 2012 when a blood
clot migrated to President Bush's lung and almost killed him. I was at
a Houston Texans football game when one of President Bush's primary
care physicians called me. "You need to come right now," she said. "This
might be it."

Ironically I was at the game with three key members of the funeral
team—Laura Pears, in charge of the family; Roxann Neumann, who
was Jim McGrath's No. 2 on his media team; and Susie Peake, who
would be in charge of the family at the Houstonian Hotel when they
were in Houston. I turned to them and simply said, "This is it." And we
got up and left.

All Christmas plans were canceled. I called the team together and we started getting ready for what might come. But it didn't. As he did so often—back to the nine lives again—President Bush rallied.

Mrs. Bush chose not to tell her children just how seriously ill their father was. She didn't want to ruin their Christmases. Especially given the fact I had alerted the funeral teams in Houston, Washington, and College Station, I felt the family needed to know what was happening. Among other concerns, I didn't want them to hear it from someone else.

So I sent them an email that began with the plea, "This falls under the broadening category of things NOT TO TELL YOUR MOTHER."

A year later, Doro's emails were hacked and published on a website called The Smoking Gun, creating a media firestorm. Lucky for me, the *Houston Chronicle* chose to publish that particular email. Mrs. Bush did not speak to me for a couple of weeks.

Another time I raced the three hours from Austin back to Houston—and got stopped for speeding along the way[1]—because of yet another "this might be it" call. Again, President Bush rallied. The next day he asked me if he had "almost bought the farm last night." I suggested he discuss that with his doctor. "Do you know the answer?" he asked. "Tell me."

I confirmed he had almost died. "I thought so," he said. Then we went on to talk about other things.

This kind of thing went on for years. In 2015, while I was at lunch with the Bushes and while President Bush was in the bathroom, Mrs. Bush confided in me she was fairly certain she was dying. She told me not to tell anyone, but she thought I should know in case I "had things to do." When her husband returned to the table, we went on talking as if she had not dropped this bombshell on me. I called their doctor, Dr. Lenz, on the way back to the office and reported the conversation. His reaction: "Well, one day but I don't think tomorrow."

---

1. I did not get a ticket. I didn't do this often, but I gave the Texas Ranger my business card and explained why I was driving 80 mph. He told me to slow down—and Godspeed.

I once left a basketful of "stuff" halfway through a shopping spree at a Target store in Maine when Evan called and said, "You need to come right now." The scene in the emergency room was grim when I arrived. A few hours later President Bush was asking for a milk shake.

The scariest "close call" was when he broke his neck in the summer of 2015 as one of his medical aides was helping him get out of bed. Unfortunately, he fell and his neck hit a railing. But once again, he rallied.

Evan recalls that taking care of him after he'd suffered that injury might have been the most difficult: "He was the hardest patient to treat when it came to pain management because he never complained about having pain. A cervical vertebrae neck fracture had to be exceedingly painful but that wasn't who George Bush was."

He was, however, very grumpy about wearing a neck brace. The day he came home from the hospital, he defiantly took it off when he and I were alone in the bedroom. I took immediate action: I called Evan. He told Evan it was hot and uncomfortable and he was not going to wear it and he didn't have to wear it.

The former Navy medic listened and then told the former commander in chief respectfully but firmly: "Sir, who am I to order you to do something? But I do want you to make informed decisions. If you do not wear this neck brace, one of two things likely will happen: (1) You will die; (2) You will be paralyzed for the rest of your life. But it is your decision."

He looked at me. He glared at Evan. Then he said, "Give me the damn brace."

We had more close calls with President Bush than Mrs. Bush, although her congestive heart failure issues almost got the best of her in the summer of 2017. An ambulance was called to Walker's Point, and as she was leaving, she told her aide, Catherine Branch,[2] to inform me that if the media found out she was in the hospital, she would kill Jean Becker. An ambulance leaving Walker's Point was always hard to hide, but especially

---

2. Catherine now lives in Dallas.

so this time, since following the ambulance were two men named President George Bush. I asked Evan and 43's chief of staff, Freddy Ford, to hustle to the hospital and try to control the situation. They obviously succeeded—the media never found out she was there.

After she came home, I dreaded telling Mrs. Bush that there were many holes in her funeral plan and we really needed to tie up the loose ends. I felt my timing was awful—this was something I should have done years earlier—as I did not want her to think that we all thought her death was imminent.

She saved the day by telling me she was so glad I had brought it up, as she had some things she wanted to change or add. However, her main concern was not really about the funeral but what would happen to her dogs. She wondered out loud if she should take them with her. She adored her Maltipoos but no one else did. They bit everyone but her. Catherine quickly assured her she would take the dogs. (For the record, Mini-Me and Bibi ended up with Linda Poepsel and her husband, Jim.)

One of the decisions Mrs. Bush made in that meeting was to ask Jon Meacham to be one of her eulogists. When I called and asked Jon on her behalf, Jon said he would be honored.

Earlier that summer, Jon had come to Maine to visit with the Bushes and had spent some time reading *Destiny and Power* aloud to them. (Mrs. Bush said it was much better than books on tape.) Jon said reading to the man about whom he had written was overwhelming. When Jon left, it was left to Evan to finish reading *Destiny and Power* to President Bush, but Jon asked that as they approached the end of the book, to let him know and if he could, he would fly back to Maine and read President Bush the final chapter of his biography.

A month or so after I called Jon about being a eulogist, Evan told me he was almost done reading *Destiny and Power* to President Bush, so I better let Jon know in case he really did want to come back and finish the book. Obviously not giving enough thought to the email, I simply wrote in the subject line: "Heads up. The end is near."

My phone rang a few minutes later and it was Jon. He could barely speak, he was so broken up. "What happened?" he asked. "I didn't think it would be this soon."

"Well, Evan has been reading him a chapter a day," I said to Jon, thinking he was being a tad melodramatic. "They are almost done."

"What the hell are you talking about?" Jon asked.

"What the hell are *you* talking about?" I countered.

"Look at the email you just sent me. 'The end is near,'" said Jon. "Is Mrs. Bush dying or not?"

Jon still reminds me now and then of that incident.

When Mrs. Bush did die the following April, we were all surprised she went first. President Bush had been frail for years; her health was sort of ebb and flow. And it was not what she'd wanted. Numerous times she had told me—really informed me—that she wanted to die the day after her husband's funeral. She once looked at me as if to say, "Why aren't you writing this down? I just gave you an order."

But her time came before his. We called in hospice for her final week so she could die at home, and one of their suggestions was that she and President Bush have a frank discussion about what was happening. He needed to give her permission to go.

So with one of their doctors, Amy Mynderse, Evan and I sat down with President Bush to tell him what hospice needed for him to do. He was a little taken aback. "This is the worst news ever," he told us. He was not convinced his wife of seventy-three years was really dying. At first I was surprised by his reaction—how could he not know?—but this was the man who had dodged death so many times, I sort of saw his point. All three of us told him that, unfortunately, she was.

I told him I hoped he would stick around a little longer. He assured me he was. "I am not ready to go," he said. "My children will need me."

We then went downstairs to the den where the Bushes sat every evening watching a little TV. Mrs. Bush was drinking her usual Manhattan. President Bush went in and said to her: "Bar, I am not worried about you." She said, "George, I won't worry about you." Then he had a martini. It was all they needed to say.

Mrs. Bush died a few days later, with President Bush holding her hand—which in itself had been a difficult feat. The Bushes' power was out for three hours the day Mrs. Bush died, which meant President Bush could not use the elevator to get to her second-floor bedroom. The Secret Service carried him up the stairs.

The power came back on about the same time she passed.

Despite his grief, President Bush was amazing during the following few days. The day before the funeral, when it seemed all of Houston got in line to pay their respects as Mrs. Bush lay in state at St. Martin's, he decided while watching the coverage on television he must go and thank as many people as possible. The funeral team at the church held the line at the door while President Bush, with Doro at his side, paid his respects to his beloved wife. Despite the solemnity of the occasion, Doro reported that her father, even at that moment, tried to lighten the mood for the both of them by repeating one of his favorite lines: "You know it's not the cough that carries you off but the coffin that they carry you off in."[3]

The doors were then reopened so he could shake hands for as long as he could. He lasted only fifteen minutes before tiring out, but certainly he gave some of the mourners the surprise of a lifetime in meeting him. (As I write this at the height of the COVID-19 pandemic, I realize Evan was a man before his time. He made all of them use hand sanitizer before they shook President Bush's hand.)

The day of the funeral, President Bush hosted a brunch—with some major help from his oldest son—for all the former presidents and First

---

3. I want to give credit where credit is due and tell you who came up with this line. The internet cites numerous people, but I believe the line originated with British comedian George Formby Sr.

Ladies and First Lady Melania Trump, along with other VIPs. He made the trip to College Station to bury his wife, then ate a late lunch with a few of us before heading back to Houston. Much to my surprise, he went out that night for Tex-Mex with the family still in town.

And then he almost died the next day.

He had developed an infection that turned into sepsis. Evan was at the house when he realized what was going on and estimated he maybe had an hour to live, his blood pressure was so low. He told the agents there was no time to call an ambulance—they needed to get to Methodist with lights and siren NOW.

I raced to the ICU, where I found Neil and Doro, with George W. on the phone. They were meeting with one of the doctors, Dr. Clinton Doerr, who was seeking advice from the family on whether they should use lifesaving measures. I couldn't quit thinking of President Bush telling Evan and me that he wanted to stick around for his kids. So after listening to Dr. Doerr explain all the options, 43 called for a vote, telling Evan and me we should participate. I voted yes to lifesaving measures. We all did. (Dr. Doerr commented he felt like he was attending a cabinet meeting.)

As I was getting ready to leave, I asked Dr. Amy Mynderse, who was also there, if I should call the staff to the office or go to Sunday evening Mass, which had been my plan. "I need for you to go to Mass," she said.

Either the medicine or the prayers or both worked, as he rallied once again. But when we left for Maine for the summer a few weeks later, the doctors told Evan and me President Bush would likely come back to Houston in a coffin.

It was a bittersweet summer, beginning with the beginning.

Given that it would be President Bush's first summer since 1945 to come to Maine without Barbara Bush and given the great love in the Kennebunkport community for the Bushes, it occurred to me the day before President Bush arrived we needed to do something special. (I had arrived a few days earlier.) With the permission of the Secret Service— who were never thrilled with giving out a president's schedule—I sent an email first thing the morning of his arrival to as many people as possible and asked them to be on the street that afternoon to welcome him home. Just like the furniture incident eleven years earlier, the town was excited to help. Dave Berg, owner of Red Apple Campground, found a stash of American flags to give out, and a host of volunteers worked the sidewalks to let people know what was happening. I ran into a group of very excited French Canadian millennials who asked me if I knew that George Bush was coming. I think I acted surprised.

A teary-eyed President Bush waved at his friends, family, and tourists as his car went through downtown. It was a good beginning.

But he missed his wife of seventy-three years. He admitted to being a little lost that first night.

His children and grandchildren came and stayed as much as they could, and it was rare that at least one or two of them—usually more like a dozen of them—were not around.

Friends and other family also rallied round. More than one flew or drove in just to see him, which I warned them not to do, given if President Bush was having an off day, we might have to cancel at the last minute. President Bush worried about that as much as I did and encouraged me to tell people to come only if they were "in the area."

Suddenly the whole world swore they were "just passing by." People like Nick Brady, a longtime close friend and President Bush's secretary of the Treasury; and country singer Lee Greenwood, who came with his wife, Kim, and sang for President Bush in his living room. It wasn't long before President Bush caught on. "Where are they all going?" he asked me one day. "Canada?" But he loved the visits.

President Bush was a great music lover, so we surrounded him with as much as we could. Besides Lee Greenwood, gospel singer Michael W. Smith came to sing for him; George Dvorsky came and sang several times. President Bush's nephew Hap Ellis would drop by with his guitar and sing a few ballads.

As you now know, another favorite pastime of President Bush's was having someone read to him, so the family and staff did so almost every day. But he especially loved when the authors themselves came. That summer we managed to bring in a stellar lineup who were also good friends: Mark Updegrove read from *The Last Republicans*; historian Jeff Engel read from *When the World Seemed New: George H. W. Bush and the End of the Cold War*; Brad Meltzer read from *The First Conspiracy: The Secret Plot to Kill George Washington*.

But maybe the sweetest book reading that summer came from the Bushes' granddaughter Ellie LeBlond Sosa, who spent hours sharing with her grandfather the book she had written: *George and Barbara Bush: A Great American Love Story*.

Also helping to keep the mood light at Walker's Point was a great addition to President Bush's life that summer—a yellow Lab called Sully, a gift from America's VetDogs, whose members train and provide service dogs for wounded warriors. He wasn't sure he should say yes to the gift, but when told it would help spotlight the program and service dogs, he agreed.

President Bush really couldn't play with Sully, but he loved that his new dog followed him wherever he went. One of his greatest joys was watching Sully roughhouse with Marvin's two dogs—Lucille Ball and Ryan Zimmerman.[4] I learned early on it was pointless to try to talk to him about anything if the dogs were at play.

For years, the great-grandchildren had been a little afraid of Mrs. Bush's snippier dogs, so they loved this much bigger but gentler soul. But Sully's favorite playmate might have been President Bush 43, who is rumored to have once snuck Sully an entire cheeseburger.

But there was a sense of sadness that hung over Walker's Point that last summer. Barbara Bush was gone, and everyone knew George Bush's time was coming. At least once a week, I found myself crying with visitors as they left the house and walked down the driveway. It almost became part of my job—comforter in chief.

"I knew this would be the last time I saw him," remembers Chris-

---

4. The human Ryan Zimmerman plays for the Washington Nationals. I am going to assume you know who Lucille Ball was.

topher Buckley, one of the last nonfamily visitors to Walker's Point. "It was a struggle to keep my emotions in check as I sat beside him, holding his hand. To usurp a Bush family saying, I loved him more than tongue could tell. Losing him was going to be like losing a father."

Sometime around Labor Day, Evan suggested to me that he and I needed to have a conversation with President Bush about where he wanted to die. Once again, he had defied all odds and not died during the summer. But along with the doctors in Maine and Houston, Evan feared he might not survive the four-hour flight back to Texas. President Bush loved the coast of Maine and Walker's Point—it was where he had gone his entire life to recharge his batteries and refresh his soul. We guessed it might be where he would want to die.

When we sat down with him, we tiptoed around the question. We offered to stay with him in Maine as long as he wished.

"Are you asking me where I want to die?" President Bush finally asked us, even then doing what he always did so well: cut to the chase.

"Yes," we told him.

"Let's go home," he said. "Let's go to Houston."

The last weekend we were to be in Maine, the Bushes' granddaughter Barbara decided to get married in a quiet, family-only ceremony at Walker's Point, with her aunt Doro officiating, so her beloved Gampy could attend.

Thankfully, we had a good way to transport President Bush back to Houston. The Bushes' friend Phil Morse always gave the Bushes his plane to get from Houston to Maine and back—a Christmas gift that kept on giving. For this last trip, Evan arranged for two Maine doctors to travel with them, but he says it was still among the most nerve-racking four hours of his job.

I left two days ahead of President Bush, determined to make it back before he did in case the doctors' fears proved true. With the help of my friend and almost fiancé, George Dvorsky—and Zeke—we drove two thousand miles in two days.

When Evan called to say they were on the ground in Houston, I cried.

One big benefit of getting President Bush back to Houston was that it meant Secretary Baker was back in our lives. He had been such a rock for President Bush during the last few years, especially the last few months. He was almost the only "best friend" left.

President Bush's longtime best friend and college roommate, Lud Ashley,[5] had died in 2010. Bob Mosbacher also had died in 2010. General Scowcroft was dealing with his own serious health issues.[6] His best friends on the world stage—Brian Mulroney and John Major—had been amazing and had "dropped in" whenever they could. But they lived somewhere else.

Which left James A. Baker III.

They had been through thick and thin as friends, then as president and secretary of state, and now as friends again.

I knew the depth of the friendship went to the bottom of the ocean, yet even I was surprised by what Secretary Baker did toward the end of Mrs. Bush's life.

The Saturday before Mrs. Bush died, President Bush decided he would fly to St. Louis for his brother Bucky's memorial service. The doctors, Evan, and I did not want him to go. It was way too big of a day for him. He insisted otherwise. So staffer Laura Pears—whose job was to find planes when necessary—called our friend Keith Mosing and asked if he could take us. Keith had been quite generous over the years, especially when we were in a pinch. The plane Keith gave us was big, so we could bring Marvin and Doro, who attended their uncle Bucky's funeral, back to Houston with us.

Then a few days before the service, Secretary Baker called and asked if there was room for him on the plane. "I was very close to Bucky," he insisted. It's not that I thought he was lying, but after working for this

---

5. More formally, Thomas Ludlow Ashley, a Democratic congressman from Ohio from 1955 to 1981. Lud's death was the first one that I saw truly devastate President Bush.

6. General Scowcroft died in August 2020.

family for nearly thirty years, this was news to me. "I loved Bucky," Secretary Baker said.

It was obvious all day to me that he went to be with his friend, who had just lost his brother and was about to lose his wife. Susan Baker went to the house to be with Mrs. Bush while the rest of us went to St. Louis. When we got there, I could tell President Bush 43 was surprised to see Secretary Baker in our entourage. I think he knew, too.

On the way home, Secretary Baker asked if I thought it would be okay if he talked to President Bush about how it feels to lose one's wife. His first wife, Mary Stuart Baker, had died in 1970, and he told me he would not have survived that without George Bush. He now wanted to do the same for him—just be there. I said, "Of course." (I could never imagine telling Secretary Baker no about anything.) I told Marvin and Doro about the conversation, and we cried as we watched the two old friends visit.

A few months later, it was no surprise that on the day President Bush died, November 30, 2018, Secretary Baker came to the house twice—once earlier in the day, when President Bush asked him where they were going. "You are going to heaven," he told his friend. "That's where I want to go," President Bush replied.

And he and Susan were there that night when he passed, with Secretary Baker occasionally rubbing President Bush's feet. Also in the room were Neil and his wife, Maria; Neil's son Pierce and stepson Alexander; the Reverend Russ Levenson; Dr. Mynderse and Dr. Doerr; and trying to stand back—myself, Jim McGrath, Evan Sisley, and Marlon Harris, the head of President Bush's Secret Service detail. And, of course, Sully.

Doro was on a plane headed down from Washington; President Bush had spoken to all his children earlier in the day. His last phone call was with his oldest son, to whom he spoke his last words: "I love you, too."

And then he was gone.

I took a deep breath.

It was 10 p.m. on a Friday, and I needed to go to work.

★   ★   ★

So how does one get ready to plan and execute a presidential funeral?

You ask for lots of help, seek advice, and learn from those who died before you.

We'll start with those who "went first":

After every funeral they attended, the Bushes would call me even before they got home with what they liked and didn't like.

- After President Nixon's, they decided to be buried at the library instead of in Kennebunkport.
- After President Reagan's, President Bush said, "No riderless horse." Too dramatic.
- After President Ford's, they called to say they loved his service and wanted to use a lot of his ideas—especially music.
- General Scowcroft also called me after President Ford's funeral to say that he and Henry Kissinger wanted me to know that they were too old to serve as honorary pallbearers. They were cold, hungry, and stiff. "No one older than eighty should be pallbearers" was their joint pronouncement.
- Mrs. Bush took me with her to Betty Ford's funeral, so we could talk about her funeral on the way home. It proved to be enormously helpful.
- President Bush 43 called me right after Senator John McCain's funeral to tell me all the eulogies, except his, were too long.
- We also had learned a lot from Mrs. Bush's funeral—which was one service on one day in one city. But it helped me get ready for the much bigger show that was about to happen. I think her parting gift to me was to give me a chance for a dress rehearsal.

As for the advice, I used as a blueprint for President Bush's funeral the extensive memos President Reagan's chief of staff, Joanne Drake, and President Ford's personal lawyer, Greg Willard, wrote me after their presidents' funerals. Not long after President Bush's, I did the same for the chiefs of staff of Presidents Carter, Clinton, Bush 43, and Obama.

What were some of my biggest pieces of advice? What can go so wrong in a presidential funeral?

Just about everything…

One big problem surfaced almost the minute President Bush died.

My first job that night, after I was sure the immediate family all knew, was to call the rest of the staff, all of whom then had calls to make—our phone tree had sixty-three names in total, and then some of them had a list of people to call. We called our team leaders in each city; I called the eulogists—all of whom started crying. I finally put Prime Minister Mulroney and Senator Alan Simpson on the phone with Secretary Baker, since he was still at the house.

Before he told the media, and therefore the world, that President Bush had died, Jim McGrath was waiting for me to give him the thumbs-up that everyone we hoped would not find out from CNN had been notified. Done.

I was feeling pretty confident about the first hour or so when I got a call from Jason Denby, a member of our Washington team headed by former advance person Therese Burch. Big problem.

The historic Mayflower Hotel in Washington—which had been the headquarters for the Reagan and Ford funerals and with whom we had met at least five times to go over the details of how many rooms we would need, staff office space, and so on—was booked. No room at the inn.

So much for that plan and that huge file.

But Jason was ready. He had been checking hotel space all that month/week and knew we might be in trouble.

So at midnight that night, Jason called me from the Omni Shoreham Hotel to get my permission to book on his credit card (we did pay him back) every single remaining room they had left, including ballroom space to accommodate check-in and security clearance for the day of the funeral. He did all this through the front desk staff, who must have wondered, "Who on earth is this?" It was a big leap to book all the remaining rooms on a personal credit card. But we did, and Jason and the Omni saved the day.

One of the biggest challenges that I already knew might be coming, thanks to the Ford and Reagan funerals, was the problem of having hundreds of empty seats in the National Cathedral.

Much to my chagrin, every single member of Congress *and* their spouses are invited to presidential funerals. A large block of tickets also goes to the White House for the current administration; to the diplomatic corps; and to all fifty governors and their spouses.

Out of 3,061 seats in the National Cathedral, I had only eight hundred to use for the very large group of Bush family and friends, and the thousands of staffers who had worked for and with him during more than thirty years of public life, including eight political campaigns.

I spent years fighting this "tradition" of state funerals and lost. At the very least, I wanted to eliminate spouses. I am praying my former fellow chiefs of staff continue the fight and win.

The problem is—a lot of these people don't show up. And if Congress is not in session—which they were not for the Ford funeral since he died the day after Christmas—it literally could be hundreds and hundreds of seats. What's worse, I was warned, I probably wouldn't know for sure until around 5 p.m. the day before the funeral how many tickets came back to us.

The Ford plan enlisted dozens of Boy Scouts to serve as ushers and to fill any last-minute empty seats. And yes, the Scouts were thrilled to do so.

So thanks to their heads-up, I was ready. Here is what I wrote to the Carter, Clinton, Bush, and Obama teams to get them ready for the same possibility:

- I overinvited. It made my team nervous. I was given eight hundred seats to fill at the Cathedral, and we invited 1,654 people. Given the age of a lot of the Bushes' friends and given that a lot of their friends—like yours—have busy lives, I assumed only 75 percent of those invited would be able to come, which was what I was told was standard. Our RSVP rate was 82 percent, so for about twelve hours, I had 213 people coming I could not seat. Yes, I was a tad nervous. I ate ten cookies. Congress RSVPs were supposed to close at noon, but I didn't hear from them until 5 p.m. Five hundred seats. Gulp. But 213 were filled immediately.

- I assigned one hundred seats to the CIA; they knew that might happen as I gave them a heads-up. So if possible, have a group of people in the wings ready to fill seats. My backup idea was sailors from the aircraft carrier. (Note: When I told my CIA contact I would need their ticket holders' names so I could put them on the "admit" list, they told me not to worry about that. Fascinating.)

- We had a "B" funeral list: people we wanted to invite, but we'd just run out of space. A lot of our "B" list were more staffers from the White House days; friends but maybe not necessarily best friends; people who previously had served on some of our nonprofit boards; and people who had called the office and complained about not being invited. When they called to protest—unless they were way out of line—they went on the "B" list.

We invited the "B" list to attend the departure ceremony at Andrews Air Force Base after the funeral. This was key, to invite them to something right away. As a result, many of them made plans to come to Washington for the departure ceremony. So we had a built-in group, ready to go. They all found out by email at six o'clock the night before they were invited to the funeral. They didn't even have to RSVP. We told them just to come pick up their tickets. (Some of them had to buy funeral clothes although I warned them this might happen; another unnamed person complained to me after the funeral if he had known there was a chance he would get into the cathedral, he maybe would have come. I was nice and didn't tell him he wasn't paying attention.)

We filled every seat, including the balconies, which the cathedral gave back to me in the eleventh hour to help.

★   ★   ★

As for getting good help—the true heroes that week were the incredible team we had. My longtime assistant, Nancy Lisenby, was my No. 2 on all things funeral, and by the end she knew more and did more than I did. All of the Office of George Bush staff were stars, heading their own teams and own projects. We also had hundreds of volunteers—many of them former staffers, especially former advance men and women—plus hotel staff, bus drivers, the Secret Service and police, church personnel, and so many others. They all found out late on a Friday night that President Bush had died, but by the time Air Force One was wheels up from Houston the following Tuesday morning for Washington, DC, we were in full operating mode.

I would love to list all their names but cannot. But I must mention Mike Wagner, head of National Events Planning for the Military District of Washington. Mike's office does inaugurations and presidential funerals. President Bush had nicknamed Mike (and his predecessor) "Dr. Death," a moniker President Bush 43 adopted by the end of the funeral. Mike was (I think) a good sport about it.

Although there were hundreds of things the Office of George Bush team had to plan, organize, and run, there were another hundred things we didn't have to do, thanks to Mike and his team. They were lifesavers. So much so I have forgiven Mike, and hopefully President Bush has also, that the military really does walk/march too slowly.

At the end of the day, what are some of my most lasting memories from funeral week?

- We'll begin with Sully. That week he became a rock star, and to this day has more than two hundred thousand followers on Instagram. It began with a photo Evan took of Sully lying in front of President Bush's casket, and ended when he got off Air Force One with the family in Washington, DC. He really was not part of the official traveling party, but now that President Bush was gone, Sully's next posting was to be Walter Reed Army Medical Center in Bethesda, Maryland. Evan and I decided the best way to get him there was to just take him with us on the plane. When we landed, I got the job of escorting Sully off, and as I stood on the tarmac waiting for the family and the casket to deplane, one of our volunteers came running up to me to say the press wanted to know if I would mind (I immediately assumed they were going to ask for an interview) getting out of the way. I was between Sully and the cameras.

• Watching the Bush family. Obviously, this was tough for them, especially since they had just lost their mom. But as always, they amazed me. And as always, they made me smile. Their oldest brother had told all of them that during the Capitol Rotunda ceremony, there would be no dramatics. No Nancy Reagan who had draped herself on her husband's casket. (Mrs. Bush also had told me several times over the years she would not "drape.") As a result, when it came time for them to pay their respects, they walked around the casket about 50 mph. Doro told me later she wanted to slow down and touch the flag, but she was afraid she would miss the motorcade to Blair House,[7] where they all were staying. However, following their father's example in Houston, they returned to the Rotunda that evening to shake the hands of some of the thousands of people who stood in line throughout the night to pay their respects to their dad.

• Senator Bob Dole insisting he get out of his wheelchair and salute the casket.

---

7. Blair House, operated by the State Department, is sort of the guesthouse for the country. It's where visiting heads of state often stay; where presidents-elect and their families stay the night before Inauguration Day; and where the family of a deceased president stays during the Washington part of the service.

- I cried watching the fifteen personal aides who had served President Bush pay their respects in the Capitol Rotunda. No group of men loved President Bush more.[8]
- The people who called and begged for tickets to the funeral. "It's the hottest ticket in town," one caller complained. It was fascinating. Yes, some of them are people you would know. I would love to tell you who, but I know President Bush would not approve. (One of my *not*-favorite things: dealing with last-minute seating hassles caused by people who didn't get along and couldn't sit next to each other. Sorry. No names.)
- Watching the former presidents gather for the funeral reminded me of President Bush admitting to me he rather enjoyed state funerals. I could tell they were enjoying their reunion while at the same time dealing with their genuine sorrow at losing one of their own. The forty-third president sat with his family, of course, and across the aisle from his presidential peers. But after he came into the church, he went over to shake their hands and thank them for coming—and to give Michelle Obama a mint. It was a bit of an inside joke gone viral when the cameras had caught him doing the same at Senator McCain's funeral earlier that year.
- President Bush 43 breaking down at the end of his eulogy, which he was determined not to do. His brother Jeb later teased him, "You made it to the one-yard line."
- On the train from Houston to College Station, a group of cowboys lined up on horseback tipped their hats as we went by. We all dissolved into tears.
- When the train pulled into College Station, thousands of Aggies were waiting to welcome their hero back to campus as the band

---

8. They were, in order of service: Will Farish, Donald Ensenat, David Bates, Joe Hagin, Don Bringle, Sean Coffey, Tim McBride, Bruce Caughman, Bill Farish, Michael Dannenhauer, Gian-Carlo Peressutti, Tom Frechette, Jim Appleby, Coleman Lapointe, and Evan Sisley.

played the "Aggie War Hymn." The relationship between President Bush and Texas A&M had been a love affair since the library and school opened in 1997. It was the perfect ending for his journey.

- The quiet of the burial itself, with just the family; the Bushes' two priests—the Reverend Levenson from St. Martin's and the Reverend Peter Cheney from St. Ann's in Maine; and two sets of best friends: Jim and Susan Baker; and Will and Sarah Farish. (Jon Meacham, Evan Sisley, and I watched from a discreet distance.) It was the perfect solemn yet sweet ending to a long few days. No cameras, no media, no onlookers. Just them.

- Most of the Bush family left straight from College Station to go home. I rode the bus back to Houston with Neil and his family, some of our staff and funeral team members, and a few others. Thanks to Neil, we told stories the entire two-hour trip. It was almost like the wake we didn't have. It was two of my favorite hours of the week.

- The last line of Jon Meacham's eulogy is still in my heart: "He was always extending a hand, always opening that big, vibrant, inclusive, all-enveloping heart. And if we listen closely enough, we can hear that heart beating even now, for it is the heartbeat of a lion—a lion who not only led us, but who loved us."

As is tradition, members of President Bush's Secret Service detail stood post at his gravesite through the night. The head of the detail, Marlon Harris, sent a message to his bosses in Washington at six o'clock the next morning to tell them the Bush detail's work was done. His final words echoed what was in the hearts of many:

"Godspeed, Former President George H. W. Bush—you will be missed by all of us."

EPILOGUE

I t was a cold, rainy Friday afternoon right before Christmas 2008, at the end of what I remember had been a long week. I had just finished a great working lunch with President and Mrs. Bush and Bush School professor Jeff Engel.[1] I say "great" with one caveat: We decided we were the only patrons of the restaurant who were (1) not attending a Christmas party lunch, and (2) not slightly inebriated.

My game plan for the rest of the day was quite simple: Get back to the office and tie up some loose ends, then go home and collapse on my couch and watch Christmas movies.

Then President Bush had a better idea. Of course.

"Jean, Bar and I are going to that new supermarket, Central Market. We hear it's something else. Why don't you go with us?"

First, it was not "new." It had opened a few years earlier, but they were just getting around to checking it out. It was a little like their

---

1. A historian and a professor, Jeff was at this point the director of the Bush School's Scowcroft Institute for International Affairs. President Bush was hoping Jeff one day would be dean of the school, but Southern Methodist University snatched him away before that happened.

watching George Clooney in reruns of *ER* on TNT. Most of us had been there, done that.

I had no interest in or intention of going to one of the most popular grocery stores in Houston on a rainy Friday afternoon when the traffic would be gridlocked and the store would be worse. Nope. Not gonna do it.

So about twenty minutes later I pulled into the parking lot at Central Market and met the Bushes inside.

They decided to split up. Mrs. Bush got a full-sized basket and was going to walk the entire store. President Bush wanted to go straight to the cheese section. I decided to go with her but she shooed me away, asking me to go help her husband so he wouldn't take forever.

Off she went and off we went. The head of the cheese department magically appeared, offering President Bush samples of this cheese and that, and recommending the best crackers to use with each. After about thirty minutes or so, he made his choices and was ready to go.

But where was Mrs. Bush?

I offered to go find her, but a Secret Service agent waved me off, discreetly saying into his radio: "Timberwolf is looking for Tranquility. Location?"[2]

A few minutes later she appeared, still pushing her full-sized basket with one large sweet potato sitting in the middle. And nothing else.

"I know exactly what you are thinking," she said, noticing my surprised look. "You are thinking this sweet potato is too big for just George and me, but we will eat it. We love sweet potatoes."

No, that was not what I was thinking at all.

President Bush did not seem to think it was odd that Mrs. Bush had bought only one thing in the largest grocery store in Houston. He felt his cheese would pair nicely with the sweet potato, so they happily declared their field trip a success and headed for the checkout.

---

2. Timberwolf and Tranquility were the Bushes' Secret Service code names, which I can now tell you only because they don't need them anymore.

The lines were long, and the people in them were starstruck. I gently suggested that I stay and purchase the items and they go home. They would have none of it, so the three of us waited to make our purchases. (I bought a poinsettia—well, President Bush paid for it.)

We then hugged goodbye and went our separate ways—them with a sweet potato and some cheese, me with my plant.

And another cherished memory.

How could I have not wanted to go?

Working for George and Barbara Bush and being part of their lives was like unwrapping a big Christmas gift at least once a week. I was never disappointed.

Yes, there were moments so huge that now I sometimes wonder if they even happened: meeting kings and queens and even a few dictators; traveling the world and visiting faraway places like Moscow and Hanoi; commissioning an aircraft carrier and opening the Olympics; and, just once, spending the night in the Lincoln Bedroom.

How lucky was I?

Yet it was moments such as our trip to the grocery store that I treasure the most, little pieces of their lives that were simple, basic, and yet the most magical.

They really had no idea what special people they were. Which of course is what made them so special.

Even President Bush's gift buying was—well, special. Over the years for Christmas he bought me, among other things, a George Foreman grill; a set of golf clubs, although I didn't play golf; a bright yellow carry-on bag (which I still use); my first iPad; a jacket he had made in Hong Kong, which was two sizes too small; and a gift certificate to Neiman Marcus to buy new clothes. I wasn't sure how to take that one.

He also once bought me a new car, because my old one had a very large dent, and I had whined to him about having to find the time to get it fixed. A few days later, a new car—the exact same model I had—

magically appeared. Problem solved. (I couldn't decide if I should whine more or less to him. I opted for less.)

He also gave the staff very generous year-end bonuses. One year he said in his handwritten note to me: "A year-end bonus for the one who saves my life every day and brings me great happiness and lots of smiles. You da woman! Love—GB."

If I saved his life, he made my life.

He was not only my boss. He was my mentor, my friend, and my biggest cheerleader. There was nothing we did not talk about, from life and death, to current events, to what was happening in everyone's life, and yes, to baseball.

I felt I could ask him anything, and I am sure he felt the same.

The most interesting question he ever asked me was very close to the end. He wanted to know if I believed in hell, and if yes, who did I think was there. I told him off the top of my head: Adolf Hitler and Saddam Hussein. (I did report this conversation to his priest, the Reverend Russ Levenson, as I felt once again I was practicing without a license.)

The funniest question he ever asked me—and he was serious: "Jean, just what is a 'Kardashian'?"

After he died, Linda Poepsel gave me a secret file she kept in her desk, marked "personal." It was filled with emails and correspondence that President Bush did not want sent to his presidential library—at least not yet.

You could say this file had replaced Don Rhodes's oven.

I was deeply touched to find in the file an email I had written him on July 19, 2007. Reading it twelve years later, I realized it described exactly how I felt about him and about being his chief of staff.

So it is how I'd like to end this journey you have taken with me by sharing something else with you from "the oven."

Sir,

Ok, please allow me to get slightly mushy and then I'll get over it.

I loved traveling with you yesterday[3] because it was a wonderful reminder (not that I needed to be reminded) of what a truly remarkable person you are. Your ability to connect with every single person you meet, young or old, to make them all feel special, to make them all feel important is amazing. You always say the exact right thing at the exact right time.

And even when you are tired, you still do this. I know you would love to quit having to make these kinds of trips, and I don't blame you and I completely support you in that desire. But when you do leave the stage, Ross Perot will finally hear that giant sucking sound he always talked about. It will be like the air being left out of a very giant tire.

You are, in two words, a rock star, and I feel very grateful and blessed to be part of your life.

---

3. President Bush and I had traveled to Philadelphia, where he attended a lunch for Points of Light and visited the National Constitution Center.

I am not sure I ever told you this but in case I didn't, I must: Many years ago when Eddie decided to become a priest, I told him I was somewhat jealous that he had figured out what his calling in life was, and I told him I feared I would go to my grave never figuring out mine. Eddie was surprised by this, because he said he assumed I knew that I had heard my calling and was doing exactly what God wanted, and that was working for one of His truly special people. That would be you. Eddie said you were my calling, and I knew then, and have known ever since, that he was right.

Love,
Jean

Afterwords

President Bush hated the word "legacy." He hated it almost as much as he hated broccoli. I learned early on never to eat the latter in his presence and to try very hard not to say the former.

But he's not here, so we are going to talk about his legacy.

At the beginning of this book, I asked the question: How did he go from losing his reelection bid in 1992 to being one of the most revered men in the country and the world when he died almost exactly twenty-six years later?

I hope by now that question has been answered through the stories I have shared, and I hope you've gotten to know the man I knew.

But now we'll let some others have their say—specifically, his six eulogists at his two funeral services.[1]

The first four were given at the state funeral service at the National Cathedral in Washington, DC.

Jon Meacham

Shortly after dawn on Saturday, September 2, 1944, Lieutenant Junior Grade George Herbert Walker Bush, joined by two crewmates, took off from the USS *San Jacinto*. The mission: to attack a radio tower on

---

1. I am using the text of the eulogies as written for delivery.

Chichijima. The weather was clear, but the air was heavy with flak from Japanese guns. The plane was hit. Smoke filled the cockpit. Flames raced along the wings. *My God*, Lt. Bush thought, *this thing's gonna go down.*

But he stayed on point. He kept the plane in its thirty-five-degree dive, struck his target, and then roared off, out to sea, telling his crew-mates to "hit the silk!" Following protocol, Lt. Bush turned the plane so that they could bail out. Only then, at about two thousand feet above the waves, did Bush parachute from the cockpit. At full force the wind propelled him backward. He gashed his head and bruised his eye on the tail as he flew through the sky.

Lt. Bush plunged deep into the ocean. His head was bleeding, his eyes were burning, and his mouth and throat were raw from salt water. Flopping onto a tiny raft, alone, the future forty-first president sensed that his men had not made it. Overcome, he wept. He felt the weight of responsibility as a nearly physical burden. At four minutes shy of noon, a submarine emerged to rescue the downed pilot. Awarded the Distin-guished Flying Cross for his heroism that day, George Herbert Walker Bush was safe.

The story—his story, and ours—would go on, by God's grace. Through the decades President Bush often asked himself: "Why me? Why was I spared?" His life was no longer wholly his own. In his mind the years he was given had to be devoted to the service of his nation, of his family, of his friends, and of his God. There were always more mis-sions to undertake, more lives to touch, more love to give.

And what a headlong race he made of it all. He *never* slowed down. He once shook the hand of a department-store mannequin in New Hamp-shire, seeking primary votes. ("Never know," he recalled. "Always gotta ask." You can hear the voice, can't you? As Dana Carvey said, the key to a Bush 41 impersonation was "Mr. Rogers trying to be John Wayne.")

George Herbert Walker Bush was America's last great soldier-statesman, a twentieth-century Founding Father. He governed with virtues that most closely resemble those of Washington and of Adams, of TR and of FDR, of Truman and of Eisenhower—of men who believed in causes larger than themselves, who favored the common good over personal gain, and who cared more for the fates of others than they did their own political fortunes.

Six-foot-two, handsome, dominant in person, he spoke with his big, strong hands, making fists to underscore his points. President Bush was a firm believer that to whom much is given, much is expected.

And because life gave him much, he gave back. He stood in the breach in the Cold War he brought to a peaceful conclusion. He stood in the breach in Washington against division and unthinking partisanship. He stood in the breach against tyranny and discrimination; on his watch a wall fell in Berlin, a dictator's naked aggression did not stand, and doors opened to the disabled across America. And he stood in the breach against heartbreak and hurt. His capacity to charm and to comfort and to reassure was an essential element of his soul. Strong and gracious, steely and shrewd, magnetic and kind, loving and loyal, he was our shield in danger's hour.

There was ambition, too, of course: loads of that. Politics, he once told me, "isn't a pure undertaking—not if you want to win, it's not." An imperfect man, he left us a more perfect union.

And it must be said that for a keenly intelligent statesman of stirring private eloquence, public speaking was not a strong suit. "Fluency in English," President Bush once remarked, "is something that I'm often not accused of." Looking ahead to the 1988 election, he observed that "it's no exaggeration to say the undecideds could go one way or another."

His tongue may have run amok at moments, but his heart and his mind were steadfast. His life code, as he said, was: "Tell the truth. Don't blame people. Be strong. Do your best. Try hard. Forgive. Stay the course."

It was—and is—the most American of creeds. Lincoln's "better angels of our nature" and George H. W. Bush's "thousand points of light" are companion verses in America's national hymn, for Lincoln and Bush both summoned us to choose the right over the convenient, to hope rather than to fear, to heed not our worst impulses but our best instincts.

In his years as vice president, he was visiting a children's leukemia ward in Krakow. Thirty-five years before, he and Barbara had lost a daughter, Robin, to the disease. In Krakow, a small boy wanted to greet the American vice president. Learning that the child was sick with the cancer that had taken Robin, Bush began to cry.

To his diary, he dictated: "My eyes flooded with tears, and behind me was a bank of television cameras. I thought, 'I can't turn around. I can't dissolve because of personal tragedy in the face of... the nurses that give of themselves every day.' So I stood there looking at this little guy, tears running down my cheek, hoping he wouldn't see, but, if he did, hoping he'd feel that I loved him."

He was always extending a hand, always opening that big, vibrant, inclusive, all-enveloping heart. And if we listen closely enough, we can hear that heart beating even now, for it is the heartbeat of a lion—a lion who not only led us, but who loved us.

Prime Minister Brian Mulroney

Do you remember where you were the summer you left your teenage years behind and turned twenty?

I was working as a laborer in my hometown in Northern Quebec, trying to make enough money to finance my years at law school. It was a tough job, but I was safe and secure and had the added benefit of my mother's home cooking every night.

On September 2, 1944—as we have just heard—twenty-year-old Lieutenant George Bush was preparing to attack Japanese war installations in the Pacific.

He was part of a courageous generation of young Americans who led the charge—against overwhelming odds—in the historic and bloody battle for supremacy in the Pacific against the colossal military might of Imperial Japan.

That's what George Bush did the summer he turned twenty.

Many men of differing talents and skills have served as president and many more will do so as the decades unfold, bringing new strength and glory to these United States of America.

And fifty or one hundred years from now, as historians review the accomplishments and context of all who have served as president, I believe it will be said that in the life of this country—which is, in my judgment, the greatest democratic republic that God has ever placed on the face of this earth—no occupant of the Oval Office was more courageous, more principled, and more honorable than George Herbert Walker Bush.

George Bush was a highly accomplished man who also had a delightful sense of humor and was a lot of fun.

At his first NATO meeting as the new U.S. President, George—who sat opposite me—took copious notes as the heads of governments spoke. We were limited in time.

It is very flattering to have the president of the U.S. take notes as you speak and, even someone as modest as me, threw in a few adjectives here and there to extend the pleasure of the experience.

After President Mitterrand, Prime Minister Thatcher, and Chancellor Kohl had spoken it was the turn of the Prime Minister of Iceland who—as President Bush continued to write—went on and on and on and on—ending only when the Secretary General of NATO firmly decreed a coffee break.

George put down his pen, walked over to me, and said: "Brian, I have just learned the fundamental principle of international affairs." "What's that?" I asked. Bush replied, "The smaller the country, the longer the speech."

In the second year of the Bush presidency, responding to implacable pressures from the Reagan and Bush administrations, the Soviet Union imploded. This was the most epochal political event of the twentieth century.

An ominous situation that could have become extremely menacing to world security was instead deftly channeled by the leadership of President Bush into the broad and powerful currents of freedom, providing the Russian people with the opportunity to build an embryonic democracy in a country that had been ruled by czars and tyrants for a thousand years.

As the Berlin Wall collapsed soon thereafter and calls for freedom cascaded across central and Eastern Europe, leaving dictators and dogma in the trash can of history, no challenge assumed greater importance for Western solidarity than the unification of Germany within an unswerving NATO. But old fears in Western Europe and unrelenting hostility by the military establishment in the U.S.S.R. and the Warsaw Pact rendered this initiative among the most complex and sensitive ever undertaken. One serious misstep and the entire process could have been compromised, perhaps irretrievably.

There is obviously no more knowledgeable or competent judge of what really happened at this most vital juncture of twentieth-century history than Chancellor Helmut Kohl of Germany himself. In a speech to a parliamentary commission of the Bundestag, he said categorically that this historic initiative of German reunification could never have succeeded without the brilliant leadership of President Bush.

Much has been written about the first Gulf War. Simply put, the coalition of twenty-nine disparate nations assembled under the aegis of the United Nations—including for the first time many influential Arab countries—and led by the United States will rank with the most spectacular and successful international initiatives ever undertaken in modern history, designed to punish an aggressor, defend the cause of freedom, and ensure order in a region that had seen too much of the opposite for far too long. This was President Bush's initiative from beginning to end.

President Bush was also responsible for the North American Free Trade Agreement—recently modernized and improved by new administrations—which created the largest and richest free trade area in the history of the world, while also signing into law the Americans with Disabilities Act which transformed the lives of millions of Americans forever.

President Bush's decision to go forward with strong environmental legislation, including the Clean Air Act that resulted in an Acid Rain Accord with Canada, is a splendid gift to future generations of Americans and Canadians to savor in the air they breathe, the water they drink, the forests they enjoy, and the lakes, rivers, and streams they cherish.

There is a word for this: it is called "leadership"—and let me tell you that when George Bush was president of the United States of America, every single head of government in the world knew they were dealing with a true gentleman, a genuine leader—one who was distinguished, resolute, and brave.

I do not keep a diary, but occasionally I write private notes after important personal or professional events. One occurred at Walker's Point in Kennebunkport, Maine, on September 2, 2001. Mila and I had been spending our traditional Labor Day weekend with George and Barbara, and towards the end he and I had a private conversation. My notes capture the moment.

I told George how I thought his mood had shifted over the last eight years. From a series of frustrations and moments of despondency in 1993 to the high enthusiasm of the Houston launch of the Presidential Library and George W.'s election as governor in November 1994, to the delight following Jeb's election in 1998, followed by their great pride and pleasure with George W.'s election to the presidency, to the serenity we found today in both Barbara and George. They are truly at peace with themselves, joyous in what they and the children have achieved, gratified by the goodness that God has bestowed upon them all, and genuinely content with the thrill and promise of each passing day.

At that, George, who had tears in his eyes as I spoke, said: "Brian, you've got us pegged just right—and the roller coaster of emotions we've experienced since 1992. Come with me."

He led me down the porch at Walker's Point to the side of the house that fronts the ocean and pointed to a small, simple plaque that had been unobtrusively installed some days earlier. It read: "C-A-V-U."

He said: "Brian, this stands for 'Ceiling and visibility unlimited.' When I was a terrified eighteen- to nineteen-year-old pilot in the

Pacific, those were the words we hoped to hear before takeoff. It meant perfect flying. That's the way I feel about our life today—C-A-V-U—everything is perfect. Bar and I could not have asked for better lives. We are truly happy and truly at peace."

As I looked over the waters off Walker's Point on that golden September afternoon in Maine, I was reminded of the lines—simple and true—that speak to the nature of George Bush and his love of family and precious surroundings.

There are wooden ships,
There are sailing ships,
There are ships that sail the sea.
But the best ships are friendships
And may they always be.

Senator Alan Simpson

I first met my dear friend in 1962 when my father, Milward Simpson, was elected to the United States Senate, and I came back to Washington with Dad to settle into his new office, being vacated by one Senator Prescott Bush—George's father!

We met again when my parents left Washington and sold their home to a brand-spanking-new Texas congressman named George H. W. Bush. George and Barbara, Mom and Pop did that sale on a handshake. Sound familiar?

I came to the Senate in 1978, and soon after that Ronald Reagan cornered me and asked me to support him for president. I said I would—not knowing my friend George would enter the fray. Hearing that, I called and said, "George, I want to tell you, I'd love to help, but I've already committed to Ronald Reagan." George's response? "Well Al, I'm sorry about that, I probably should have let you know sooner. And actually, a guy doesn't get many calls from a friend who says they can't support you!" Sound familiar? Of course it does, because in George

Bush's theme of life, during all the highs and lows, there's a simple credo, "What would we do without family and friends?" When he became vice president, our enjoyable relationship was refreshed, and the four of us had many pleasant times together.

Now my life in Washington was rather tumultuous. I went from the A social list to the Z list, and never came back up to the A! In one dark period I was feeling pretty low and all my wounds were self-inflicted. George called me early one morning (always early in the morning!), country music playing in the background. He said, "I see the media is shootin' you pretty full of holes"—actually he said it a bit more pungently!! He said, "Why don't we go up to Camp David? You and Ann come over—and we'll have a weekend together." At that time his popularity rating was 93 percent. And mine was .93 percent! Off we went, the media all gathered as we headed to Marine One. George said, "Now wave to your pals over there in the media, Al!" They didn't wave back! Next morning he's rattling through all the U.S. papers, and he looks up and says, "Ah-hah, here's the one I'm looking for!" A picture of Barbara and Ann, and George with his arm and hand on my back. Later, we're having a sauna, and I said, "George, I'm not unmindful as to what you are doing. You are propping up your old wounded-duck of a pal, while you are at the top of your game, you reach out to me while I'm tangled in rich controversy and taking my lumps." He said, "Yup. Well, there were staff members who told me not to do this. But Al, this is about friendship and loyalty." Sound familiar?

We had an awful lot of fun, too. Always a delight to be in the president's box at the Kennedy Center, slip off to a play at the National Theater or the Warner with the Bushes. Outside the president's box one evening there was a massive six-foot vase with an extraordinary glaze (you know the difference between a vase and a "vahse"? Thirty-five bucks!). George walked up to it and said, "Al, wait I think that's Etruscan. I noticed that blue-grayish glaze from that period, a clay that could only be found during that era." And I said, "No, no, George, the patina there gives me the perception that it was possibly older, perhaps of Greek origin with that particular herbal paste before firing."

Folks of course gathered around, mumbling about these "expert" observers. Barbara and Ann finally came by and said, "Get out of here. Both of you. Get back in that box!"

Well, it was impressive for a while! Then of course one night we four went to see Michael Crawford, singing the songs of Andrew Lloyd Webber. All four of us were singing as we went back to the White House, "Don't cry for me, Argentina!" and tidbits from the *Phantom* and other magic of Webber. A few days later he's getting hammered by the press for some extraordinarily petty bit of trivia, and suddenly he sings out, "Don't cry for me, Argentina!" The press then thought he was surely losing his marbles!

These honored guests here before us who have held this noble post know well of the slings and arrows of outrageous fortune. His was a class act—from birth to death. He housed the strong sinews in mind and body gained from an extraordinary mother (we compared our mothers as "velvet hammers" and, of course, certainly most awesome fathers).

The history books will—and are—treating him most fairly while uncovering other powerful traits: his great competitiveness, raw courage, and self-discipline. Recall the Andrews Air Base conclave where congressional participants drafted a remarkable bill that dealt with two-year budgeting, entitlement reform, comprehensive and catastrophic health care, Social Security solvency, and much more—but it required a critical ingredient called "revenue." Translated into the word "taxes"— translated into the words, "Read my lips"—and the group went to George Bush and said, "We can get this package done, but we must have some revenue." And he said, "What I've said on that subject sure puts a helluva lot of heat on me." They all said, "Yes, but we can get it done— and it will be bipartisan." George said, "Okay. Go for it—but it will be a punch in the gut." Bob Dole, a loyal warrior for George, took it back to the Senate, where we won a strong bipartisan vote and it went over to the House where his own party turned on him—surely one of the main factors assuring his return to private life! But he often said, "When the really tough choices come, it's the country—it's not me, or the Democrats, or the Republicans, it's for our country—that I fought for."

He was a man of such great humility. Those who travel the high road of humility in Washington, DC, are not bothered by heavy traffic! He had one serious flaw known by all close to him. He loved a good joke—the richer the better—and he'd throw his head back and give that great laugh—but he never could remember a punch line! Ever!

The punch line for George Herbert Walker Bush is this: "You would have wanted him on your side!" He never lost his sense of humor. Humor is the universal solvent against the abrasive elements of life. He never hated anyone. He knew what his mother and my mother always knew: "Hatred corrodes the container it's carried in." The most decent and honorable person I ever met was my friend George Bush. One of nature's noblemen. His epitaph? Perhaps just a single letter—the letter *L* for "Loyalty." It coursed through his blood. Loyalty to his country, loyalty to his family, loyalty to his friends, loyalty to the institutions of government, and always, always—a friend to his friends!

None of us were ready for this day. We mourn his loss from our own lives, and what he was to each of us. That is so personal, so intimate, so "down inside." It would have been so much easier to celebrate his life with him here! But he is gone. Irrevocably gone. We have now loosed our grip upon him, but we shall always retain his memory in our hearts. God has come now to take him back. We all knew on one unknown day he would return to his God. Now we give him up. We commend him to your loving hands. Thank you for him. God rest his soul.

President George W. Bush

Distinguished guests, including our presidents and First Ladies, government officials, foreign dignitaries, and friends: Jeb, Neil, Marvin, Doro, and I, and our families, thank you all for being here.

I once heard it said of man that "the idea is to die young as late as possible."

At age eighty-five, a favorite pastime of George H. W. Bush was firing up his boat, the *Fidelity*, and opening up the three 300-horsepower engines to fly—joyfully fly—across the Atlantic, with Secret Service boats straining to keep up.

At ninety, George H. W. Bush parachuted out of an aircraft and landed on the grounds of St. Ann's by the Sea in Kennebunkport, Maine—the church where his mom was married and where he'd worshipped often. Mother liked to say he chose the location just in case the chute didn't open.

In his nineties, he took great delight when his closest pal, James A. Baker, smuggled a bottle of Grey Goose vodka into his hospital room. Apparently, it paired well with the steak Baker had delivered from Morton's.

To his very last days, Dad's life was instructive. As he aged, he taught us how to grow old with dignity, humor, and kindness—and, when the Good Lord finally called, how to meet Him with courage and with joy in the promise of what lies ahead.

One reason Dad knew how to die young is that he almost did it— twice. When he was a teenager, a staph infection nearly took his life. A few years later he was alone in the Pacific on a life raft, praying that his rescuers would find him before the enemy did.

God answered those prayers. It turned out He had other plans for George H. W. Bush. For Dad's part, I think those brushes with death made him cherish the gift of life. And he vowed to live every day to the fullest.

Dad was always busy—a man in constant motion—but never too busy to share his love of life with those around him. He taught us to love the outdoors. He loved watching dogs flush a covey. He loved landing the elusive striper. And once confined to a wheelchair, he seemed happiest sitting in his favorite perch on the back porch at Walker's Point contemplating the majesty of the Atlantic. The horizons he saw were bright and hopeful. He was a genuinely optimistic man. And that optimism guided his children and made each of us believe that anything was possible.

He continually broadened his horizons with daring decisions. He was a patriot. After high school, he put college on hold and became a Navy fighter pilot as World War II broke out. Like many of his generation, he never talked about his service until his time as a public figure forced his hand. We learned of the attack on Chichijima, the mission completed, the shoot-down. We learned of the death of his crewmates, whom he thought about throughout his entire life. And we learned of his rescue.

And then, another audacious decision; he moved his young family from the comforts of the East Coast to Odessa, Texas. He and Mom adjusted to their arid surroundings quickly. He was a tolerant man. After all, he was kind and neighborly to the women with whom he, Mom, and I shared a bathroom in our small duplex—even after he learned their profession—ladies of the night.

Dad could relate to people from all walks of life. He was an empathetic man. He valued character over pedigree. And he was no cynic. He looked for the good in each person—and usually found it.

Dad taught us that public service is noble and necessary; that one can serve with integrity and hold true to the important values, like faith and family. He strongly believed that it was important to give back to the community and country in which one lived. He recognized that serving others enriched the giver's soul. To us, his was the brightest of a thousand points of light.

In victory, he shared credit. When he lost, he shouldered the blame. He accepted that failure is part of living a full life but taught us never to be defined by failure. He showed us how setbacks can strengthen.

None of his disappointments could compare with one of life's greatest tragedies, the loss of a young child. Jeb and I were too young to remember the pain and agony he and Mom felt when our three-year-old sister died. We only learned later that Dad, a man of quiet faith, prayed for her daily. He was sustained by the love of the Almighty and the real and enduring love of our mom. Dad always believed that one day he would hug his precious Robin again.

He loved to laugh, especially at himself. He could tease and needle, but never out of malice. He placed great value on a good joke. That's why he chose Simpson to speak. On email, he had a circle of friends with whom he shared or received the latest jokes. His grading system for the quality of the joke was classic George Bush. The rare 7s and 8s were considered huge winners—most of them off-color.

George Bush knew how to be a true and loyal friend. He honored and nurtured his many friendships with his generous and giving soul. There exist thousands of handwritten notes encouraging, or sympathizing, or thanking his friends and acquaintances.

He had an enormous capacity to give of himself. Many a person would tell you that Dad became a mentor and a father figure in their life. He listened and he consoled. He was their friend. I think of Don Rhodes, Taylor Blanton, Jim Nantz, Arnold Schwarzenegger, and perhaps the unlikeliest of all, the man who defeated him, Bill Clinton. My siblings and I refer to the guys in this group as "brothers from other mothers."

He taught us that a day was not meant to be wasted. He played golf at a legendary pace. I always wondered why he insisted on speed golf. He was a good golfer.

Well, here's my conclusion: He played fast so that he could move on to the next event, to enjoy the rest of the day, to expend his enormous energy, to live it all. He was born with just two settings: full throttle, then sleep.

He taught us what it means to be a wonderful father, grandfather, and great-grandfather. He was firm in his principles and supportive as we began to seek our own ways. He encouraged and comforted, but never steered. We tested his patience—I know I did—but he always responded with the great gift of unconditional love.

Last Friday, when I was told he had minutes to live, I called him. The guy who answered the phone said, "I think he can hear you, but hasn't said anything most of the day." I said, "Dad, I love you, and you've been a wonderful father." And the last words he would ever say on earth were "I love you, too."

To us, he was close to perfect. But not totally perfect. His short game was lousy. He wasn't exactly Fred Astaire on the dance floor. The man couldn't stomach vegetables, especially broccoli. And by the way, he passed these genetic defects along to us.

Finally, every day of his seventy-three years of marriage, Dad taught us all what it means to be a great husband. He married his sweetheart. He adored her. He laughed and cried with her. He was dedicated to her totally.

In his old age, Dad enjoyed watching police show reruns, volume on high, all the while holding Mom's hand. After Mom died, Dad was strong, but all he really wanted to do was to hold Mom's hand, again.

Of course, Dad taught me another special lesson. He showed me what it means to be a president who serves with integrity, leads with courage, and acts with love in his heart for the citizens of our country. When the history books are written, they will say that George H. W. Bush was a great president of the United States—a diplomat of unmatched skill, a commander in chief of formidable accomplishment, and a gentleman who executed the duties of his office with dignity and honor.

In his inaugural address, the forty-first president of the United States said this: "We cannot hope only to leave our children a bigger car, a bigger bank account. We must hope to give them a sense of what it means to be a loyal friend, a loving parent, a citizen who leaves his home, his neighborhood and town better than he found it. What do we want the men and women who work with us to say when we are no longer there? That we were more driven to succeed than anyone around us? Or that we stopped to ask if a sick child had gotten better, and stayed a moment there to trade a word of friendship?"

Well, Dad—we're going to remember you for exactly that and so much more.

And we're going to miss you. Your decency, sincerity, and kind soul will stay with us forever. So, through our tears, let us see the blessings of knowing and loving you—a great and noble man, and the best father a son or daughter could have.

And in our grief, let us smile knowing that Dad is hugging Robin and holding Mom's hand again.

* * *

These eulogies were given at the funeral at St. Martin's Episcopal Church in Houston.

Secretary of State James Baker

My friends, we're here today in the house of the Lord to say goodbye to a man of great faith and integrity—a truly beautiful human being. And to honor his noble character, his life of service, and the sweet memories he leaves for his friends, his family, and our grateful nation.

For more than sixty years, George Herbert Walker Bush has been my friend and my role model. Today, as we entrust his soul to heaven, his name to history, and his memory to our hearts, I must begin with an apology.

Jefe, I am about to do something you always hated, and your mother always told you not to do—boast about yourself.

I will do this because it *must* be done. And because, as a lawyer, I see that thing beloved by all lawyers—a loophole.

"Don't brag about yourself," you once wrote. "Let *others* point out your virtues, your good points."

Well, today, Mr. President, I am that *other*, with the special privilege and joy of sharing your good points.

George Bush was a charter member of the greatest generation. As we gather here to salute him, his incredible service to our nation and the world are already etched in the marble of time.

After becoming the youngest naval aviator, he served in increasingly responsible positions on behalf of his country—congressman, ambassador to China and to the United Nations, director of the CIA, and vice president.

Then (as history will record) he became one of our nation's finest presidents and, beyond any doubt, our nation's very best one-term president!

For millions and millions across the globe, the world became a better place because George Bush occupied the White House for four years.

He was not considered a skilled speaker. But his deeds were eloquent. And he demonstrated their eloquence by carving them into the hard granite of history.

They expressed his moral character. And they reflected his decency, his boundless kindness and consideration of others, his determination always to do the *right* thing and always to do that to the very *best* of his ability. They testify to a noble life, well-lived.

He possessed the classic virtues of *our* civilization and of *his* faith—the same virtues that express what is best about America. These same ideals were known to, and shared by, our Founding Fathers.

George Bush was *temperate* in thought, in word, and in deed. He considered his choices and chose wisely.

The Berlin Wall fell in November 1989, less than one year into his presidency. It was a remarkable triumph for American foreign policy.

As joyous East and West Germans danced on the remains of that hated Wall, George Bush could have joined them, metaphorically, and claimed victory for the West, for America. And frankly, for himself. But he did not!

He knew better. He understood that humility toward—and not humiliation of—a fallen adversary was the best path to peace and reconciliation. And so, he was able to unify Germany as a member of NATO notwithstanding the initial reservations of France, the United Kingdom, and the Soviet Union.

Thus, the Cold War ended, not with a bang but with the sound of a halyard rattling through a pulley over the Kremlin on a cold night in December 1991 as the flag of the Soviet Union was lowered for the very last time.

Need we ask about George Bush's *courage*? During World War II, he risked his life in defense of something greater than himself.

Decades later, when Saddam Hussein invaded Kuwait in August 1990 and began to brutalize Kuwaitis, George Bush did not waver. "This will not stand," he said. And he got the rest of the world to join him in reversing that aggression.

Yes, he had the courage of a warrior. But when the time came for prudence, he always maintained the *greater* courage of a peacemaker. He ended the wars in Central America. He signed two nuclear arms reduction treaties and brought Israel and all of its Arab neighbors together face-to-face for the first time to talk peace.

His *deeds for his fellow man* always spoke for him. "Give someone else a hand," he would say, and he did. "When a friend is hurting, show that you care." And he did. "Be kind to people." And he was.

To the parents of a young son lost to cancer he wrote: "I hope you will live the rest of your lives with only happy memories of that wonderful son who is now safely tucked in—God's loving arms around him."

His wish for a kinder, gentler nation was not a cynical political slogan. It came honest and unguarded from his soul.

After they left the White House, George and Barbara Bush continued to display their compassion for others. Their dedication to the Points of Light, the Barbara Bush Foundation for Family Literacy, and countless other charities is a model for *all* former first families—past, present, and future.

To these virtues, we can add one more source of his character: his *family.*

As a friend once put it, George Bush believed family "is a source of both personal strength and the values one needs to face life."

And of course, history has shown that few families have accomplished as much as his. Barbara wrote the book on how to be a great First Lady. His legacy lives on with his children, who have contributed so very much to make our nation great. And who knows what the future will bring for his grandchildren and their children?

I have always been proud that George described our relationship as one of big brother and little brother.

He used to say that one of the things he liked best about me was that I would always tell him what I thought—even when I knew he didn't want to hear it. Then, we would have a spirited discussion about the issue. But he had a very effective way of letting me know when the discussion was over.

He would look at me and say: "Baker, if you're so smart, why am I president and you're not?"

He was a leader...and he knew it!

My hope is that in remembering the life of George Herbert Walker Bush and in honoring his accomplishments, we will see that we are really praising what is best about our nation, the nation he dearly loved and whose values he embodied.

There is more to say than time permits. And anyway, when measured against the eloquence of George Bush's character and life, our words are inadequate.

And so, I conclude with *his* words, written some years ago to his old tennis buddy:

"We have known each other a long time," he wrote to me. "We have shared joy and sadness, and time has, indeed, gone swiftly by. Now it races on even faster. That makes me treasure even more this line of William Butler Yeats about 'where man's glory begins and ends,' namely with friends.

"My glory is I have you as 'such a friend.'"

To which I reply on behalf of his friends here today, across America, and throughout the world:

We rejoice, Mister President, that you are safely tucked in, now and through the ages, with God's loving arms around you.

Our glory, George, was to have had you as our president...and as "such a friend."

George P. Bush

Good morning. Today I stand before you as the oldest grandson of the man I simply knew as "Gampy."

George Herbert Walker Bush was the most gracious, most decent, and most humble man I will ever know.

We are here to give thanks for his extraordinary life, but *I'd* like to talk about things he was thankful for—the things that, to him, mattered most.

My grandfather was thankful for his family.

When he began running for president in 1988, my grandfather released a campaign book outlining his views for the future. The book opened with "A Letter to a Grandson." It was addressed to me and recounted our most recent summer together in Maine.

"P," the letter read, "I've been thinking about it a lot—the most fun was the big rock boat, climbing out on it, watching you and Noelle playing on it. Near the end of summer, when the moon was full and the tides were higher, there was that special day at high tide when it almost seemed like the boat was real."

In those few words my grandfather said more about his life than I could ever say today. Here was a man gearing up for the role of a lifetime—and yet his mind went back to his family. This was a book about policy issues—and yet he still found time to write about an imaginary boat he built with his grandson.

He would wake up around 5 a.m. to review security briefings and grab his first coffee of the day. When the coast was clear, all of the grandkids would do our best to snag a spot on his bed with Ganny while they read the paper.

We all grew up in awe of my grandfather—a larger-than-life figure fly-fishing off the rocks in Maine while talking up where the blue fish were running. He would be the first to host intense horseshoe matchups between family and Secret Service or any willing head of state, while encouraging trash talk like "power outage" if you were short, or "Woodrow Wilson" if you were long on your throw. His typical spread included BBQ, tacos, or pork rinds with hot sauce—of course with a healthy dose of Blue Bell ice cream. Always the competitor, each night closed with Gampy challenging us to the coveted "first asleep" award.

In classic Gampy fashion, he would write letters of encouragement—whether one of us had a hard semester at school, one of us (*not me*) drove his boat *Fidelity* into the rocks, or one of us (*definitely not me*) ended up in Ganny's crosshairs.

At the close of one summer, after he had left public service, Gampy wrote an email to all of us: "The only thing wrong with the last five months is that none of you were here enough. Next year, promise this old Gampster that you will spend more time with us here by the sea. As you know I have had to give up fly fishing off the rocks, but there is plenty left to do—plenty of wonderful things. I think of all of you an awful lot. I just wonder how each of you is doing—in life, in college, in school. If you need me, I am here for you, because I love you very much."

In the Psalms, God makes this promise: "With long life, I will satisfy him and show him my salvation." Today, we know that Gampy did enjoy a long life; and we know he is enjoying the beginning of his next life, rejoining those whom he lost but now, by grace, has found again.

My grandfather was thankful for his country.

My grandfather was grateful to lead a country where people can go as far and as fast as their dreams can take them; a country that celebrates individuals alone or working together to improve the condition of their fellow man on a voluntary basis—a bright hope for America he evoked so brilliantly when he spoke of a Thousand Points of Light.

He often spoke about the timeless creed of "duty, honor, country" that has sustained the republic for over 240 years.

But this wasn't something he just talked about...it was something that he lived. He flew fifty-eight combat missions in the Pacific, was shot down, and rescued at sea. Yet he never saw his own heroism as being any greater than anyone else's. I know this because I experienced it personally. Gampy was so proud when my cousin Walker joined the Marines and I joined the Navy, and he was even prouder when we served overseas. In no way did our service compare to his; yet we could never convince him of that.

In our times together, our big, wonderful, and competitive family saw the personal goodness that led to his historical greatness. He left a simple yet profound legacy to his children and grandchildren and to our great country—service. When the last words on George H. W. Bush are written, they will certainly include this: The fulfillment of a complete life cannot be achieved without service to others.

Finally, my grandfather was thankful for his God.

Gampy once said: "God is good, but His love has a cost: We must be good to one another." It was his faith and his love for others that drove him, that fulfilled him, and that led him to a calling in public life.

Toward the end of his service as president, at a Prayer Breakfast here in Houston, he reflected on his time aboard the submarine *Finback* after being shot down during World War II—he went up topside one night on the deck, stood watch, and looked out at the dark. He said the sky was clear; the stars were brilliant like a blizzard of fireflies in the night. There was a calm inner peace. Halfway around the world in a war zone, there was a calm inner peace: God's therapy.

Today, after ninety-four years, the heavy hand of time has claimed the life of my Gamps. But in death, as in life, my grandfather has won—for he has exchanged his earthly burdens for a heavenly home and is at peace.

Yes, George Herbert Walker Bush was the most gracious, most decent, and most humble man I will ever know. And it's the honor of a lifetime to share his name.

God bless you, Gampy. Until we meet again—maybe out on that rock boat we built together.

Acknowledgments

First and foremost, this book would not exist if not for the extraordinary life of George Herbert Walker Bush (and of course Barbara Bush, too). If he had been a complete bore, there would be no stories, no adventures, no insights to share. In many ways, he wrote this book. I'm just his conduit between heaven and earth.

I also could not have written this book without the support of George W., Jeb, Neil, and Marvin Bush and Doro Bush Koch. Jeb, Marvin, and Doro read the first draft and gave me invaluable advice and direction. President George W. Bush gave me advice when sought, and Neil was great on fact-checking when I needed him.

President George W. Bush's chief of staff, Freddy Ford, also read an early draft and proved himself to be an outstanding editor and discerning reader. He saved me from myself more than once.

But he was not alone. My other black-belt readers were my sisters Millie Aulbur and JoAnn Heppermann; author and friend Dava Guerin; and former colleagues Laura Pears, Nancy Lisenby, and Melinda Lamoreaux. At times I was almost irritated by how many mistakes (almost all of them minor, really) they caught and the suggestions they made. The publishing industry could hire any of them. They are really good at this. This book is so much better because they were on the team. Above all else, they were my loudest cheerleaders, which I needed a time or two.

I fear the list goes on. I am most grateful to Jim McGrath, Chase

Untermeyer, Mark Updegrove, Jeff Engel, and Jim Cicconi, who also read the book and who also gave me good ideas on stories to include or maybe not to include. (Sorry, no examples on those we decided to take out.) As published authors and/or people who knew George Bush well, their input was invaluable.

Jon Meacham deserves his own paragraph, since it's possible that after ten years of researching and writing about George Bush, no one knows the man better. His encouragement and advice were—well, again, invaluable. I hope he knows how much I appreciate his friendship and support.

I asked Secretary James Baker to read only the parts of the book that mentioned him, but he read it from cover to cover. When we tried to talk about it, we ended up having a good cry instead. It was one of my favorite "feedback" calls.

When the rest of the team just could not read this book one more time, Linda Poepsel came to the rescue and read the galley for me, to catch all the things no one else had yet caught.

As I mentioned in the Author's Note, the George H. W. Bush Library was closed the entire time I was writing *The Man I Knew.* So I never had a chance to spend days on end surrounded by boxes of records and files to fact-check this book.

But the library team, headed by director Warren Finch and deputy director Robert Holzweiss; head archivist Debbie Wheeler; archivist Doug Campbell; and audiovisual archivist Mary Finch, came to the rescue. Working from home—and, toward the end, going into the office and pulling a file or two—they were truly amazing on how much fact-checking they were able to pull off in the middle of a pandemic. As always, I am most grateful to them.

In addition to the library team, I double-checked my memory and the facts with a huge group of folks who played important roles in some of the stories told. Did they remember what I remembered? Except for a tweak here and there, they mostly did. Whew.

First and foremost, I am profoundly grateful to President Bush's post–

White House personal aides, to whom I sent dozens and dozens of fact-checking emails. My guess is no one was happier when the book was done. In the order in which they served: Michael Dannenhauer, Gian-Carlo Peressutti, Tom Frechette, Jim Appleby, Coleman Lapointe, and Evan Sisley.

Also most helpful were Mrs. Bush's aides: Peggy White, Nancy Huang, Quincy Crawford, Kara Sanders, Brooke Sheldon, Michele Stanton, Kristan King Nevins, Amanda Sherzer, Hutton Higgins, Catherine Branch, and Neely Brunette.

The rest of this huge cast of fact-checkers are, in alphabetical order: the Reverend Ed Becker, Sally Bradshaw, Ann Brock, Christopher Buckley, the Reverend Peter Cheney, George Clooney, Tom Collamore, Mary Kathryn Cooper, Jason Denby, George Dvorsky, Marlin Fitzwater, Tina Flournoy, Tony Freemantle, Jamie Gangel, Bob Gates, Joe Hagin, Valerie Jarrett, Ginny Mulberger, Pat Mulvey, Dr. Martin Murphy, Chris Needels, Roxann Neumann, Ann Pendley, Gregg Petersmeyer, Diane Quest, Topper Ray, Karl Rove, Dr. Andy von Eschenbach, Mark Welsh, Kevin Wensing, Greg Willard, John Williams, and Donna Zaccaro.

David Priess kindly fact-checked everything about the CIA, and Marlon Harris did the same for everything about the Secret Service. They not only kept me honest but prevented me from telling stories out of school. Two retired Navy admirals did the same: Chip Miller and Brian "Lex" Luther.

I began this note by saying this book would not have been possible without President Bush and the Bush family. I will end by talking about another group of people without whom this book would not exist: the team at Twelve.

First and foremost, I owe a huge debt of gratitude to Sean Desmond, who first believed in this book and then guided me every step of the way. Simply put, he is a brilliant editor. I cannot imagine writing for anyone else.

The rest of the team at Twelve includes Jarrod Taylor, who designed this wonderful cover and book layout and put up with all my nitpicks;

the marketing and publicity team—Brian McLendon, Megan Perritt-Jacobson, and Estefania Acquaviva; and Rachel Kambury, who patiently answered all my emails and kept me on track and on deadline.

I owe both gratitude and apologies to the copyediting team, led by Carolyn Kurek. Because I was a journalism major and then a newspaper writer for ten years, the Associated Press stylebook will forever be imbedded in my DNA. I can't help it. The AP stylebook does not always agree with how books are edited. So for all the capitalizations and digital numbers you had to constantly correct—I am sorry. For all the mistakes you caught—I am most grateful. I will be embarrassed for the rest of my life that I got the official name of the Houston Livestock Show and Rodeo wrong but a team in New York got it right.

It really does take a village.

P.S.: My apologies to the hundreds of friends and relatives of George Bush who are not in this book. Sean kindly reminded me a time or two that nothing drags down a book's narrative more than endless lists of people. So I wasn't able to work everyone into the dialogue. Please know I tried. If only you had done something like run naked across the yard at Walker's Point…

About the Author

Jean Becker was chief of staff for George H. W. Bush from March 1, 1994, until his death on November 30, 2018. She previously served as deputy press secretary to First Lady Barbara Bush from 1989 to 1992. Before joining the Bush White House staff in 1989, Ms. Becker was a newspaper reporter for ten years, including a four-year stint at *USA Today* where her duties included covering the 1988 presidential election and being a Page One editor. Her book about Mrs. Bush, *Pearls of Wisdom*, became a *New York Times* best-seller when it was released on March 3, 2020. She lives in Houston, Texas.